ASIATISCHE FORSCHUNGEN

MONOGRAPHIENREIHE
ZUR GESCHICHTE, KULTUR UND SPRACHE
DER VÖLKER OST- UND ZENTRALASIENS

Begründet von Walther Heissig

Herausgegeben von Thomas O. Höllmann

Band 162

2024

Harrassowitz Verlag · Wiesbaden

Peoples of Pingcheng (398–494):

Cultural Diversity and Interaction

Edited by
Thomas O. Höllmann
and Shing Müller

2024

Harrassowitz Verlag · Wiesbaden

Bibliografische Information der Deutschen Nationalbibliothek
Die Deutsche Nationalbibliothek verzeichnet diese Publikation in der Deutschen
Nationalbibliografie; detaillierte bibliografische Daten sind im Internet
über https://dnb.de abrufbar.

Bibliographic information published by the Deutsche Nationalbibliothek
The Deutsche Nationalbibliothek lists this publication in the Deutsche
Nationalbibliografie; detailed bibliographic data are available in the internet
at https://dnb.de.

For further information about our publishing program consult our
website http://www.harrassowitz-verlag.de
© Otto Harrassowitz GmbH & Co. KG, Wiesbaden 2024
Printed on permanent/durable paper.
Printing and binding: Prime Rate Zrt.
Printed in Hungary
ISSN 0571-320X   ISBN 978-3-447-12308-2
eISSN 2940-3642   eISBN 978-3-447-39624-0

Contents

Preface

The study of Chinese history during the era of disunity from the 4th to the 6th century is a rather complex and intriguing challenge. Although cultural exchange between states and confederations in Central and East Asia had existed long before this period, the foreign impact on China seems to have been far less dramatic and massive. This concerns not only the trading of objects and the migration of ethnic groups, but also the influence on a great variety of cultural traits. The period was not only hallmarked by political instability and social unrest, it was also accompanied by long-term climate cooling that changed the living conditions.

The result was on the one hand a tremendous, and partially forced, mobility and a continuous coexistence of communities of different cultural backgrounds, and on the other an increasing ability to accept otherness and to innovate. As Albert E. Dien pointed out in the introduction to volume 2 of *The Cambridge History of China* "it was the very disorder, a collapse of central authority, that provided the conditions enabling such important advances which make the Six Dynasties period such a significant one in Chinese History".[1]

During the last twenty years, the construction boom has had far-reaching consequences for archaeological fieldwork. The number of excavations has increased dramatically, providing new insights into the formation of Northern Cultures influenced by both Han traditions and the contributions of inhabitants regarded as "barbarians" by Chinese historiographical sources.

For this reason, in 2015 the Institute for Chinese Studies of LMU Munich established the research project "Cultural Diversity in Northern China during the Fifth and Sixth Centuries", supported by a generous research grant from the German Research Foundation (DFG). From the beginning, Shing Müller served as investigator-in-charge, bearing the main load of coordinating the project and editing the results of the study. I would like to express my deepest gratitude to Shing Müller, who was also responsible for the organization of an international conference on "Culture and Cultural Diversity in Early Medieval China" in 2017. The papers were published under the title "Early Medieval North China: Archaeological and Textual Evidence" two years later.

Right from the start, Zhang Qingjie, the former director of the Archaeological Institute of Shanxi Province, was our major cooperation partner in China. He not only facilitated visits to important sites, museums, and collections in Shanxi, but also introduced the members of our research team to colleagues in neighboring provinces and autonomous regions. Thus, we had the opportunity to discuss our ideas with archaeologists, historians, and art historians in Shaanxi, Ningxia and Inner Mongolia. Many thanks to him as well for his continuous inspiration and help.

---

1 Albert E. Dien and Keith N. Knapp. ed. 2019. *The Cambridge History of China*, Volume 2: *The Six Dynasties, 220–589.* Cambridge: Cambridge University Press, 1.

Both Shing Müller and Zhang Qingjie contributed to this book. The focus is on the excavations of 5th century Pingcheng (Datong), the second capital of the Northern Wei Dynasty. This setting was chosen because of its dense population with inhabitants of diverse origins and a high degree of cultural complexity that could be researched within a manageable timeframe.

I feel indebted to all members of the Archaeological Institute of Shanxi Province, the Datong Archaeological Institute, the Datong Museum, the Museum for Northern Dynasties Arts at Datong, and the Yungang Academy, who supported the research project and shared their knowledge with us. Sincere thanks go finally to Mary Wong-Sommer for her careful proofreading and help with the translation.

Thomas O. Höllmann

The Brick Inscriptions of Yifu Mogui and Yifu Qiangui of the Northern Wei Dynasty

Zhang Qingjie

Shanxi Datong University, Archaeological Institute of Shanxi Province

In spring 2016, several dozen inscribed tomb bricks bearing the names of Yifu Mogui 乙弗莫瓌 and his son Qiangui 乾歸 of the Northern Wei Dynasty were acquired by the Museum of Northern Dynasties Arts in Datong 大同北朝藝術博物館. Yifu Mogui's bricks with a burnished surface and a dark grayish-blue color resemble those commonly encountered during the Northern Wei period. There are three sizes of them: 26.8 cm × 13 cm × 4 cm, 26.5 cm × 13.5 cm × 4 cm, and 25 cm × 13 cm × 4 cm. Every brick has a plain reverse and a front with a slightly raised (0.2 cm) border framing a rectangular depression (approximately 20 cm long and 5.2 cm wide), into which the inscriptions are impressed. Three inscriptions can be distinguished. These bricks were allegedly discovered several years earlier during railway construction in Yingxian 應縣 of Suozhou 朔州, Shanxi province. Another two tomb bricks with engraved texts were also included in the same acquisition. Both are of similar quality to Yifu Mogui's bricks but are slightly larger (29 cm long, 15 cm broad, 5.2 cm high) and bear the name Yifu Qiangui.

Despite the damage, these brick inscriptions provide novel information not contained in the transmitted historical works. A careful study and interpretation of the inscriptions can shed new light on the history of this family, the processes of cultural convergence, and the history of the Northern Dynasties period in general.

Brick inscriptions of Yifu Mogui

The inscriptions were written in a Northern Wei calligraphic style. Their contents vary to some degree:

Mogui inscription I:

(Tomb) Brick of Yifu Mogui, Palace Attendant, General-in-Chief Conquering the East, Commander Unequalled in Honor, Chief Commandant of Attendant Cavalry, Yuzhen and Prince of Xiping (present-day Xining in Qinghai).[1] 侍中、征東大將軍、啓府儀同三司、駙 / 馬都尉、羽真、西平王乙弗莫瓌專。/ (Fig. 1)

---

1 Note of trl.: The translation of the official titles is based on Hucker, Charles O. *A Dictionary of Official Titles in Imperial China*. Stanford: Stanford University Press, 1985, and De Crespigny, Rafe. *Official Titles of the Former Han Dynasty*. Canberra: ANUP, 1967.

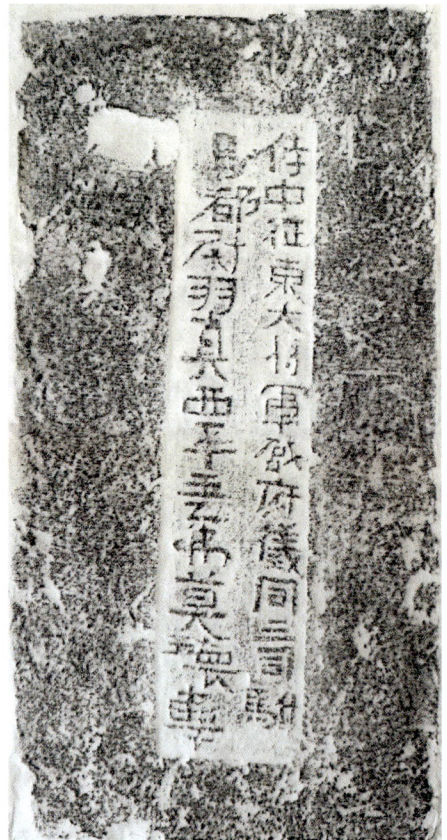

Figure 1 Mogui Inscription I. *Left*: photo, *right*: rubbing.

Mogui inscription II:

(Tomb) Brick of Yifu Mogui, Palace Attendant, General-in-Chief Conquering the East, Commander Unequalled in Honor, Chief Commandant of Attendant Cavalry, *Yuzhen* and Prince of Xiping. (The tomb was) built on the twenty-first day of the fourth month in the fourth (*wuxu*) year of the Tai'an Era of Dai (state) the Great [i.e., the Great Dai] (5/19/458 CE). 侍中、征東大將軍、啓府義[儀]同三司、駙 / 馬都尉、羽真、西平王乙弗莫瓌專。/代大太安四年四月廿一日，歲在戊戌造 (Fig. 2)

Mogui inscription III:

(Tomb) built on the twenty-first day of the fourth month in the x (*wuxu*) year of the Tai-x Era of the Great Dai. (Tomb) Brick of Yifu Mogui, Palace Attendant, General-in-Chief Conquering the East, Commander Unequalled in Honor, Chief Comman-

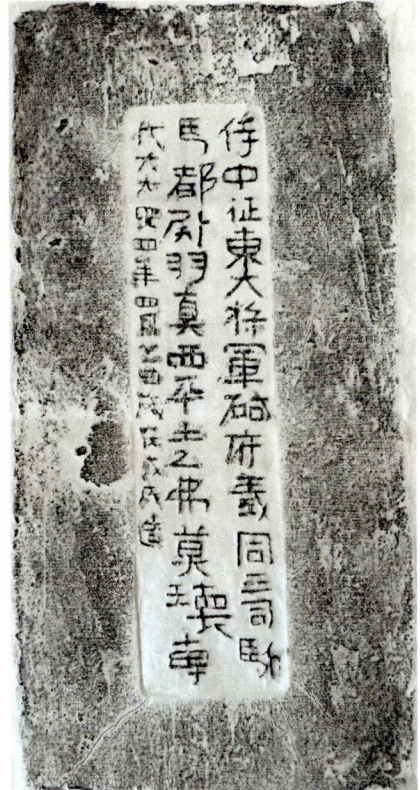

Figure 2 Mogui Inscription II.

dant of Attendant Cavalry, *Yuzhen* and Prince of Xiping. 大代太□□年四月廿一日，歲在戊戌造。/ 侍中、征東大將軍、啓府儀[儀]同三司、駙 / 馬都尉、羽真、西平王乙弗莫瓌專。/ (Fig. 3)

Several variants of characters were used in the inscriptions, such as 啓 for qi 啟 and 義 or 儀 for 儀 (both used in the combination for the honorary title "Unequal in Honor" 儀同三司), as well as 專 for 磚 (brick). The same variant qi 啓 was also written on the epitaph of Qinwen Jichen 欽文姬辰 (died 474 CE), the consort of Sima Jinlong 司馬金龍 (died 484 CE).[2] Additionally, the "Great Dai" (da dai 大代) in Inscription II was written "Dai, the Great" (dai da 代大). The two illegible characters in Mogui inscription III after "Da Dai Tai xx" 大代太□□ can be reconstructed from Mogui inscription II and be read as "the fourth year (of the Tai'an Era of the Great Dai)" (大代太)安四(年) (458 CE).

2　Yin Xian 1999: 165, fig. 4.

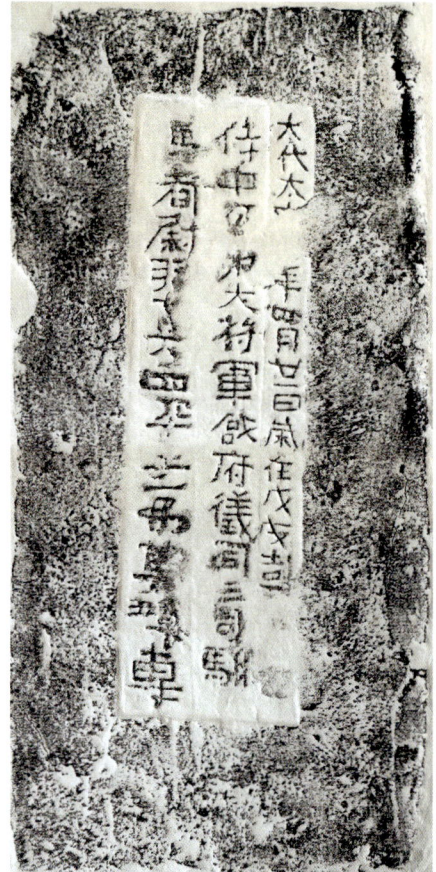

Figure 3 Mogui Inscription III.

Brick inscriptions of Yifu Qiangui

Both inscriptions for Qiangui are similar. Inscription I is well preserved, while Inscription II is damaged since the brick has broken apart. The characters on both bricks bear a typical Northern Wei calligraphic style as well.

Qiangui inscription I:

(Front) In the ninth (*yichou*) year of the Taihe Era (485) of the Great Dai, in the second half of the first (*jisi*) month, on the second (*gengwu*) day, to Yifu Qian[gui], General-in-Chief [Conquering] the East Commissioned with Extraordinary Powers, Chief of the Qin Region, Chief Commandant of Attendant Cavalry, *Yuzhen* and

Prince of Xiping, (Reverse) this inscription was dedicated by his eldest son, Erhu, and (his) wife, Aruo[yide], the Elder Princess of Yangping. (Head) conquer. (Front) 大代太和九年，歲在乙丑正月 / 己巳朔，二日庚午，使持節 / 東大將軍、秦州刺史、駙馬 / 都尉、羽直、西平王乙弗乾 / (Reverse) 歸。元息睿(貳) 庸(虎)，坴 (妻) 陽平 / 長公主阿若〔益得〕銘 / 記。(Head) 征 (Fig. 4)

Qiangui inscription II:

(Front) In the ninth (*yichou*) year of the Taihe Era of the Great Dai (485), in the second half of the first (*jisi*) month, on the second (*geng x*) day, [to Yifu Qiangui], General-in-Chief Conquering the East Commissioned with Extraordinary Powers, Chief of Qin Region, Chief Commandant of Attendant Cavalry, *Yuzhen* and the [Prince] of Xiping, (reverse) this inscription was dedicated by his eldest son Erhu and his wife Aruoyi(de), the Elder Princess of Yangping. (Front) 大代太和九年，歲在乙丑 / 正月己巳朔，二日庚，使持 / 節、征東大將軍、秦州刺史 / 駙馬都尉、羽真、西平 / (reverse) 王, 乙弗乾歸。元息睿(貳) / 庸(虎), 婁(妻) 陽平長公主 阿若 / 益 [得] 銘記 (Fig. 5)

The character *zheng* 征 for "conquer" in Qiangui I's military title "General-in-Chief Conquering the East" was left out by the time of engraving but was later replenished at the head side of the brick (Fig. 4 above). The sexagenery cycle character *wu* 午 following *geng* 更 was absent in Qiangui II, but it can be reconstructed according to Qiangui I. A rubbing of Qiangui II is impossible due to the extreme fragility of the brick.

　　Qiangui Inscription I bears the name of Qiangui's son, Erhu 貳虎, which is written 睿庸. The character *lu* 坴 above Yangping 陽平 in Line 1 on the back of this brick is probably a variant for *qi* 妻 ("wife"), or it was erroneously written (Fig. 4 *below*). The character 妻 for wife is clearly given in Qiangui inscription II (Fig. 5 *left*).

Yi Gui and Yifu Mogui

Yifu Qiangui does not appear in the dynastic chronicles. However, a certain Yi Gui 乙瓌, who received a biographical chapter in both the *History of the Northern Dynasties* (hereafter: *Bei shi* 北史) and the *Book of the Northern Wei Dynasty* (hereafter: *Wei shu* 魏書) in different lengths, bore official titles and noble ranks that are remarkably similar to those mentioned in Qiangui's inscription. Yi Gui and Yifu Mogui were without a doubt one and the same person. The name Yifu Mogui was obviously used prior to Emperor Xiaowen's 孝文帝 reform in 496, in which all tribesmen were to change their multisyllabic to monosyllabic names in Chinese style.[3] After this date, Yifu Mogui was recorded as Yi Gui.

　　In some early Northern Dynasties stone inscriptions, Yīfu 乙弗 was also written Yīfu 一弗. Two Yīfus (一弗) appear on the stele commemorating Emperor Wencheng's 文成帝 (r. 452–465) southern inspection (*Nan xun bei* 南巡碑). The first, carved in the first register on the reverse, bears the personal name Bu-x-x (the second and third characters are illeg-

---

3　*Wei shu* 7B.179; *Zizhi tongjian* 140.4393–94.

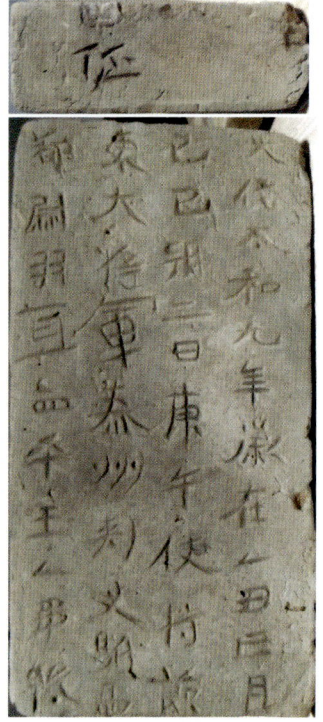

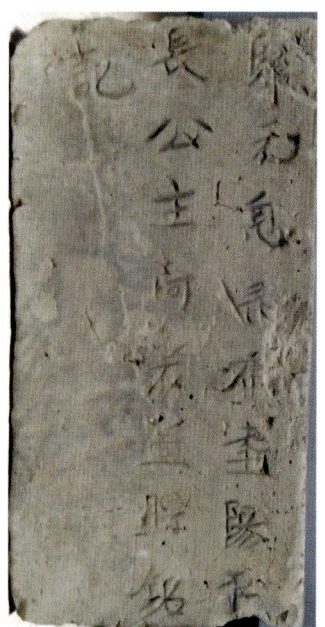

Figure 4
Qiangui
Inscription I.
Above: Front
and head;
below:
reverse.

Figure 5 Inscribed tomb brick of Yifu Qiangui; Inscription II. *Left*: front; *middle*: reverse; *right*: detail of Line 2 on the reverse.

ible). The inscription states that he was "Palace Attendant, Specially Promoted to the Chariot and Horse General-in-Chief, Grand Guardian of the Heir Apparent, Prime Minister, and Prince of Taiyuan," 侍中特[進]車騎大將軍□太子太保尚書太原王一弗步□□. The combination of the titles and noble ranks identifies him as Yi Hun 乙渾 recorded in the *Wei shu*.[4] The second Yīfu with the personal name Afuzhen 阿伏真 and the noble title "Baron of Jiangcheng" 江乘男 was found carved in the same register. Another Yīfu appears in one of the twenty Northern Wei inscriptions of the Longmen caves 龍門二十品. This was a woman who donated a Buddha statue to her deceased husband Zhang Yuanzu, which, in turn, immortalizes her name.[5] Yao Weiyuan clearly demonstrated decades ago that Yīfu 一

---

4   Zhang Qingjie and Li Biao 1997: 72.

5   The famous inscription"Commemoration of the Making of a Buddhist Votive Image dedicated to Zhang Yuanzu by Yīfu" 一弗為張元祖造像記 states: "In the twentieth year of the Taihe Era [496], the Gentleman-Attendant of the [Imperial] Sedan-Chair Zhang Yuanzu unfortunately died. His wife [née] Yīfu made for [him] one image, with the wish that the deceased husband was to be reborn directly in the Buddha Land" 太和廿年, 步輦郎張元祖不幸喪亡, 妻一弗為造像一軀, 願令亡夫直升佛國. [Note of the translator: The translation follows that of Kate A. Lingley, "Lady Yuchi in the First Person: Patronage, Kinship, and Voice in the Guyang Cave," *Early Medieval China* 18 (2012), 39, n. 48, with minor modifications.]

弗 and Yīfu 乙弗 were factually variants of the same name.[6] It is not necessary to go into
details on this subject again.

Biographies in the *Wei shu* and the *Bei shi*

The biographies of Yifu Mogui, i.e., Yi Gui, and his offspring in the *Wei shu* and *Bei shi*
vary considerably. In light of the discoveries of the brick inscriptions, it would be beneficial
to examine the transmitted records more closely and compare them with the inscriptions.
For a better understanding of the differences, a textual comparison between the versions in
Wei shu and *Bei shi* is given in Table 1.

Table 1. Biographies of the Yifus in the *Wei shu* and the *Bei shi*

	Wei shu 44.991–92	*Bei shi* 25.911–12
莫瓌	乙瓌，代人也。其先世統部落。世祖時，瓌父匹知慕國威化，遣瓌入貢，世祖因留之。瓌便弓馬，善射，手格猛獸，膂力過人。數從征伐，甚見信待。尚上谷公主，世祖之女也。除鎮南將軍、駙馬都尉，賜爵西平公。從駕南征，除使持節、都督前鋒諸軍事。每戰，身先士卒，勇冠三軍。後除侍中、征東將軍、儀同三司、定州刺史，進爵為王。又為西道都將。和平中薨，時年二十九。贈太尉公，謚曰恭。	乙瓌，代人也。其先世統部落。太武時，瓌父匹知遣瓌入貢，帝留之。瓌善騎射，手格猛獸。尚太武女上谷公主，除駙馬都尉，賜爵西平公。從駕南征，都督前鋒諸軍事，勇冠三軍。後進爵为王，又為西道都將。薨，年二十九，贈太尉公，謚曰恭。
Mo-gui	Yi[fu Mo]gui was a man of Dai. His ancestors were tribal leaders for generations. Pizhi, the father of [Mo]gui, greatly admired the superiority of the [Northern Wei] state. Thus, he instructed [Mo]gui to bring tributes to Emperor Shizu (r. 423–452). Shizu then asked him to stay. [Mo]gui was proficient in horseback riding. He was an excellent archer and, thanks to his exceptional physical strength, was able to fight with bare hands with wild beasts. He participated in Shizu's numerous military campaigns, which earned him Shizu's trust and respect. After marrying Princess of Shanggu, daughter of Shizu. [Thereafter,] he was appointed General Pacifying the South and Chief Commandant of Attendant Cavalry and was granted the noble rank Duke of Xiping. For his part in	Yi[fu Mo]gui was a man of Dai. His ancestors were tribal leaders for generations. During the reign of Emperor Taiwu (i.e., Shizu), Pizhi, the father of [Mo]gui, instructed [Mo]gui to bring tributes to [the Northern Wei court]. The emperor asked him to stay. Gui was proficient at horseback riding and archery and was able to fight with bare hands with fierce beasts. After marrying Princess Shanggu, the daughter of Taiwu, he was appointed [thereupon] Chief Commandant of Attendant Cavalry. The noble rank Duke of Xiping was bestowed on him. He participated in the military campaign against the South led by the emperor [Taiwu], and was endowed

6   Yao Weiyuan 1962, 165, note 6.

	the military campaign against the southerner led by the emperor [Shizu], [Mogui] was endowed with the title He Who Commissioned with Extraordinary Powers and Commander-in-Chief of the Vanguard in all Military Matters. He led the charge personally in each battle and was always the bravest man of all armies. Later, he was promoted to Palace Attendant, General Conquering the East [who was] Unequalled in Honor, Inspector of the Dingzhou, and his noble rank was elevated to Prince. He also served as General-in-Chief of the Western Circuit. He expired in the Heping period (460–465) at the age of twenty-nine. Upon his death, the title Defender-in-Chief was conferred on him, and he was named posthumously Gong [Reverent One].	with the title Commander-in-Chief of the Vanguard in all Military Matters. He was the bravest man of the whole armies. Later, his noble rank was elevated to Prince. He also served as General-in-Chief of the Western Circuit. He expired at the age of twenty-nine. Upon his death, the title Defender-in-Chief was conferred on him, and he was named posthumously Gong [Reverent one].
乾歸	子乾歸，襲爵。年十二，為侍御中散。及長，身長八尺，有氣幹，頗習書疏，尤好兵法。復尚恭宗女安樂公主，除駙馬都尉、侍中。顯祖初，除征西將軍、秦州刺史，有惠政。高祖初即位，為征西道都將，又為中道都將。延興五年卒，時年三十一。贈左光禄大夫、開府儀同，謚曰康。	子乾歸襲爵。乾歸有氣幹，頗習書疏，尤好兵法。尚景穆女安樂公主，除駙馬都尉、侍中。獻文初，為秦州刺史，有惠政。孝文即位，為中道都將。卒，謚曰康。
Qian-gui	(The son) Qiangui inherited the noble rank. At the age of twelve, [Qiangui] was granted Courtier-Attendant. He grew up to be eight feet tall and was a strong and capable man. He had skills in writing and reporting, but the art of military strategy was his greatest passion. After marrying Gongzong's daughter, Princess Anle, he was appointed Chief Commandant of Attendant Cavalry and Palace Attendant. In the early years of Xianzhu (r. 465–471), he was appointed General Conquering the West and Inspector of the Qin Region, where he ruled benevolently. When Gaozu (r. 471–499) ascended the throne, he was appointed General-in-Chief Attacking the Western Circuit and General-in-Chief of the Central Circuit. He expired in the fifth year of the Yanxing Era (475) at the age of thirty-one. The titles Left Grand Master for Splendid Happiness and Commander Unequalled in Honor were bestowed on him. The posthumous title 'Kang' [Laudable One] was conferred on him.	Qiangui, the son, inherited the noble rank. Qiangui was a strong and capable man. He had skills in writing and reporting, but the art of military strategy was his greatest passion. After marrying the daughter of Emperor Jingmu (i.e., Gongzong), Princess Anle, he was appointed Chief Commandant of Attendant Cavalry and Palace Attendant. In the early years of Xianwen, he was appointed Inspector of the Qin Region where he ruled benevolently. When Xiaowen ascended the throne, he was appointed General-in-Chief of the Central Circuit. The posthumous title "Kang" [Laudable one] was conferred on him after his death.

	Wei shu 44.991–92	*Bei shi* 25.911–12
海	子海，字懷仁。少歷侍御史散、散騎侍郎，卒時年四十一。贈散騎常侍、衛將軍、濟州刺史，謚曰孝。	子海，字懷仁，位散騎侍郎。卒，謚曰孝。
Hai	Hai was [Qiangui's] son. His courtesy name was Huairen. At a young age, [Hai already] held several positions, such as Honorific Attendant Censor and Gentleman Cavalier Attendant. [Hai] expired at the age of forty-one. The titles Cavalier Attendant-in-Ordinary, General of the Guards [of the palace] and Inspector of Ji Region were bestowed on him. The posthumous title Xiao [Filial one] was conferred on him.	Hai was [Qiangui's] son. His courtesy name was Huairen. His [highest] position was Gentleman Cavalier Attendant. The posthumous title Xiao [Filial one] was conferred on him after his death.
瑗	子瑗，字雅珍。尚淮陽公主，高祖之女也，除駙馬都尉。汝南王友，固辭不拜。歷濟南太守，時為逆賊劉桃攻郡，瑗逾城獲免。後都督李叔仁討桃平之，瑗乃還郡。後除司農少卿，銀青金紫左右光禄大夫，中軍將軍，西兗州刺史。天平元年，舉兵應樊子鵠，與行台左丞宋顯戰，敗死，時年四十六。	海子瑗，字雅珍，尚孝文女淮陽公主，除駙馬都尉，累遷西兗州刺史。天平元年，舉兵應樊子鵠，戰敗死。
Yuan	[Hai's son] was Yuan. His courtesy name was Yazhen. After marrying Princess of Huaiyang, Gaozu's daughter, he was appointed Chief Commandant of Attendant Cavalry. The Prince of Ru'nan attempted to develop a close relationship with him but was met with reluctance. During the time [Yuan] was governor of Jinan, the rebel Liu Tao attacked the commandery. Yuan jumped over the city wall and barely escaped with his life. Only after commander-in-chief Li Shuren defeated Tao was Yuan able to return to his commandery. Later, he was appointed Vice Minister for the National Treasury, Grand Master of the Palace with Silver Seal and Blue Ribbon as well as with Gold Seal and Purple Ribbon to Left and Right, General of the Capital Army, and Inspector of the Western Yan Region (present-day western Shandong and eastern Henan). In the first year of the Tianping Era (534), Yuan led a troop to aid Fan Zihu in the campaign [against Gao Huan] but lost the battle against Song Xian, the Left Assistant Director of the local Branch Department of State Affairs and was killed. He was forty-six years old.	Hai's son was Yuan. His courtesy name was Yazhen. After marrying Xiaowen's daughter, Princess of Huaiyang, he was appointed the Chief Commandant of Attendant Cavalry. He was promoted several times and was elevated to Inspector of the Western Yan Region. In the first year of the Tianping Era (534), Yuan led a troop to aid Fan Zihu. He was defeated and killed [in the battle].

諧	瑗弟諧，字遵和。武定中，司馬。	-
Xie	Yuan's younger brother of was Xie, whose courtesy was name Zunhe. During the Wuding Era (543–550) he was appointed Commander.	-
琛	諧弟琛，字仲珍。解褐司空參軍事。稍遷東平、濟陰二郡太守，散騎常侍。卒時年四十九。	-
Chen	Xie's younger brother of was Chen, whose courtesy name was Zhongzhen. Initially, he did not hold an office but was later appointed Administrative Aide in the Ministry of Works. Later, he was elevated to governor of the Dongping and the Jiying commanderies, and the title Cavalier Attendant-in-Ordinary was bestowed upon him. He expired at the age of forty-nine.	-

Inscriptions vs. records in *Wei shu* and *Bei shi*

The tomb inscriptions and the entries in the *Wei shu* and *Bei shi* differ in several points. These are presented in Table 2.

Table 2 Differences between Mogui's inscriptions and the records in *Wei shu**

Mogui	Tomb Inscriptions	*Wei shu*
Last offices	侍中、征東**大**將軍、**啓府**儀同三司、**駙馬都尉**、**羽真**、**西平**王 Palace Attendant, General-**in-Chief** Conquering the East and **Commander** Unequalled in Honor, **Chief Commandant of Attendant Cavalry**, *Yuzhen* and Prince **of Xiping**.	侍中、征東將軍、儀同三司、**定州刺史**，進爵為王。**又為西道都將**。 Palace Attendant, General Conquering the East [Who was] Unequalled in Honor, **Inspector of the Ding Prefecture**, with the noble rank elevated to Prince. He also served as the **General-in-Chief of the Western Circuit**.
Dates	代大太安四年四月二十一日，歲在戊戌造 (The tomb was) **built** on the **21st day of the fourth month in the fourth (*wuxu*) year of the Tai'an Era of the Great Dai** (5/19/458)	和平中薨 (He) expired **during the Heping Era** (460–465)

* The differences are highlighted with underlined bold type.

As shown in Table 2, the titles mentioned in the *Wei shu*, the "Inspector of Ding Prefecture 定州刺史" and "General-in-Chief of the Western Circuit" 西道都將, are missing in the inscription. On the other hand, the title *Yuzhen* 羽真 in the inscription was not recorded in the *Wei shu*. The grades for the ranks and honorific titles are given differently in the *Wei shu* and inscription. For example, the "General Conquering the East" 征東將軍 and "[He Who was] Unequalled in Honor" 儀同三司 were recorded in the *Wei shu*. However, the titles were graded higher in the inscription as the "General-in-Chief Conquering the East" 征東大將軍 (inscription) and the "Commander Unequalled in Honor" 啟府儀同三司.

According to the "Former Enactment for State Offices and Their Servants" 前職員令 implemented in the seventeenth year of the Taihe period (493), the "General-in-Chief Conquering the East" and the "Commander Unequalled in Honor" were ranked Grade 1 and thus would match better with Mogui's noble rank as Prince of Xiping.[7] The information in the inscription therefore appears to be more credible. It appears that the *Wei shu* records were incomplete or even inaccurate.

Two different dates are given in both sources as well. According to the *Wei shu*, Yifu Mogui died "during the Heping (460–465) era," while the Mogui inscription II bears an exact date of 5/19/458, which referred to the date of the tomb construction. The reason for this early construction of the tomb, at least two years before his death, is unknown. It is very likely that he was seriously ill or had suffered a severe injury.

Not mentioned in the brick inscriptions at all is Princess of Shanggu, who was according to the *Wei shu* and *Bei shi* the consort of Yifu Mogui. After whose death, the princess remarried another high minister and dignitary Xiu Shi 宿石 (died 471).[8]

The differences between the brick inscription and the biography of Yifu Qiangui, the son, in the *Wei shu* are even more pronounced, as is illustrated in Table 3.

Table 3. Differences between the brick inscription of Qiangui and the *Wei shu*

Wei shu 44.991	Qiangui Inscription II
子乾歸，襲爵。……復尚恭宗女**安樂公主**，除駙馬都尉、侍中。顯祖初，除**征西將軍**、秦州刺史，有惠政。高祖初即位，為**征西道都將**，又為**中道都將**。**延興五年卒**，時年三十一。贈左光禄大夫、開府儀同，**諡曰康**。	**大代太和九年**，歲在乙丑正月己巳朔二日庚午，**使持節**、**征東大將軍**、秦州刺史駙馬都尉、**羽真**、西平王……。元息貳虎，妻**陽平長公主**阿若益[得]銘記。
[Mogui's] son was Qiangui, who inherited [Mogui's] noble rank [i.e. Prince of Xiping]. [Qiangui] was **married to the daughter of Emperor Gongzong, Princess Anle**, (…) In the first years of Emperor Xianzhu, he was appointed **General Conquering the West** and Inspector of the Qin Region. (…). After Emperor Gaozu ascended the throne, he was appointed **General-in-Chief Conquering the Western Circuit** as well as **General-in-Chief of the Central Circuit**. He **expired in the fifth year of the Yanxing Era** (475) (…).	In the **ninth (*yichou*) year of the Taihe Era** (485) of the Great Dai, (…) in memory of Yifu Qiangui, **[He Who was] Commissioned with Extraordinary Powers**, **General-in-Chief Conquering the East**, the Inspector of the Qin Region, Chief Commandant of Attendant Cavalry, *Yuzhen* and Prince of Xiping, this inscription was written by his eldest son Erhu and **his consort** Aruoyi(de), **Elder Princess of Yangping**.

7   Zhang Hequan and Hou Rui 2012.
8   *Wei shu* 30.724–25; *Bei shi* 25.917–18.

The first discrepancy between the two sources on Qiangui is related to his consort: The *Wei shu* names Princes Anle, daughter of Gongzong, as his wife, while the brick inscription refers to an "Elder Princess of Yangping." Both sources also provide inconsistent information about his posts and titles. In fact, the only title appeared both in the *Wei shu* and the inscription is "Chief of the Qin Region". The military posts mentioned in the *Wei shu* (see Table 3) are lacking in the inscription. Again, titles retained in the inscription like "He Who was Commissioned with Extraordinary Powers," "General-in-Chief Conquering the East" and "*Yuzhen*" are not mentioned in the *Wei shu*. Lastly, the dates are different. According to the *Wei shu*, Qiangui died "in the fifth year of the Yanxing Era (475)," whereas the inscription gives the "ninth year of the Taihe Era (485)" as the date of endowment of the inscription. These inconsistencies will be examined in the following.

Consort

Was Qiangui married to the Princess of Anle or the Elder Princess of Yangping? The Princess of Anle is documented in the *Wei shu*, but not the Elder Princess of Yangpig. Indeed, a Princess of Yangping found, as the consort of a Yuwen Ce 宇文測 (484–537), entry into the history.[9] She was the daughter of Emperor Xuanwu 宣武帝 (486–515; r. 499–515), and thus at least fifteen or sixteen years younger than the Elder Princess of Yangping mentioned in Qiangui's inscription. It is possible that the Elder Princes was not included in the dynastic chronicles, as this occurred occasionally during the period. For example, an Elder Princess of Jiankang, who did not appear in the historical records, is known only through the discovery of her epitaph ("Epitaph of the Elder Princess of Jiankang, Shuxi of the Great Juqu" 建康長公主大沮渠樹爲之銘), which bears the date of the fourth year of the Yanxing Era (474).[10] The information provided by tomb inscriptions are generally reliable, for they were contemporary records. As regards Yifu Qiangui, the carver could not have confused "Princess of Anle" with "Elderly Princess of Yangping". It is therefore possible that the lady was first invested with the title "Princess of Anle", which was later changed to "Elder Princess of Yangping."

Titles

Qiangui's military titles recorded in the *Wei shu* were all related to the western direction, such as General Conquering the West, Chief of the Qin Region (Qinzhou, present-day Tianshui in Gansu), and General-in-Chief of the Western Circuit. His last military post was the general-in-chief of the Central Circuit. Despite the fact that he inherited the position as General-in-Chief of the Western Circui from his father, which frequently happened during the Northern Wei, it was not mentioned in the brick inscription. One possible explanation is that family members decided to leave out all the military titles.

The General-in-Chief of the Western Circuit was a high-ranking military official during the Pingcheng period of the Northern Wei dynasty (398–493) but was rarely mentioned in historical sources. The *Wei shu* refers to only two additional individuals who bore this title. These were the facilitator of Emperor Xiaowen, the powerful Minister of Works (*sikong* 司空), Mu Liang 穆亮 (c. 450–502), and the close confidant of Emperor Xiaowen and his

---

9 *Bei shi* 57.2071; *Zhou shu* 24.455.
10 Yin Xian 2016, 77, pl. 2.

Chamberlain for the Imperial Stud (*taipu* 太僕), Yuwen Fu 宇文福. Both men were appointed Generals-in-Chief of the Western Circuits in 493,[11] shortly before the emperor's
military expedition against the Southern Qi dynasty.

Interestingly, both the *Wei shu* and the *Bei shi* do not refer to the General-in-Chief of
the Central Circuit, which appeared to be of the same rank as the General-in-Chief of the
Western Circuit, responsible, however, for different regions.

The title *Yuzhen* appears both in dynastic chronicles and brick inscriptions and was
clearly of steppe origin. The stele of Hulü Da Nagui 斛律大那瓌 of Eastern Wei time
(dated to 538), which was discovered several years ago in the City of Taiyuan, mentions
that Nagui's "sixth-generation forefather" also bore the *Yuzhen* title.[12] This "forefather"
was probably the "great-grandfather" of Hulü Jin 斛律金 mentioned in the *Bei shi*.

> "(Hulü Jin) was a member of the Chi'le tribe in Shuozhou. Beihouli, his great-
> grandfather submitted himself to the Northern Wei Emperor Daowu (371–409). The
> emperor elevated him to the position of Great *Yuzhen* and conferred upon him the
> noble rank Duke of Mengdu." (斛律金) "朔州敕勒部人也。高祖倍侯利，魏道武
> 時內附，位大羽真，賜爵孟都公"[13]

Unfortunately, the responsibilities of the *Yuzhen* title-bearer have not been satisfactorily
determined.[14] Given that Mogui passed on this title to his son, it seems that *Yuzhen* was
hereditary. The sources indicate that the majority of the holders of the *Yuzhen* title were
those who submitted themselves to Tuoba sovereignty, the remaining were a small number
of royal members. Since the "Former Enactment for State Offices and Their Servants" of
493 and the inscription on the stele "Mourning for Bi Gan" ("*Diao Bi Gan bei*" 吊比干碑;
494) do not contain this title, it is likely that the title had already been eliminated by the end
of the Pingcheng period. When the history of the Northern Wei was compiled one century
later, the original meaning of *Yuzhen* was no longer understood.

Dates

The third problem concerns the dates. There is a ten-year difference between the *Wei shu*
record and Qiangui's brick inscription. There are two possible explanations for this dis-
parity. The first would be that the *Wei shu* made a mistake, while the brick epitaph is
reliable. The alternative is that the date of death was correctly given in the *Wei shu*. In this
case, it would mean that Yifu Qiangui, although already died in 475, was not entombed
until ten years later. Until then, his body was only encoffined.

---

11 *Wei shu* 42.943; 44.1000.

12 Hulü Nagui was the father of the Northern Qi general Hulü Jin 斛律金 (488–567). The titles on the stele
read "Stele of the Minster of Works, Commissioned with Extraordinary Powers and Commander-in-
Chief of the Ding, Ying and Cang Prefectures, and Inspector of the Ding Prefecture" 使持節[都]督定瀛
滄三州諸軍事定州刺史司空公之碑. The line of concern reads: "the sixth-generation forefather Qi …
was elevated to the General-in-Chief of the Guards of the Palatial Inner Quarters, *Yuzhen*, and Minister
of the Department of State Affairs" 六世祖器，……除衛大將軍、羽真、尚書公. The readings and
interpretation of the stele inscription are work in progress.

13 *Bei shi* 54.1965.

14 Zhang Qingjie and Guo Chumei 1999: 61–62.

One further issue is that the honorary official titles and posthumous names mentioned in the dynastic chronicles are absent from the brick inscriptions of both Yifus. Since an honorific official title and a posthumous name were regarded as imperial homage to the dead and were generally asked for by the family, it is unlikely that these honors would not be recorded in epitaphs. Thus, it is possible that both were conferred upon the Yifus after a considerable period of time. There are several similar cases during the early Northern Wei dynasty. Shizu (r. 423–452), for example, conferred the posthumous title of 'Lord Wenkang (Culture and Tranquility)' 文康公 upon Zhang Gun 張袞 (338–410).[15] Similar *ex post* actions for the clansmen or officials of the past also occurred during the reigns of Emperors Taiwu (r. 423–452), Wencheng (r. 452–465) and Xiaowen (r. 471–499).

Other members of Mogui's lineage

The Northern Wei strongman Yi Hun (d. 466), appearing as Yīfu Bu-x-x on the afore-mentioned stele "Commemoration of the Southern Inspection" (of Emperor Wencheng), was active, according to the *Wei shu*, slightly later than Yifu Mogui. During the reign of Emperor Xianwen 獻文 (r. 465–471), Yi Hun rose to Grand Defender (*taiwei* 太尉) and Chancellor (*chengxiang* 丞相) of the State, which ranked much higher than those of Yifu Mogui. Qiangui and Yi Hun belonged to the same Yifu clan but were of two different lineages. At the height of his career, Yi Hun dominated the court and politics.[16] Yifu Qiangui clearly did not attempt to ally himself with Yi Hun. Consequently, when Yi Hun, who had been accused of planning a coup d'état, was executed by Empress Dowager Feng in the first year of the Tian'an period (466), Qiangui was not implicated. On the contrary, Qiangui received more prestigious titles and promotions.

A number of Mogui's descendants were more famous than he was. One was the consort of the Western Wei Emperor Wendi 文帝 (r. 535–551), Empress Wen 文皇后. Her biography in the *Bei shi* offers some interesting insights into the origin of the Yifu clan.

> "The Empress Wen, née Yifu, of Emperor Wendi was a native of Luoyang in Henan. Her forefathers were tribal lords under the Tuyuhun. They lived in Qinghai and called themselves the 'Kings of Qinghai'. After Liangzhou was conquered, the high ancestor Mogui brought his tribesmen to [the territory of the Northern Wei]. [Mogui] was appointed Inspector of the Ding Prefecture and was given the title Duke of Xiping. For three generations beginning with Mogui, sons were wedded to princesses, while daughters were frequently imperial consorts. The entire family received dignity and respect. [Empress'] father was Yuan. The title '[He Who is] Unequalled in Honor' and Inspector of the Yan Prefecture was bestowed upon him. [Empress'] mother was the Elder Princess of Huaiyang, the fourth daughter of Emperor Xiaowen." 文帝文皇后乙弗氏，河南洛陽人也。其先世為吐谷渾渠帥，居青海，號青海王。涼州平，后之高祖莫瓌擁部落入附，拜定州刺史，封

---

15 *Wei shu* 24.614.
16 *Wei shu* 6.126.

西平公。自莫璝後，三世尚公主，女乃多為王妃，甚見貴重。父瑗，儀同三
司、兗州刺史。母淮陽長公主，孝文之第四女也。[17]

The epitaph stone of Yifu Yu 乙弗玉, unearthed in Taiyuan and now in the Museum of
Northern Dynasties Arts (Fig. 6), provides additional details about the offspring of Yifu
Mogui:

> "Her tabooed name was Yu, and her courtesy name was Run. She was a native of
> Luoyang, Henan. Her great-great-grandfather, (Yifu) Hai, was Chief Commandant
> of Attendant Cavalry, Cavalier Attendant in Ordinary, Left Grand Master for
> Splendid Happiness, Filial Duke of Xiping. Her great grandfather, Yuan, was Chief
> Commandant of Attendant Cavalry, Minister of Works, Loyal Duke of Xiping. Her
> grandfather, Ziwen, was Chief of the Qin and the Yu Regions of the [Eastern] Wei,
> General of the Palace Guard, Duke of Dingtao, and her father, Yi'en, was Governor
> of the Tang Commandery of Sui, Cadet to the Right Accompanying the Heir
> Apparent, Duke of Dingtao." 夫人諱玉，字潤，河南洛陽人也。高祖海，魏駙馬
> 都尉、散騎常侍、左光禄大夫、西平孝公。曾祖瑗，魏駙馬都尉、司空公、西
> 平忠公。祖子文，魏秦豫二州刺史、直閣將軍、定陶公；父遺恩，隨（隋）唐
> 州刺史、東宮右庶子、定陶公。[18]

Following the records in the *Bei shi* and Yifu Yu's epitaph, we may trace Mogui's
ancestors back to the generations in Qinghai as tribal lords under the Tuyuhun. These Yifus
were probably related to a Yifu Wudiguo 乙弗勿敵國 mentioned in the *Bei shi*,[19] who was
subjugated by Juqu Mengxun 沮渠蒙遜 (r. 401–433), King of the Northern Liang 北涼
(397–439), between 405 and 418. As the military power of the Western Qin 西秦 (385–
400, 409–431) became more threatening, the [*note of transl.*: same? another?] leader Yifu
Wudiyan 乙弗烏地延 submitted to the Western Qin with one hundred thousand households
only two years later. The Yifu later split into two groups. Tuozi 他子, a son of Wudiyan,
moved eastwards with five thousand households to the Xiping Commandary 西平郡 of the
Western Qin. The other group was led by Tigu 提孤, a cousin of Tuozi. Tigu fled the
Western Qin and migrated to the mountainous regions surrounding the Qinghai Lake,
where he and his followers were living a pastoral way of life.[20] The Tuyuhun conquered
this group and granted the Yifus of the Tigu branch the status of tribal chiefs under their
sovereignty. The family of Yifu Mogui clearly stemmed from this branch, as Mogui's
father, Pizhi, was indeed a tribal leader under the Tuyuhun. Pizhi later succumbed to the
Northern Wei during the Taiyan 太延 Era (435–440), when Emperor Taiwu used military
force to (re-)open the Western Regions.

What the later generations is concerned, we know, for example, that Yifu Yuan had two
sons. The aforementioned Yifu Ziwen is known only through the epitaph of Yifu Yu.[21] The
other son, Yifu Hui, was mentioned in the *Bei shi*:

---

17 *Bei shi* 13.506.
18 Zhang Jianhua and Liu Guohua 2016: 25.
19 *Bei shi* 96.3189.
20 See *Jin shu* 125.3125.
21 See above the epitaph of Yifu Yu.

Figure 6 Epitaph of Yifu Yu. *Above*: the cover stone; *below*: the biography stone

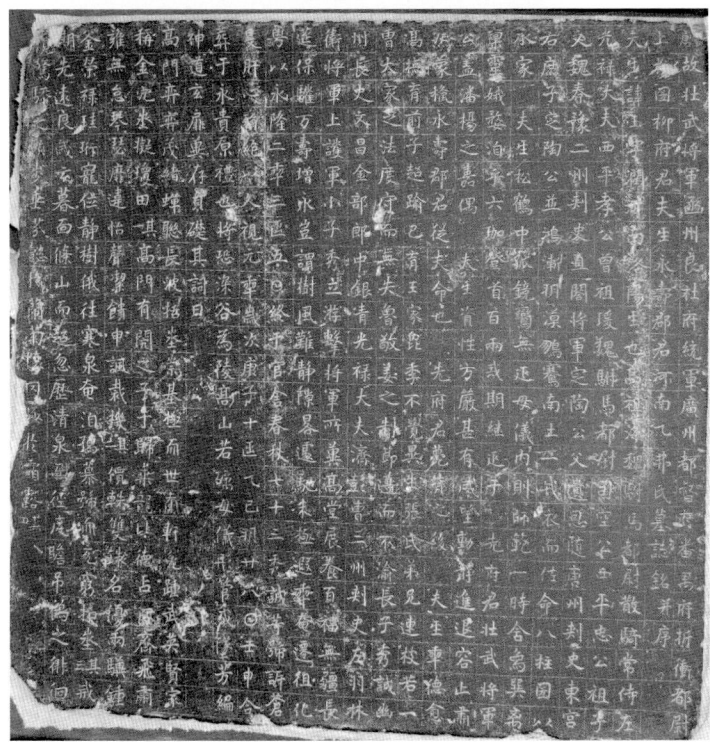

"Yifu Hui was a native of Luoyang in Henan, and an elder brother of the Empress Wen. After Wendi succeeded to the throne, [Hui was] granted the title Commander Unequalled in Honor [and serving as] Palace Attendant, Inspector of the Secretariat, Duke of Weichang County, and Minister of the Personnel Bureau." 乙弗繪，河南洛陽人，文帝皇后之兄也。文帝即位，位開府儀同三司、侍中、中書監、魏昌縣公，又為吏部尚書。[22]

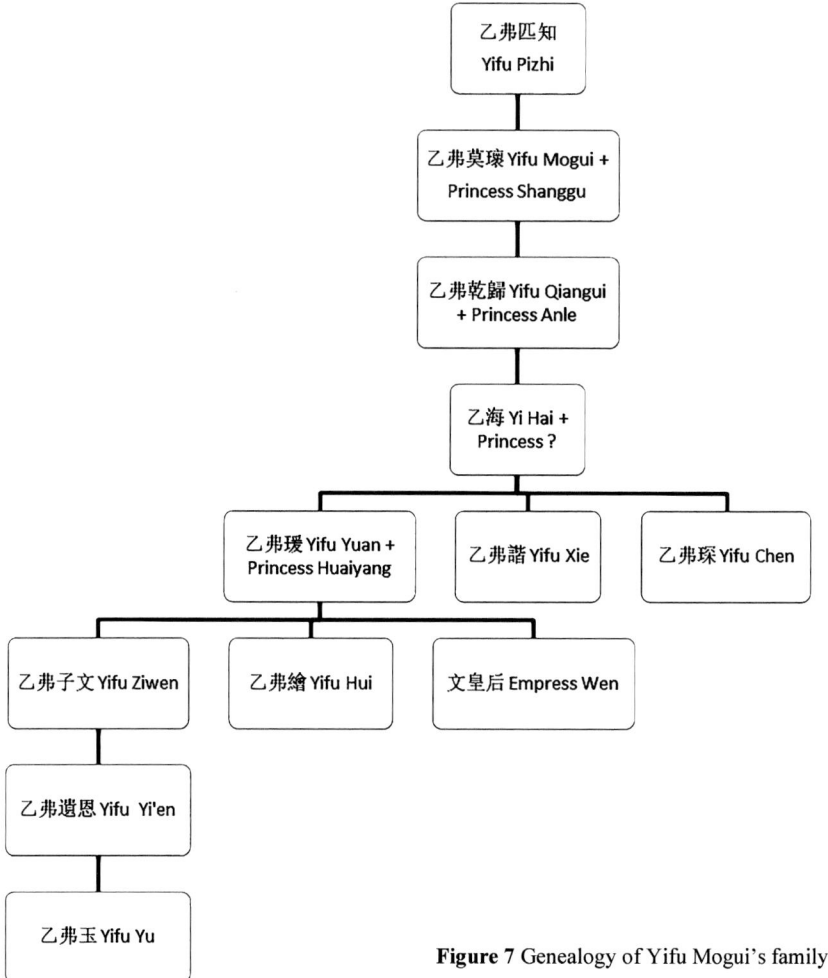

Figure 7 Genealogy of Yifu Mogui's family

22 *Bei shi* 80.2693.

Putting all information together, we can trace back eight generations of Yifu Mogui's family, starting with Pizhi (Fig. 7). Sons from four generations were married to imperial princesses, and a daughter became an empress. The family apparently remained prominent for a considerable period of time.

Other Yifu branches

Genealogical studies of nomadic peoples during the Northern Dynasties period are often complicated by the various descending lines, for example, Yifu Lang 乙弗朗 of the east. Lang's forefathers were, according to the *Bei shi*, "members of the eastern [Xianbei] confederation and tribal leaders for generations. One of them moved to Dai after following the [Tuoba] Wei. He eventually settled in Shangle."[23] Since the Tuyuhun were a splinter group from the eastern Xianbei confederation which later migrated to the west, it appears that one branch of the Yifu followed the Tuyuhun to the Qinghai region, while the other branch remained in the east and later joined the Tuoba. Yifu Lang belonged to this eastern branch, as well as Yifu Li, King of Koguryo, and the above-mentioned Yi Hun. However, both the eastern and western branches of the Yifus shared the same ancestry.

Some Yifus of the later Northern Dynasties period were not related to either Yifu branches. During the Western Wei/Northern Zhou Dynasties, the multisyllabic surnames of the nomadic style were restored and bestowed on meritorious individuals, including Han Chinese. For example, the surname Yifu was bestowed on Zhao Gui 趙貴 (?–557), a Chinese of Tianshui 天水, by the Western Wei Emperor Yuwen Tai 宇文泰 (507–556).[24] A similar case is that of Hua Shao 華紹, whose epitaph was recently unearthed in Xi'an. Shao received the surname Yifu in 551, possibly because of his support of Yuwen Tai in consolidating the latter's power and overthrowing Gao Huan 高歡, the overlord of the Eastern Wei. After this, Yifu Shao, or Hua Shao, was dispatched several times as envoy to the Eastern Turks. A late example is a née Yifu (d. 643) of Tang times. Her epitaph, found in Gansu, tells that she came from a Zhao 趙 family of Tianshui 天水. Since her husband was a Yang 楊, it can be surmised that Yifu had been bestowed on a male member of her family several generations earlier, and the descendants, in this case both sons and daughters, kept the bestowed surname down to the Tang Dynasty.[25]

There are more Yifus in the Northern Dynasties period. However, their origins cannot be traced due to a lack of information. A certain Yifu Chou 乙弗醜 was mentioned in the Biography of Xue Guyan 薛孤延 of the *Bei Qi shu*.[26] Additionally, a Yifu Feng 乙弗鳳, Master of the Palace Militia, a Yifu Kugen 乙弗庫根, a Yifu Ya 乙弗亞 were all only mentioned once in the dynastic chronicles.[27] These names can only be listed here until new archaeological information becomes available for future research.

---

23 *Bei Shi* 49.1810.
24 *Zhou shu* 59.2104.
25 See the "Epitaph of Lady Yifu, Wife of the late Director of Shipping of the Tang Dynasty" 唐故都水使者楊公夫人乙弗氏墓志銘. Cf. http://blog.sina.com.cn/s/blog_97d0a3970102yyou.html; accessed August 11, 2019.
26 *Bei Qi shu* 19.255.
27 Yifu Feng, *Bei shi* 57.2060; *Zhou shu* 3.49; Yifu Kugen, *Bei shi* 49.1795; Yifu Ya, *Bei shi* 62.2210.

本文乃中國國家社科基金冷門絕學《山西北朝石刻遺存文獻搶救性整理研究》項目 21VJXT004 階段性成果 (This is an interim outcome of Project 21VJXT004, "The Salvage Study of the Surviving Northern Dynasties Stone Inscriptions in Shanxi," which is sponsored by the "Unusual and Unique Learning" Program of the National Social Science Foundation of China.)

Bibliography

Bei Qi shu 北齊書. Compiled by Li Baiyao 李百藥 (565–648). Beijing: Zhonghua shuju, 1972.

Bei shi 北史. Compiled by Li Yanshou 李延壽 (Tang) et al. Beijing: Zhonghua shuju, 1974.

Jin shu 晉書. Compiled by Fang Xuanling 房玄齡 (579–648) et al. Beijing: Zhonghua shuju, 1974.

Wei shu 魏書. Compiled by Wei Shou 魏收 (507–572). Beijing: Zhonghua shuju, 1974.

Yao Weiyuan 姚薇元. 1962. *Beichao hu xing kao* 北朝胡姓考. Beijing: Zhonghua shuju.

Yin Xian 殷憲. 1999. "Bei Wei zao qi Pingcheng muming xi" 北魏早期平城墓銘析, *Beichao yanjiu* 北朝研究 1: 163–192.

——. 2016. *Beichao yishu yanjiuyuan cangpin tulu* 北朝藝術研究院藏品圖錄: *Muzhi* 墓誌. Beijing: Wenwu chubanshe.

Zhang Hequan 張鶴全 and Hou Rui 侯瑞. 2012. "Lue lun Bei Wei qianqi zhuwang suo ling jiangjun hao de qianzhuan yu chuanxi" 略論北魏前期諸王所領將軍號的遷轉與傳襲. *Gudai wenming* 古代文明 1: 56–62.

Zhang Jianhua 張建華 and Liu Guohua 劉國華. eds. 2016. *Shanxi sheng yishu bowuguan guancang muzhi jicui* 山西省藝術博物館館藏墓誌集萃. Taiyuan: Shanxi Jingji chubanshe.

Zhang Qingjie 張慶捷 and Guo Chumei 郭春梅. 1999. "Beiwei Wencheng di 'Nan xun bei' suo jian Tuoba zhiguan chutan" 北魏文成帝《南巡碑》所見拓跋職官初探, *Zhongguo shi yanjiu* 中國史研究 1999.2: 57–69.

—— and Li Biao 李彪. 1997. "Shanxi Lingqiu Bei Wei Wenchengdi 'Nan xun bei'" 山西靈丘北魏文成帝 '南巡碑', *Wenwu* 文物 12: 70–80.

Zhou shu 周書. Compiled by Linghu Defen 令狐德棻 (583–666). Beijing: Zhonghua shuju, 1971.

Zizhi tongjian 資治通鑒. By Sima Guang 司馬光 (1019–1086). Beijing: Zhonghua shuju, 1976.

The Inhabitants of Pingcheng (398–494):
An Archaeological Survey

Shing Müller

The displacement of peoples in northern China was never greater than after the fall of the Western Jin Dynasty in 316. A cold period setting in around the 270s–350s in East Asia prompted the migration of various peoples southward from the cold steppes in search of food and shelter.[1] These movements and the accompanying military confrontations brought the misgoverned Western Jin Dynasty to an end. The royal Sima family, along with other high officials and members of great families, as well as millions of commoners, fled across the Huai River and settled in southern China. Many others took flight to the northeast or northwest. A long period of chaos, with many ephemeral non-Chinese polities, known as "the Sixteen Kingdoms period," now began.[2] The results were massive migrations of refugees due to wars, crop failures, and famines, or forced relocations of captives. The relocations, especially, after each successful war of one kingdom against another, were politically and militarily motivated. The forced migrations culminated in the fifth century in a series of conquests of the remaining kingdoms by the Northern Wei Dynasty (386–534) of the Tuoba Xianbei 拓跋鮮卑.[3] The captive soldiers, members of the upper echelons and craftsmen of the defeated kingdoms as well as their families were deported to Pingcheng 平城 and its vicinity. Pingcheng, present-day Datong, was proclaimed in August 398 as the

---

1 For other records of environmental catastrophes see Liu Zhaomin 1994, 86–99; Zheng Jingyun 2005; Chin 2008. For specific studies of the movements of the non-Chinese groups see de Crespigny 1977; 1978; Tang Changru 1955, 382–450; Ma Changshou 1985; Miller 2015.

2 Holcombe 2019. Some scholars estimate that at least two million steppe people entered northern China while some three million people, i.e., one tenth of the northern population, fled south; see, for example, Lee 1978, 29. Andrew Chittick (2020, 77 and Appendix B), on the other hand, argues that only several hundred thousand people moved from the Central Plains to the south in the early fourth century. It is not the purpose of this paper to examine the scale of migration but only to emphasize the drastic depopulation of some northern regions and the rapid demographic changes that occurred as regards centers of resettlement. The fact that, after the fall of the Western Jin (316), burials in Luoyang and Henan dropped to a minimum and remained low until the fifth century speaks for an evacuation of the region. See below.

3 For an introduction to the history and culture of the Tuoba Xianbei and the Northern Wei Dynasty, see Dien 1991; Dien 2007a; Holcombe 2013: 15–34; Pearce 2019. The Early Medieval Chinese "Tuoba" (t^hakbat after Pulleyblank's reconstruction in idem. 1991, 314 and 27) may have pronounced something like *taɣβač or Taghbach. According to Shimunek (2017, xxvi, 52) and Beckwith (2005: 9), the commonly adopted Tabghatch in modern western literature derived from the metathesized form taβɣač given in the Old Turkic runic inscription found in Orchon. The transcription of Xianbei has been reconstructed as *särbi by Pulleyblank 1983, 453 (see further references there). Since this article if primarily about archaeological finds, I will adhere to the conventional transcriptions like Tuoba and Xianbei.

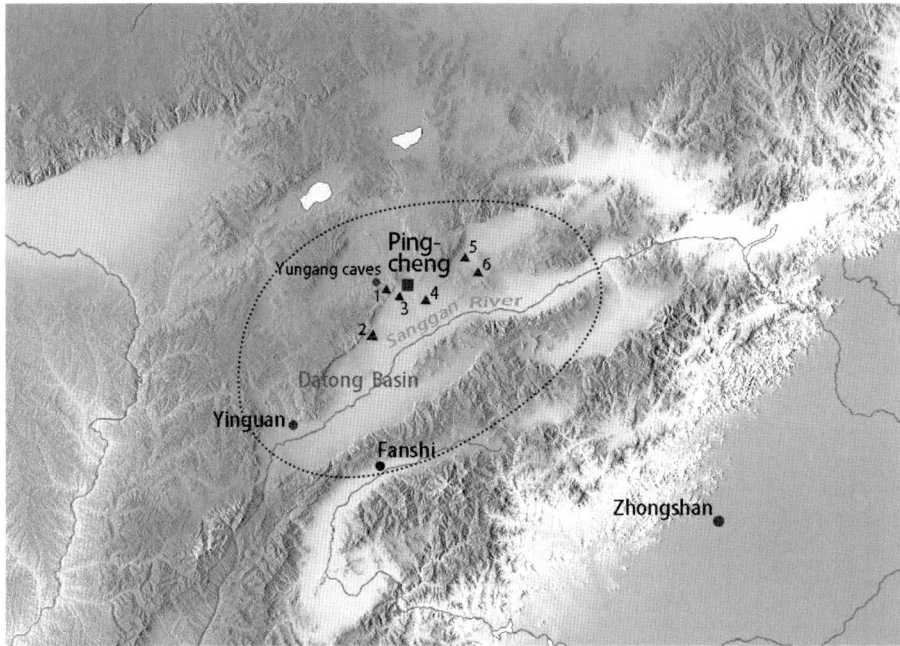

Figure 1 The Datong Basin of the upper Sanggan Valley. The dotted circle indicates the approximate area of the domain. The triangles are the tomb sites outside of the city limit: 1. Yungang Town 雲岡鎮, 2. Huairen 懷仁, 3. Tongjiawan 仝家灣, 4. Hudong 湖東 and Chenzhuang 陳莊, 5. Yanggao 陽高, 6. Xiashenjing 下深井.

capital (*jing* 京), and the Datong Basin on the upper Sanggan 桑乾 Valley was declared the imperial domain (*ji* 畿) of the young Northern Wei State (Fig. 1).[4]

Pingcheng County 平城縣 in the present-day Datong Basin was established at the beginning of the Western Han as a defense base against the Xiongnu. Directly below the Northern Wei stratum of relics, archaeologists have discovered thick strata datable to this Han period, with sherds of vessels, roof tiles, and eave ends (*wadang* 瓦當) imprinted with inscriptions such as Pingcheng 平城, as well as stone bases for pillars, coins, and ash pits. The findings demonstrate an enduring and intensive operation of this frontier outpost, as well as the fact that, after Han times, the site was not inhabited again, at least not by a sedentary population, until the Northern Wei.[5] During the third and fourth centuries, Ping-

---

4   *Wei shu* 110.2850: "(The domain reaches as far as the) Dai Commandery (Weixian 蔚縣, Hebei) in the east, Shanwu (Youyu 右玉, Shanxi) in the west, Yinguan (Shuozhou 朔州, Shanxi) in the south, and Canhe in the north (location uncertain, possibly present-day Yanggao 陽高, Shanxi)" 東至代郡, 西及善無, 南極陰館, 北盡參合. Cf. Sun Jingguo 2012: 25; Pearce 2019: 160–61. For the Sanggan River, the major upper course of the Lei River 灅水, see *Shuijing zhu* 13.1127–33.

5   Shanxi sheng et al. 2005: 486–88, 497–99; Shanxi and Datong 2016: 10–16.

cheng was not only in ruins but also probably had barely any remaining architecture. Construction of the Northern Wei capital did not begin on a larger scale until warfare to unify northern China ceased in 439. Even then, Pingcheng most likely still looked like "a huge refugee camp, periodically swelled by some new forced migration of conquered peoples."[6]

Pingcheng was built quickly.[7] The city planning was possibly modelled on Ye 鄴 of Cao Wei 曹魏 (220–265) and Shi Zhao 石趙 (319–351) times.[8] The walled wards (*fang* 坊) in the city for residents, arranged on grid patterns, later served as models for the planning of Luoyang and Chang'an of the Sui and Tang periods. This city planning also impressed contemporary visitors from the Southern Qi, who reported that large wards contained 400 to 500 households, and small ones 60 to 70.[9] The same source, however, does not mention the total number of wards. Shiozawa Hirohito suggests that the idea of ward arrangement originated with the manner of campsite formation typical of pastoralists. The encampment of the Mongols was, for example, organized according to tribal and social differences, and each unit was surrounded with fences or palisades—an arrangement in which we can perhaps recognize the basic idea of wards.[10]

In its heyday, the population in Pingcheng and its vicinity is said to have reached one million, and the wealthy households were vying with one another for larger and more splendid mansions.[11] Only shortly afterward, in the third quarter of the fifth century, Pingcheng again lost approximately half of its population to large-scale defections of tribesmen as well as to starvation and emigration caused by famines occasioned by several dramatically cold years.[12] Regardless, from 399 to the beginning of the 480s, the population of forced migrants who arrived in waves in Pingcheng and its vicinity ranged between 4,000 and 25,000, with the highest concentration occurring in the first half of the fifth century.[13] To summarize, the Pingcheng of the Tuoba Xianbei was rebuilt on the Han ruins. People from all different regions moved there during its history, which spans nearly one hundred years.

Those who were resettled in Pingcheng included tribesmen of the steppe in the north and the Ordos region (the Gaoju, the Rouran, and the Southern Xiongnu), the northeastern forest-steppe in southern Manchuria (the Murong and Koreans), western pastoralists in the Guan-Long region (present-day southern Shaanxi, Ningxia, and eastern Gansu), north-western city dwellers from Guzang 姑臧 (present-day Wuwei) or farther west, and, lastly, Chinese, such as the inhabitants of the Qing 青 and Qi 齊 commanderies of the Southern Qi state in the present-day Shandong area.

---

6 Soper made this disparaging remark (1960: 51) based on the pejorative description in *Nan Qi shu* 57.984.
7 The construction of Pingcheng based on written sources has been discussed often. One of the best such discussions is that of Jenner 1981, 18–37. For a nearly contemporary description of the imperial buildings in Pingcheng, see *Shuijing zhu* 13.1141–51.
8 Li Ping 2011, 355–56.
9 *Nan Qi shu* 57.985.
10 Shiozawa Hirohito 2007: 19–21.
11 Masana Maeda 1994, 78; *Wei shu* 60.1338: "北都富室，競以第宅相尚."
12 *Wei shu* 110, 2856; Masana Maeda 1994, 81–85; Sun Jingguo 2012: 29; Pearce 2019: 172, 175.
13 Jenner 1981, 19–20; Su Bai 1991, 177–78; Sun Jingguo 2012: 28 and Table 2; Pearce 2019: 164–68.

Where and how did these people live and how did they subsist? Only a few written sources provide information. Even less aboveground constructions of Pingcheng remain. The Qing scholar Yang Shoujing 楊守敬 reconstructed the city based on the Commentary on the Water Classics (*Shui jing zhu* 水經注) of Li Daoyuan 酈道元.[14] But the archaeological findings contradict his model. A recently unearthed palatial area, including a palace hall foundation and a granary, is believed to be positioned along the northern wall of the Inner City (*zhong cheng* 中城) but within the northern wall of the Outer City.[15] There are some hints in documents about an Inner City that was surrounded by bastions for use in emergencies such as sudden attacks from the steppe. The Ming city walls partially overlap the Inner City walls.[16] Since no tombs have been found to the north of Mingtang 明堂 to date, it is possible that this ritual building, the remains of which are located to the north of the present-day Southern Ring Road 南環路, was the southern limit of the Outer City (Fig. 2).[17] Remnants of the eastern outer city wall were located on the right bank of the Yu River, but no traces of the western wall survive. Shiozawa argues that during the early fifth century, the western area within the city limits, and possibly also outside it, was reserved as a camping ground for nomads, which was arranged in the ward system, mentioned above. According to his analysis, apart from the ritual space in the western suburb, written records do not indicate any imperial buildings or monasteries in this part of the city. He also refers to a record in the Book of Wei stating that "(as the Rouran army approached Pingcheng in 439, the commander) Mu Shou 穆壽 offered no other strategy than to build a West Gate." This, in Shiozawa's opinion, is a sign that the western wall was rather weakly constructed, if at all.[18]

The only available written information specifying the physical size of the city gives a circumference of 32 *li*, approximately 3.6 km on each side.[19] The total area can be calculated to roughly 13 km^2. If one million people were all living within the walled city, then each person, including the emperor, would have had an average living space of 13 m^2. But this calculation neglects the necessary constructions such as houses, ward walls, roads, markets, and even the imperial city itself. In fact, it is likely that a large part of Pingcheng's population lived in the suburbs.

In the fifth century, all of northern Shanxi, including the Datong Basin, was arid and cold, making the region more suitable for pastoral activities. Sun Jingguo proposes that Pingcheng was primarily inhabited by members of the Tuoba confederation and newly conquered pastoral tribes. In addition to their labor and services, the latter were also supposed to defend the imperial city against an attack from the north. According to Sun, written sources indicate that livestock breeding and hunting were the primary forms of subsistence economic activity in the northern Sanggan Valley.[20]

---

14 See Tseng 2013, 19–20.
15 Shanxi sheng et al. 2005; Shanxi and Datong 2016. Cao Chenming 2010; Wang Yintian 2008; Yin Xian 2012; Zhang Qingjie 2010.
16 Cf. Wang Jiang 2021: 59 and further references there.
17 Wang Yintian et al. 2001.
18 Shiozawa Hirohito 2007: 20–24. *Wei shu* 27.665.
19 *Wei shu* 3.62. The figures were given for the seventh year of the Taichang 泰常 period (422 CE) of Emperor Mingyuan 明元, Tuoba Si 拓跋嗣.
20 Sun Jingguo 2012: 28–32.

Agriculture was, however, practiced as well, both by semi-pastoralists and sedentary people. In the early days, the most important domestic policy measure was the allocation of land to individuals. This was then succeeded by the "equal field" system.[21] The suitable region was the fertile southern Sanggan valley. Many agro-pastoralists settled there from the outset. An agricultural zone lay further south with Fanshi 繁畤 (close to present-day Xinzhou 忻州) as center. After Tuoba Gui 拓跋珪 defeated the Later Yan kingdom in February 398, "360,000 commoners and clerks (*min li* 民吏) from the six prefectures east of the [Taihang] Range (山東六州), various barbarians (雜夷) such as the Tuhe 徒何 and the Koreans 高麗, as well as 100,000 artisans, were relocated to fill the capital 京."[22] Since Pingcheng was proclaimed the capital six months later, Li Ping concludes that the famous relocation was not intended to repopulate Pingcheng but rather Fanshi.[23] In 469, the "conquered people from Qi (present-day Shandong)" 平齊民 of the Liu Song Dynasty were moved to Yinguan 陰館 (Fig. 1). The records indicate that a considerable number of the subjects of the Eastern Jin and Southern Dynasties were settled in the domain and other fertile regions of northern China. The final large-scale relocation was reported in 481, following the Tuoba's victory over the Southern Qi. This is the only account of southern Chinese captives being brought directly to Pingcheng City.[24]

If the southern part of the domain was densely populated in the fifth century, as suggested by written sources, this is not reflected in the archaeology. One explanation is that areas outside of the modern city of Datong have only been occasionally archaeologically investigated. Another issue is the dating of the findings, which will be examined further below.

The brief review above demonstrates the demographic wax and wane, the diverse cultural and regional origins of the immigrants, and the likely changes in ethnic compositions of Pingcheng.[25] The large-scale fifth-century cemeteries (Fig. 2) vividly illustrate the fact that the city was once densely populated. The archaeological findings further confirm the complexity of the material remains in Pingcheng. However, the predominant consensus in archaeological studies today is that most of the city's inhabitants were of the Tuoba Xianbei, who were, in the opinion of archaeologists, a homogeneous human group with a common descent, language, and culture, as well as common anthropological characteristics. Discussions generally focus on the assimilation of *the* Tuoba Xianbei into Chinese culture. A notion of linear development serves here as a guideline: The Tuoba, it is argued, picked up cultural elements directly from their Chinese subjects in Pingcheng, from the contemporary Southern Dynasties ruled by Chinese, or, less directly, from the people of Hexi

---

21 Su Bai 1991, 177, Table 2, Entry 413 CE. Xiong 2019, 312–14.

22 *Wei shu* 2.32. The passage is far from clear. The same event is mentioned again in *Wei shu* 110.2849–50, where "more than 100,000 families" 十萬餘家 is given for the relocated persons from the east of the Range, the Tuhe and the artisans together. Assuming there were four to five persons in each family, altogether some four to five hundred thousand people were moved to the domain at this time. The transliteration here follows the *Zizhi tongjian* 110.3463 as cited in the collation notes (*jiaokan ji* 校勘記) of the *Wei shu* 2.46–47, note 9.

23 Li Ping 2011, 48–49; Sun Jingguo 2012, 27–28. *Zizhi tongjian* 110.3463 speaks only of "to Dai."

24 Su Bai 1991, 178; Holcombe 2013, 19–20.

25 Zhang 2018, 31–38.

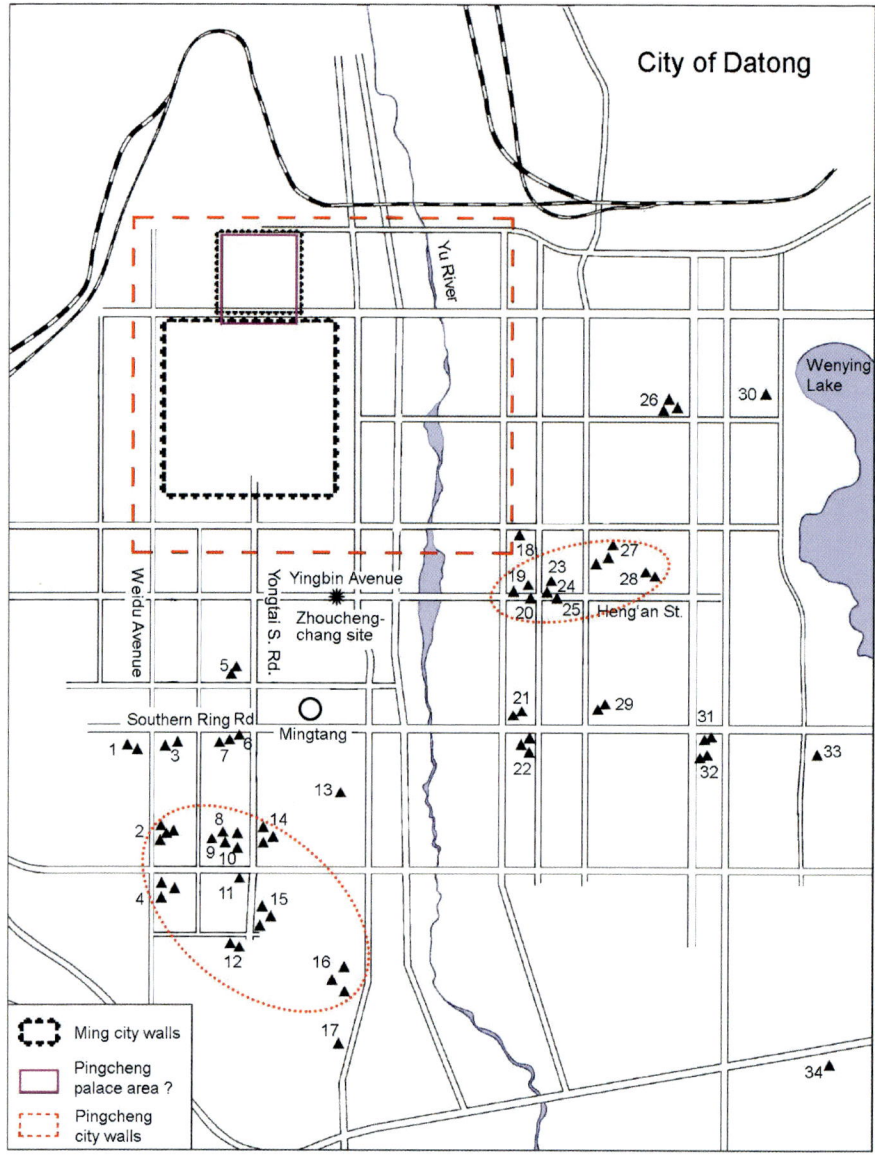

(present-day western Gansu) or present-day Liaoning, where Chinese culture was well preserved.[26] This cultural transformation toward "Chineseness," brought about by the reforms of the sinophile Emperor Xiaowen 孝文帝 (467–499) and his foster grandmother Empress Dowager Wenming 文明太后 (441–490), is considered to be archaeologically tangible, as evidenced by the use of south-oriented square-chambered brick tombs furnished with figurines (see below). In contrast, Wei Zheng and Cui Jiabao conclude in their survey that each graveyard in Pingcheng displayed its own distinct burial character. Thus, Wei and Cui acknowledge that Pingcheng was inhabited by various ethnic groups, and they imply that residents with similar cultural backgrounds were inclined to be interred in their own respective territories.[27] In any case, this view that Pingcheng's population was perpetually diverse, is clearly a minority view among archaeologists.

As historians have frequently discussed, a simple process of "Sinicization" proves problematic. This is also true for the "Sinicization" issue in archaeological studies since material remains have only been selectively evaluated. It is equally misleading to refer to the "non-Chinese" components of the Pingcheng findings as those of the "Xianbei" or "Tuoba," as this leaves their archaeological remains unrecognized. The process, therefore, constructs an archaeological "super Xianbei" human group that most likely did not exist. Recent Western studies on Pingcheng cultures have, consequently, redirected their focus

◀ **Figure 2** Conjectural city limits of Pingcheng (broken magenta line) and the position of the palace area (solid pink line). The triangles are tomb sites within the present-day city limit. 1. Jinniu Building Center 金牛建材園 cemetery; 2. Electric Welding Factory (Dianhan-chang 電焊廠) cemetery; 3. Yunboli cemeteries 雲波里 (including Yunbo Street 雲波路 cemetery and Huayu Building Plot 華宇工地 cemetery); 4. New Southern Station 新南站 cemetery; 5. Jinmao Garden Estate 金茂園 cemetery; 6. Hongqi Estate Lot 51 紅旗街 51 地塊 cemetery; 7. Xinwang Estate 新旺 cemetery; 8. Dongxin Square Estate 東信廣場 cemetery; 9. Jingang Estate Garden 金港園 cemetery; 10. Chemical Fiber Factory 化纖廠 cemetery; 11. Jiaotong Estate Garden 交通苑 cemetery; 12. Second Electric Powerplant 二電廠 cemetery; 13. Liuquan South Street 柳泉南街 cemetery; 14. Magnesium Plant 金屬鎂廠 cemetery; 15. Qilicun 七里村 cemeteries (including 2001 and 2020 excavations and Biguiyuan 碧桂園 cemetery); 16. Zhijiabao 智家堡 cemetery (1997 and 2001 excavations); 17. Tiancun 田村 tomb; 18. Qijiapo 齊家坡 tomb; 19. Tanghua City Estate 唐華城 cemetery; 20. Yingbin Avenue 迎賓大道 cemetery; 21. Bolanjun Estate 鉑藍郡 cemetery; 22. Shaling 沙嶺 cemetery; 23. Yudong Police station 御東公安局, tomb of Zhang Zhilang 張智朗; 24. Yuchang Fine Housing 御昌佳園 cemetery (including Heng'anjie 恆安街 M13); 25. Shubo Temple 水泊寺 cemetery; 26. Yanbei Teacher's College 雁北師院 cemetery; 27. Yufu 御府 cemetery; 28. Yuecheng Dijing Estate 悅城帝景 cemetery; 29. Shaling Building Supplies Market 沙嶺建材市場 cemetery (including Yulong City Estate 御龍城 projects I–III); 30. Wenyinglu 文瀛路 tomb; 31. Xinggang City Estate 星港城 cemetery; 32. Yudong New District Estate 御東新區 cemetery (only Jia Bao's 賈寶 tomb is reported); 33. Shijiazhai 石家寨, tomb of Sima Jinlong 司馬金龍; 34. Xiaonantou Village 小南頭村, tombs of Yuan Shu 元淑 and Gao Kun 高琨.
Map redrawn from Cao Chenming 2016: 62, Fig. 1.

---

26 See, for example, Lin Sheng-chih 2008, 2019; Mukai Yusuke 2010; Ni Run'an 2011a; 2011b; 2014; 2016; 2017, especially chapter 4; Wei Zheng 2017; 2019; Wang Yanqing 2006; Zhang Feng 2015.
27 Wei Zheng and Cui Jiabao 2020.

onto cultural interactions between ethnic groups and onto the identity-finding of these latter at different levels due to inter-ethnic communications.[28]

The Xianbei were a steppe confederation in which only the core members stayed stable, while the majority of members, generally the subjugated tribesmen, remained only for a brief time before breaking away again.[29] The same was also true of the Tuoba, who emerged as a strong regional power during the third century.[30] Thus, the appellation Tuoba—and this is true, on a higher level, of the Xianbei—does not promise a consistent and homogeneous human and cultural constitution. Even though the first inhabitants of Pingcheng were members of the Tuoba confederation, they nonetheless had diverse and distinct cultural backgrounds. In addition, historical records, as demonstrated above, clearly indicate that the human components of Pingcheng were exceedingly complex as a result of several forced migrations and varied from time to time, depending on their influx and outflow. Thus, the Pingcheng burials should be explored from a different angle than they have hitherto been: Instead of asking how Chinese culture and which specific regional Chinese culture influenced *the* Tuoba members, this paper examines the grave deposits, burial architecture, and pictorial materials in tombs. Tomb furnishings and grave goods are the outcomes of ritual acts that demonstrate how an individual would like to be perceived within his own group (self-distinction) or in a larger community (a collective identity). If this method produces meaningful results, it is possible to provide a rough picture of the cultural groups in Pingcheng based on their material cultures, and, as a result, detect changes in mortuary customs over time.

In order to do this, it is necessary to obtain a more detailed periodization of the Pingcheng burials than is currently available. The dating of fifth-century Datong burials by excavators is, in most cases, unsatisfactory. In most cases, a tomb will be dated "between the founding of Pingcheng (398) and the move to Luoyang (493)," i.e., the entire Pingcheng period.

This paper starts with the classification of the Pingcheng tombs into five periods, using only those with sufficient information for an evaluation. Based on this periodization, the mortuary customs and their changes over time are discussed. The second section of the paper examines some specific features of Pingcheng burials and their use to convey the identities of interred individuals. The emphasis is on tomb paintings and clay figurines, which provide more information through their iconography and spatial configuration than individual grave goods. Topics of interest include artistic themes that reveal regional or cultural backgrounds or demonstrate the (desired) social standing of the deceased. As identity is not static and can adapt in response to changing social contexts or undergo modifications over time, this paper also tracks some individual cases to observe how cultures blended, and new identities emerged. Although the available data are insufficient to assess gender issues, individual burials do provide some fragmentary information about

---

28 See, for example, Tseng 2013 and Zhang 2018.

29 Core members are defined by their proximity to the (constructed) main lineage. For the heterogeneous nature of the steppe organizations in the pre-Mongol period see Golden 2018, 317–20, 324–27; for the structure of the Xianbei and the complexity of the member components see Kradin 2010, 323–31.

30 Tuoba Shamo Han 拓跋沙漠汗 (possibly: Shamo Khan of the Tuoba), was the first person whose name carried the prefix "Tuoba." See *Zizhi tongjian* 77.2459–60 for the year of 261.

the different social positions of women in Pingcheng, which will be briefly discussed at the end of this section.

Current studies on the Pingcheng burials tend to focus on "attractive" findings, such as those with murals, figurines, funerary beds or houses inside tomb chambers, or inscriptions. Although the majority of finds are the simple earthen tombs, they have not received the attention they deserve in research. One of the main reasons is that most excavation data on earthen tombs are not published. As a result, we are still unable to gain a clear picture of Pingcheng's society with all its complexity. To avoid a one-sided presentation of the material remains in Pingcheng, this paper attempts to take into account the very few reports of simple earthen burials. However, a large part of the analysis still relies on the "attractive" findings, simply because they are better documented.

Considering that most of the inhabitants in Pingcheng were migrants or their descendants, it is often surprising to observe how quickly these peoples adapted to a new and ever-changing living environment without the support of their familiar surroundings and items of practical use.[31] They maintained their traditional customs and incorporated elements from other cultures encountered in Pingcheng. Moreover, they developed a collective identity and created, through imitation and modification new materials, forms, patterns, and techniques that were distinctively Pingcheng. Excavations in Datong over the past two decades have unearthed surprising materials that regularly challenge our existing picture of this "barbarian capital" between steppe and agrarian zones. This study aims to provide a more current understanding of Pingcheng's material culture, and it is certainly not the last.

Finds in fifth-century Datong

Of the excavated fifth-century burials in Northern China, those from Shanxi make up the lion's share, with those in Datong and its vicinity accounting for 99% of the Shanxi burials. When only those reported or briefly mentioned tombs are considered, burials in Shanxi jumped from 3 (reported) in the fourth century to 296 in the fifth century (Fig. 3).[32]

The graphic depicts merely a trend throughout the third, fourth, and fifth centuries, but it illustrates the sudden growth that must have been caused by migrations. One should be cautious about drawing any very firm conclusions from the tomb numbers since too many burials were discovered but not published or, in certain cases, problematically dated. For example, the number of fourth- and fifth-century burials in Hebei, northern China's key agricultural region, is so low that it is possible that the figure does not reflect reality. Two

---

31 Robin Fleming (2021) examined the aftermath of the economic, political, and material dislocation in Roman Britain during 400 CE, as well as the following restructuring of a new material culture in depth. Her description of the "fundamental changes in the structure of everyday life" (ibid., 6) that the peoples of Roman Britain had experienced is equally applicable to the human beings who were relocated to Pingcheng.

32 Data collection ends in January 2023. The figures given in Fig 3 only apply to tombs that can be dated with confidence. When, for example, some 200 "Wei-Jin" tombs were excavated from a site, but only data of thirteen tombs were published and five of thirteen could be securely dated to Western Jin times, only five will be counted.

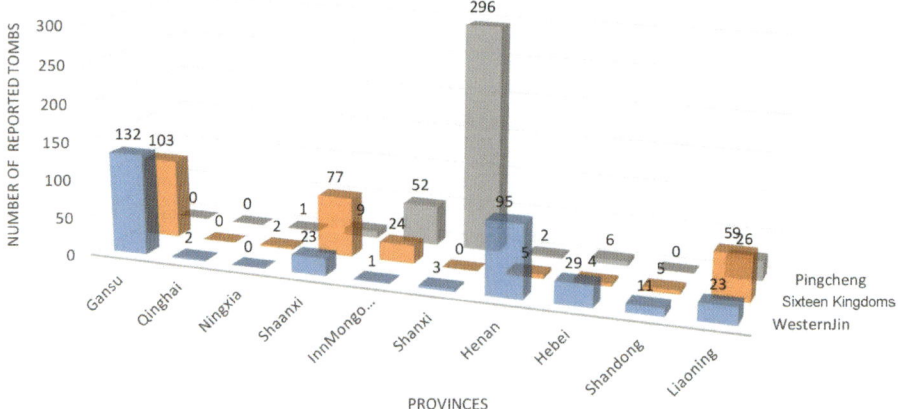

Figure 3 Numbers of excavated northern tombs of the Western Jin, Sixteen Kingdoms (ca. fourth century) and Pingcheng Periods (398–493); data collected until January 2023.

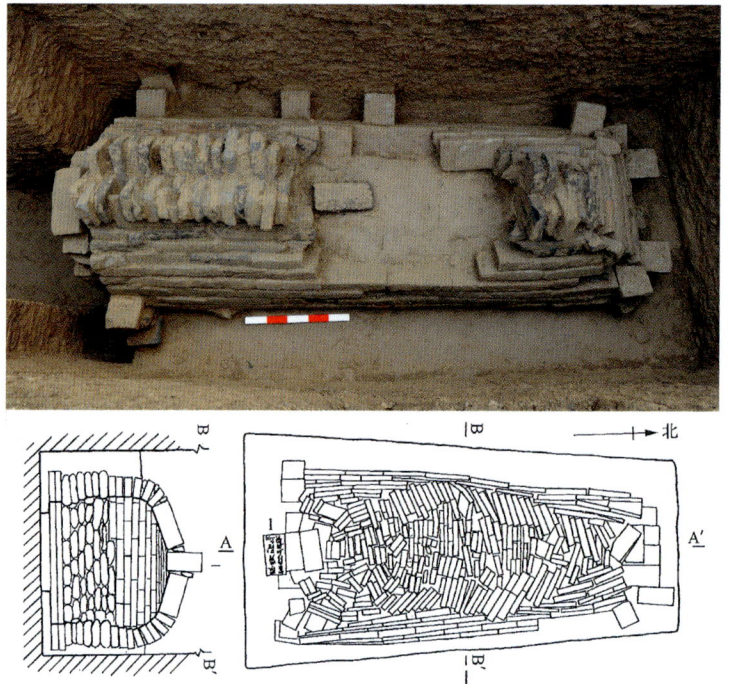

Figure 4 Western Jin tomb M13 in Fangshan (*above*) and Northern Wei tomb (dated 469) in Yan-shang (*below*), both in Beijing. *After Beijing shi 2017: 9, Fig. 11 and Li Weimin 2012, 174, Fig. 41. Courtesy of the Chinese Academy of Cultural Heritage.*

brick inscriptions carrying dates from the Pingcheng period (Fig. 4) demonstrate that some of the "typical Western Jin" burials with a simple brick chamber and a barrel vault in northern Hebei may have been dated too early.[33] The example also suggests that some fifth-century tombs in Hebei retained, more or less, the legacy of the previous Western Jin Dynasty and thus did not conform to the contemporaneous mortuary customs in Pingcheng, and that many "Western Jin tombs" in that region should be re-evaluated.[34]

Currently, over thirty cemeteries with an aggregate of nearly 3,000 tombs in and around Datong are known; almost two-thirds are found in the southern area (Fig. 2).[35] Until now, only two graveyards have been reported on in detail: the *Datong nanjiao Bei Wei muqun* 大同南郊北魏墓群 (hereinafter *Datong nanjiao*) and the *Datong Yanbei shiyuan Bei Wei muqun* 大同雁北師院北魏墓群 (hereinafter *Yanbei shiyuan*).[36] The *Datong nanjiao* contains results bearing on the 167 tombs found in 1988 in a graveyard in the compound of what was then an electric welding factory (hereinafter Dianhanchang 電焊廠) south of Datong, and the *Yanbei shiyuan* results bearing on 11 tombs found in 2000 at the site of the Yanbei shiyuan (Yanbei Normal College, now Datong University of Shanxi) east of the Yu River 御河. In several other cemeteries, only certain individual graves have been fully described. Exceptional or representative features or artifacts are exemplified, but often without archaeological contexts. The data bearing on the burials are thus extremely fragmentary.

Until now, only the *Datong nanjiao* authors have worked out a periodization of the Pingcheng tombs based on ceramic chrono-typology and other dating criteria.[37] These criteria have been validated by experts such as Mukai Yusuke by comparing them with finds with dates from recent excavations. Other scholars, on the other hand, have criticized them.[38] The ceramic sequence generated by the authors of the *Datong nanjiao* is divided into five periods, defined in political-historical terms:

---

33 Li Weimin 2012, 174–75.

34 For more "Western Jin" graves, see Beijing shi 2017. Many of them contain typical Xianbei trapezoidal coffins and should probably be dated slightly later than the Western Jin period. Similar graves persisted in Hebei even into the early six century, see Beijing shi and Yanqing xian 2012: 26–29.

35 Six master theses and one doctoral dissertation on analyses of human skeletal remains from recently excavated but not reported large Northern Wei graveyards in Datong mention the size of each cemetery that is otherwise not available: Dongxin (> 1000 tombs, Fig. 2, no. 8), Huayu (70 tombs, Fig. 2, no.3), Jingangyuan (90 tombs, Fig. 2, no. 9), Jinmaoyuan (67 tombs, Fig. 2, no. 5), Shuibosi (118 tombs, Fig. 2, no. 25), Xinggangcheng (42 tombs, Fig. 2, no. 31), Yuchang jiayuan (135 tombs, Fig. 2, no. 24), and Yufu (> 70 tombs, Fig. 2, no. 27). See Li Pengcheng 2018, Fan Xin 2020, Cui Hexun 2021, Li Jiaxin 2021, Li Pengzhen 2021, Wang Yu 2021, and Ruansun Zifeng 2022. Other cemeteries are partially reported: Biguiyuan (> 600 tombs, Fig. 2, no. 15), Tongjiawan (58 tombs, Fig. 1, no. 3), Qilicun (including the 2001 campaign with 34 tombs and the 2020 campaign with 86 tombs, Fig. 2, no. 15), Shaling xincun (26 tombs, Fig. 2, no. 22), Shaling jiancai shichang (13 tombs, Fig. 2, no. 29), Yanbei shiyuan (c. 100 tombs, Fig. 2, no. 26), Yudong xinqu (44 tombs, Fig. 2, no. 15), Yunbolu (29 tombs, Fig. 2, no. 3), Zhijiabao (of the 2021 campaign with 67 tombs, Fig. 2, no. 16). Several cemeteries, such as Nos. 1, 4, 10 and 13 in Fig. 2, are only mentioned in the map provided in Cao Chenming 2016 (p. 62).

36 Shanxi daxue et al. 2006; Liu Junxi 2008.

37 (1) Tomb shapes and their orientations; (2) Tomb stratigraphy; (3) Grave-goods assemblage; (4) Styles of the decorative motifs, such as clouds and half-palmette scrolls. Shanxi daxue et al. 2006, 435–71.

38 Mukai Yusuke (2010: 139, 143) agrees with the chrono-typology of the ceramics between Periods II and IV. Wei Zheng 2011 proposes a new periodization of the Dianhanchang tombs. Some of his criteria cannot be proven. Wei's dating is not widely accepted. Cf. the critique by Ni Run'an 2017, 136–38.

Period I: before 398 (i.e., before Pingcheng was proclaimed capital),[39]

Period II: 398–439 (i.e., from the founding of Pingcheng as capital to the unification of Northern China),

Period III: 440–476 (i.e., from the unification of Northern China to the death of Emperor Xianwen),

Period IV: 477–493 (from the beginning of the Taihe era to the abandonment of Pingcheng and the move to the new capital Luoyang),[40]

Period V: after 493.

Mukai Yusuke concludes that there was a specific local development in the style and decoration of Pingcheng ceramics and that the ceramic sequence derived from the Dianhanchang burials may serve as a relatively objective standard for all Pingcheng burials. I therefore compared the ceramics of as many undated tombs as possible with the sequence table of the *Datong nanjiao* and classified them into the five periods listed above. This method indeed has numerous shortcomings; the most obvious of which is that not all vessels in a tomb were produced at the time of the burial, and some may be much older. Ceramics, on the other hand, are the only available and, to a certain extent, reliable materials from the Pingcheng finds that can be used for rough dating. As previously stated, the information bearing on numerous burials is either incomplete or unavailable, and many tombs have been severely looted. My chronological attribution (Appendix I) is only provisional and will certainly be challenged by future studies.

The burial sites in present-day Datong (Figs. 1–2) stretched, as mentioned above, from south of Mingtang and east of the Yu River to a vast southeast area. The reason for the lack of burials in the old Datong city area, in its north as well as its west, is not clear. According to the Book of Wei (*Wei shu*), Tuoba Dao 拓跋燾 (Emperor Taiwu) prohibited burials within the city in 445,[41] implying that Pingcheng's inhabitants could bury their dead within the city walls in periods prior to this imperial interdiction. Current archaeological surveys have not yet detected burials in this area (roughly the old Datong city). Likewise, the area west of Pingcheng is nearly free of burials.[42] Only individual tombs of the very late or post-Pingcheng period have been found at the Xiaozhan Village 小站村 or west of it.[43] The imperial ritual space for the Sky Sacrifice and the camping ground for nomads suggested by Shiozawa may be responsible for this phenomenon. In any case, future excavations may offer new insights into the subject.

---

39 368, as given in Shanxi daxue et al. 2006, 472, is presumably a typo of 398, the year when Pingcheng became capital.

40 The authors in Shanxi daxue et al. 2006, 472 give 496 as the year for the move of the capital to Luoyang, which was actually 493.

41 *Wei shu* 114.3033; Cao Chenming 2016: 65.

42 Cao Chenming 2016: 64.

43 For example, the tomb of Fenghetu 封和突 (501) and several tombs in the mountainous area, Ma Yuji 1983; Datong bowu 2019b.

Several recent studies examining the forensic aspects of human skeletal remains provide estimates of age at death, stature, and body mass, as well as information on bone and dental diseases.[44] Most of the samples were taken from pit and catacomb tombs. The sex ratio is 1:1.06 (male/female); the average height of the individuals found in these burials varies between 164 and 170 cm for males and between 152 and 157.5 cm for females; the average body weight was between 65 and 68 kg for males and between 51 and 58.6 kg for females; and the average age at death ranges from 29.32 to 36.77 for males and 27.47 to 33.30 for females. What is more interesting is the observation that there were very few bone injuries due to violence. Most of the bone fractures were healed and were not directly responsible for death.[45]

Tomb typology, interior decoration, and orientation

Chinese archaeologists have worked out a detailed tomb typology based on the Dianhanchang burials according to the construction and materials involved. There are five major types, and two of which have additional three and four subtypes. This typology can be applied to all the excavated Pingcheng tombs. For the purposes of this paper, a slightly modified list of six major types will be sufficient to describe the findings.[46] Four of these, i.e., burial pits (竪穴土坑墓), catacomb tombs with a trapezoidal or rectangular chamber (帶墓道窄室土洞墓),[47] earthen-chambered tombs with a square chamber (長斜坡方形墓室土洞墓) and brick-chambered tombs (長斜坡墓道磚室墓) are most common (Figs. 5.1–2, 4–5). Additionally, there are a few of the "cleaver/knife-shaped" tombs (刀把型墓) and double-chambered tombs of bricks with long dromoi (長斜坡墓道磚雙室墓). A "cleaver/knife-shaped" tomb is similarly constructed as a catacomb tomb, but with a ramp and an entrance placed laterally. Its floorplan recalls the shape of a knife (Fig. 5.3). The knife-shaped and the catacomb tombs generally display different grave orientations and grave-good assemblages. They are treated, in this paper, as types in their own right. Both catacomb and knife-shaped tombs are simply constructed. The chambers are mostly less spacious and do not contain any built-in structures. Only in one case have we found a brick-built funerary bed in a knife-shaped tomb. Several catacomb tombs contain a niche on a side wall close to the entrance of the chamber. These were used for placing offerings of food and drinks, and sometimes a lamp as well. The difference between a catacomb and an earthen-chambered tomb is sometimes minimal. The latter is commonly equipped with an entrance corridor (甬道) and has a square or nearly square chamber. A small subgroup of

---

44 Cui Hexun 2021, for the Huayu site.

45 This is a summary from the following studies. As mentioned above, the archaeological data of the sites are not yet published. Li Pengcheng 2018 (Shuibosi); Fan Xin 2020 (Jingangyuan site); Cui Hexun 2021 (Huayu site); Li Jiaxin 2021 (Yufu site); Li Pengzhen 2021 (Dongxin site); Wang Yu 2021 (Jinmaoyuan site); Ruansun Zifeng 2022 (Yuchang site).

46 One tomb type consisting of an earthen chamber placed laterally to a vertical entry shaft (竪井墓道橫穴土洞墓) has been listed as a major category as well in Shanxi daxue et al. 2006, 6. So far, however, this has only been reported once in Datong. Therefore, this type will not be discussed in the present paper.

47 The catacomb tomb type contains two subtypes: one has a long sloping ramp (長斜坡墓道), the other has a vertical entrance shaft leading to the ground surface (竪穴墓道). Since the available data do not yield any difference in burial practices between both subtypes. I will not treat them separately.

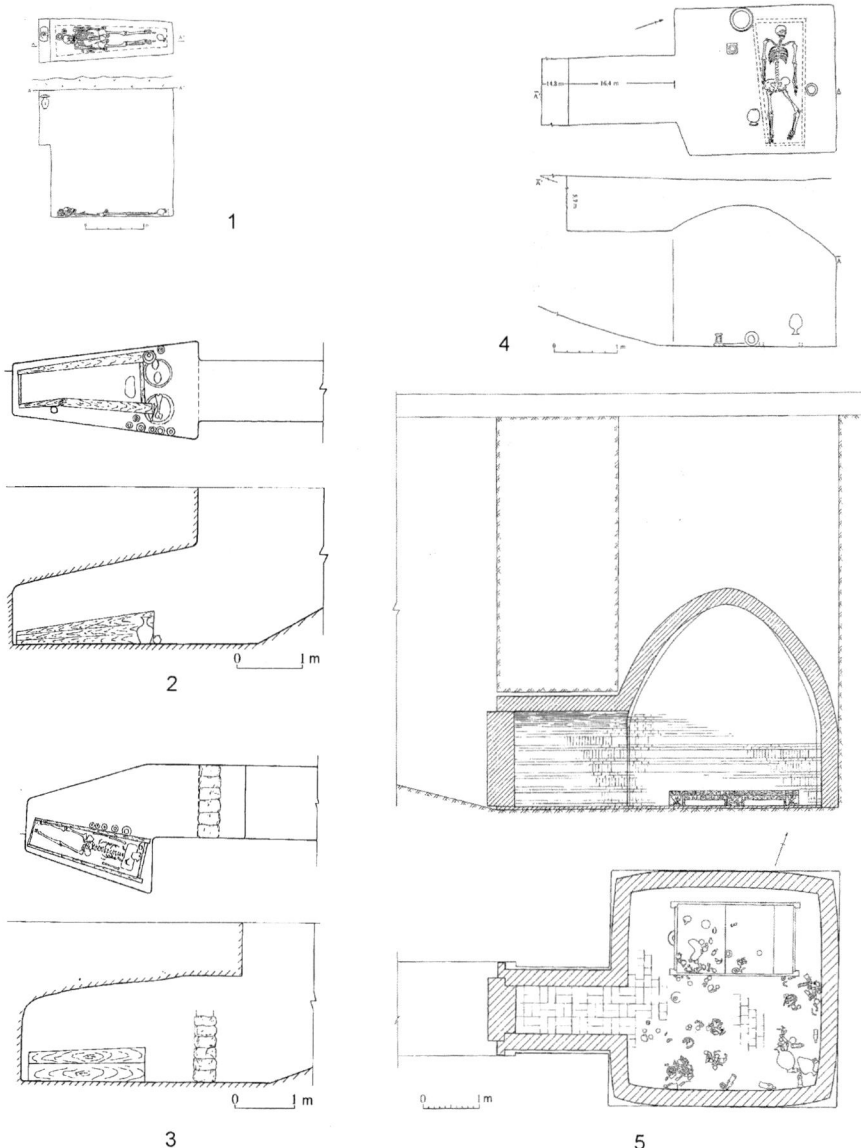

Figure 5 Tomb types in Pingcheng. (1) earthen pit; (2) earthen catacomb tomb; (3) "knife-shaped" earthen catacomb tomb; (4) earthen-chambered tomb; (5) brick-chambered tomb.

Figures adopted from: (1, 4): Shanxi daxue et al. 2006, 12, Fig. 7A and 346, Fig. 145A; (2–3): Datong kaogu 2006a: 26, Fig. 2–3; (5) Datong kaogu 2010: 2, Fig. 2. With permission of the Datong Archaeological Institute.

the earthen-chambered tombs have a chamber that is barely larger than its content: a stone funerary house. At least five of the eight stone funerary houses were discovered in this subtype, all of which can be dated or assigned to Period III. Another three or more (of stone or wood) are found in brick chamber tombs (one can be dated to Period III and two to Period IV, with the rest revealing little information helpful to dating). Therefore, the presence of a funerary house is not decisive for establishing a tomb type.

Most brick tombs are single-chambered, with only a few featuring a side chamber. Six brick tombs have two or more chambers. They were basically built using the same technique as the single-chambered brick tombs but are much larger.[48] Some had very long dromoi.[49] A medium-sized tomb such as Tongjiawan 仝家灣 M7 (L/W/H 3.62/3.66/3.48 m) was built with 4759 bricks. The mausoleum Yongguling 永固陵 of Empress Dowager Wenming was built with estimated 200,000 bricks (the walls were 1.30 m thick) and the tomb of Sima Jinlong with 50,000.[50] The bricks of the latter two tombs, as well as those of the tomb of the Prince of Danyang, were custom-made, which explains, in addition to the great wealth involved, their extraordinary status. Thus, I have treated the tombs with two or more chambers as a category of their own. Table 1 lists the number of Pingcheng burials that can be periodized. These are also the burials that are used for the analysis in this study.

Table 1 Pingcheng burials according to their architecture and period

Period / Tomb types	I (pre-398)	II (399-439)	III (440-476)	IV (477-493)	V (post-493)	Un-datable	Total
Pits	-	5	2	4	-	(10)	11
Catacomb	3	31	58	40	8	(24)	140
Knife-shaped	-	1	14	11	2	(9)	28
(w/ a funerary bed)	-	-	-	-	-	*(1)*	*1*
Earthen, square-chambered	-	-	12	4	1	(5)	17
(w/ a funerary bed)	-	-	-	-	-	*(1)*	*1*
(w/ a funerary house)	-	-	*5*	-	-	-	*5*
Brick, single-chambered	-	5	9	26	10	(16)	50
(w/ a funerary bed)	-	-	*1*	*6*	-	-	*7*
(w/ a funerary house)	-	-	*1*	*2*	-	*(2)*	*3*
(w/ a side-chamber)	-	-	-	*5*	-	*(1)*	*5*
Brick, 2 or more chambered	-	-	1	4	1	-	6
Total	3	42	96	89	22	(64)	252

(n): number of undatable tombs; italics: number of the subtypes

---

48 The floor area of the tomb chambers of Sima Jinglong is about 65 m², that of Yongguling about 59 m², and that of the Prince of Danyang about 140 m² (these estimates do not include the areas of the corridors); Huairen xian 2010: 19–21, Wang Yintian 2010: 47.
49 The longest dromos of a Pingcheng tomb measures 28.1 m (Sima Jinlong's tomb, Shanxi and Shanxi 1972: 20). The longest dromos thus far measured (39.25 m) is that of the Lincheng tomb in present-day Hebei (Hebei and Lincheng 2001). Both of Period IV.
50 Datong and Shanxi 1978: 30; Shanxi and Shanxi 1972: 10; Shanxi and Datong 2015: 5.

It is worth noting that the Xianbei tombs of Han times, such as those found in the Hulun Buir region, were typically earthen pits, whereas catacomb tombs were widespread from the second century onwards in southern Inner Mongolia, in the region once considered to be the territories of the Southern Xiongnu.[51] In my data collection, of the 252 datable Pingcheng tombs or those that can be attributed to a period, earthen pits make up only a small proportion, while catacomb tombs form the majority throughout the entire Pingcheng period. The number of brick tombs greatly increased during Period IV. Although brick-chambered tombs are considered to represent an advanced form of sepulchral architecture, they emerged rather early (Period II). Square earthen chamber tombs, on the other hand, occurred mainly in Period III, while knife-shaped tombs in Periods III and IV.[52] Both types declined drastically after Pingcheng was no longer the capital.

Knife-shaped tombs were not observed in the northern China plain before the Northern Wei period. From the fifth century onwards, this tomb type gradually became established, especially in the northern and northwest regions. In fact, between the first century BCE and the first or second century CE, knife-shaped tombs with a short entrance ramp leading to the corner of a large rectangular tomb pit are observed in the Tarim oases, for example, at Sampula 山普拉 near Khotan, or at Zhaghunluk 扎滾魯克 near Jumo 且末. During the Sixteen Kingdoms period, they are also evidenced in the Dunhuang region, for example, in Qijiawan 祁家灣.[53] However, most of these were multiple burials accommodating many bodies and cannot be considered direct forerunners of the knife-shaped graves in Pingcheng. Single or multiple burials in tombs of similar shapes of the "Kangju" (K'ang-chü) people with laterally placed ramps dated from the first to the fourth century CE were sighted in southern Kazakhstan and the Tashkent region.[54] The relationship between the earlier "knife-shaped" tombs and those in Pingcheng needs to be further studied.

Most earthen and brick-chambered tombs have a square or slightly elongated floor plan. Many brick-chambered tombs have lightly bulging walls. Most tomb ceilings had been destroyed by the time they were excavated. The few preserved ceilings indicate that most brick-chambered tombs had a corbelled cloister vault (疊澀四角攢尖頂). Very few were built with a "true" vault.[55] Only two tombs in Yanggao 陽高, east of present-day Datong, have "fan-like" vaults (四隅券進式穹隆頂), which are otherwise only found in the south (Fig. 6).[56] This may indicate that specialized southern Chinese brick masons were active in the greater Pingcheng area, particularly in the Yanggao region.[57] Domed ceilings do not yet occur in Pingcheng, but do so later in the City of Ye of Northern Qi times.

---

51 See, for example, Wu Songyan 2012.
52 For an earlier study of the burials during the Pingheng period, i.e., including burials in other regions, see Mukai Yusuke 2010.
53 Dai Chunyang and Zhang Long 1994, 48–52.
54 Zadneprovskiy 1994, 462 Fig. 4.
55 For example, the tomb chambers of Sima Jinlong (484). Shanxi and Shanxi 1972: 20.
56 Similar to the "squinch vaults." There are four vault springers, i.e., the initial stone of an arch, at the four upper corners of the chamber walls. From the vault springers there are masoned four "fan-like" arches, which meet one another in the middle lines of the four arched ceiling panels. This is attested to for Tongjiawan M7 (Period II; Shanxi and Datong 2015: 4–5) and for the tomb of Yuchi Dingzhou's wife (457, Period III; Datong kaogu 2011c). Appendix I, Nos. 17, 18, 21. See Fig. 1, nos. 3 and 5 for the sites. For the distribution in China, Xu Yongli 2018, 44–52.
57 Wei Zheng and Cui Jiabao 2020: 138.

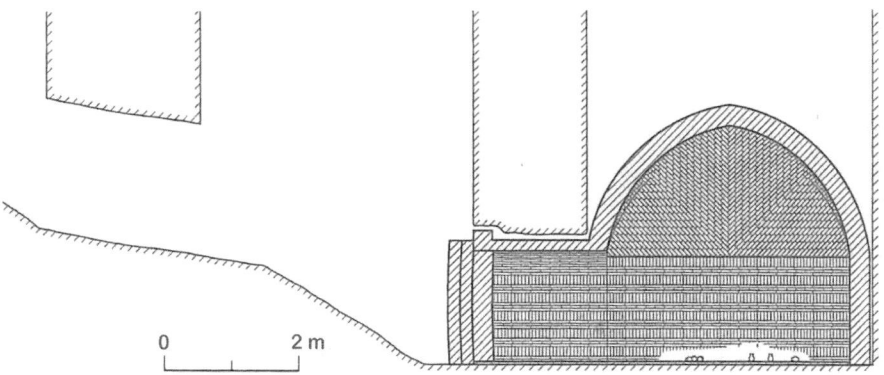

0   2 m

Figure 6 A "fan-like" vault, Tongjiawan M7.
After Shanxi and Datong 2015: 5, Fig. 2. With permission of the Datong Archaeological Institute.

While the brick tombs with two or more chambers are solitary and located away from graveyards, the remaining tomb types are present in almost all Pingcheng burial grounds, indicating that large graveyards were indeed communal and not restricted to homogeneous groups with similar mortuary customs. The available data are insufficient for a study of how graveyards grew. The impression is that tombs with different ritual customs intermingled with each other without recognizable patterns. However, there were plenty of small clusters of similar burials, which may indicate family groupings.[58] Since burials seldom intersected with each other, several scholars conjecture that this was the result of "cemetery management" (by the authorities?).[59] But the phenomenon could also indicate that burials originally had their markers on the ground. Latecomers, regardless of which cultural background they originated from, might, then, have been trying to avoid disturbing the existing tombs.

It appears that, during the early fifth century, the inhabitants of Pingcheng buried their dead primarily in two loci: south of Datong around the Dianhanchang cemetery and east of Datong along the present-day Yingbin dadao avenue on the eastern bank of the Yu River (Fig. 2, nos. 2 and 20). Both were dominated by catacomb tombs. The animal offerings of cattle, sheep/goats, horses, or dogs in these tombs were not attested to in northern Chinese tombs of previous ages. Their occupants could have had pastoral backgrounds.

Funerary paintings in the form of wall or coffin painting appeared unexpectedly early (Period II) in catacomb and brick chamber tombs. The number of painted tombs increases considerably in Period III, which can be explained by the sudden occurrence of funerary houses. Five of these were painted. In addition, five tombs bore wall paintings, and another four tombs and painted coffins. The number of tombs with paintings decreases in Period IV

---

58 Mukai Yusuke 2010: 148.
59 See, for example, Ni Run'an 2018: 89 and Wei Zheng and Cui Jiabao 2020: 128.

(Table 2.1). Some chamber tombs of Period IV were built with bricks stamped with decorative motifs in relief, similar to those in contemporaneous southern China, for example, in Nanjing or Xiangyang. The chambers in Wenming's and Xiaowen's (a ceno-taph) tombs are plain, with only keystones bearing lotus flowers in high relief. But their entrances to both tombs were adorned with large stone reliefs. Although rare, stone reliefs for tombs were not restricted to imperial use.[60]

Table 2.1 Number of tombs with paintings (including murals, paintings on coffins and funerary houses) and bricks with relief decoration

Period / Tomb types	II (398-439)	III (440-476)	IV (477-494)	V (post 494)
Earthen pits	-	-	-	-
Catacomb				
w/ a painted coffin	DHCM185	DHCM229, DHCM253, ZJB1997M-1	DHCM238	-
Knife-shaped	-	-	-	-
Earthen chamber				-
w/ a painted funerary house	-	ZJB1997M, Lü Xu (456), Xie Xing's wife (459), Zhang Zhilang (460), Xing Hejiang (469)	-	-
Brick, single chamber				
w/ mural paintings	YBL-09DYM1, SLM7, YBDDM16	QLC2020M29, YBL-2019HuayuII, Liang Bahu (461), WYLM1	Xiashenjing	-
w/ a painted coffin	EDCM37, SLM7		-	-
w/ a painted funerary house			Jia Bao, Song Saozu (both 477)	
w/ bricks w/ motifs			Yang Zhongdu (484)	
Brick, ≥2 chambers				
w/ mural paintings				CZM1
w/ a painted coffin		HD1986M1		
w/ bricks w/ motifs and paintings in corridors			Danyangwang	
w/ stone reliefs	-	-	Yongguling, Wanniantang (both 484)	-
Total no. of tombs	5 (SLM7 in 2 cases)	13	8	1

---

60 The funerary house of Lü Xu (456) is decorated with painted reliefs. Several large stone coffins in the collection of the Yungang Museum and in the deposit of the Datong Archaeological Institute are also carved, but all without provenience and cannot be dated.

Table 2.2 Number of tombs with clay figurines

Period / Tomb types	III (440-476)	IV (477-494)	V (post-494)
Earthen pits	-	-	-
Catacomb	-	-	-
Knife-shaped			
w/ figurines	-	YCJYM113, YBDDM76	-
Earthen chamber			
painted funerary house; w/ figurines	Zhang Zhilang (460)	-	-
plain funerary house; w/ figurines	YBLM10	-	-
Single chamber of bricks			
w/ a painted funerary house and figurines	-	Jia bao (477), Song Shaozu (477)	-
w/ bricks w/ motifs and figurines	-	Yang Zhongdu (484)	-
w/ only figurines	1998TCM1	YBSYM2, XSJM1, YGM18	-
Single chamber of bricks and with a side-chamber			
w/ a painted coffin and figurines		EDCM36	
w/ only figurines	-	YBDDM75, YBSYM52	-
≥2 chambers of bricks			
w/ mural paintings and figurines	-	-	CZM1
w/ stone reliefs and figurines	-	Yongguling (484)	-
w/ figurines only	-	Sima Jinlong (484)	-
Total	3	13	1

Only tombs with datable information and known tomb types are listed here. Figurines were not evidenced in burials before Period III. For keys, see Appendix I.

The absence of clay figurines in earthen pits and catacomb tombs throughout the Pingcheng period indicates that figurines did not belong to the funerary rituals of this part of the steppe peoples and were not acceptable for them. The earthen construction and the small size of a tomb chamber are not decisive factors, since even some very modest earthen tombs from the Western-Jin period contained figurines.[61] When figurines emerged in Pingcheng in Period III, they only appeared in earthen or brick chamber tombs. In Period IV, it was predominantly chamber tombs of bricks that featured figurines. Interestingly, two late knife-shaped tombs also contained figurines,[62] suggesting that their occupants were flexible enough to accept other burial practices. However, they modified the types and arrangements of figurines to meet their individual needs (see below).

While the use of clay figurines intensified in Period IV, the number of murals and painted coffins in tombs declined. However, they did not disappear. Although tombs with

---

61 Luoyang shi 2005.
62 See also Appendix II, nos. 9–10.

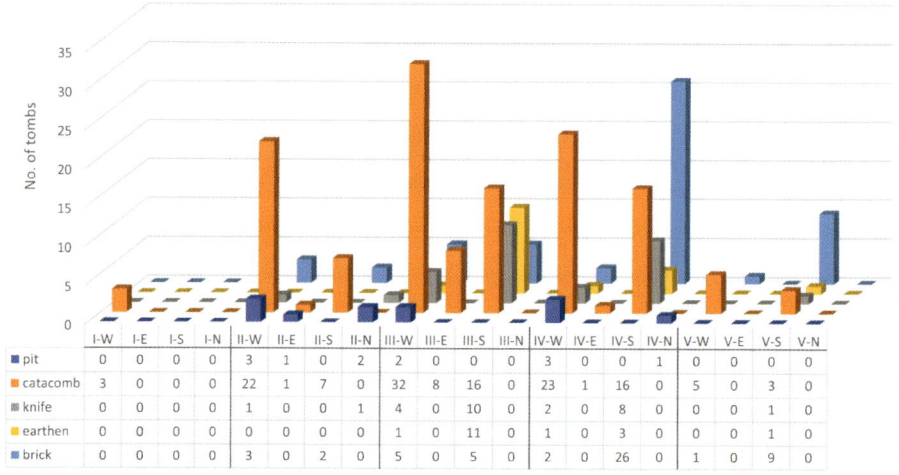

	I-W	I-E	I-S	I-N	II-W	II-E	II-S	II-N	III-W	III-E	III-S	III-N	IV-W	IV-E	IV-S	IV-N	V-W	V-E	V-S	V-N
■ pit	0	0	0	0	3	1	0	2	2	0	0	0	3	0	0	1	0	0	0	0
■ catacomb	3	0	0	0	22	1	7	0	32	8	16	0	23	1	16	0	5	0	3	0
■ knife	0	0	0	0	1	0	0	1	4	0	10	0	2	0	8	0	0	0	1	0
■ earthen	0	0	0	0	0	0	0	0	1	0	11	0	1	0	3	0	0	0	1	0
■ brick	0	0	0	0	3	0	2	0	5	0	5	0	2	0	26	0	1	0	9	0

Figure 7 Change in tomb orientation in Pingcheng over time according to tomb type. I to IV indicates the periods, W: westwards, E: eastwards, S: southwards, N: northwards.

mural paintings, funerary houses, or tomb figurines attract the attention of scholars, the figures in Table 2 illustrate clearly that they were rare. I will discuss the most important motifs in tomb paintings and certain figurine assemblages further below.

Tomb orientation

By comparing the pre-Pingcheng Xianbei tombs with the tombs in Pingcheng, arranged in the chronology they had established, the authors of the *Datong Nanjiao* concluded that the tombs in Pingcheng shifted from facing west to south over time, which pioneered the south-ward tomb orientation common in Luoyang. The concept meets broad approval, and the phenomenon is attributed to the recognition of the Chinese ritual system, in which the south played a central role, by the increasingly Sinicized Xianbei. [63] Further, archaeologists consider a southerly orientation to indicate a later burial date.

Since more tombs have been excavated since 2000, it would be interesting to test the validity of this concept. Fig. 7, which depicts the tomb orientations in relation to the types and chronology of the known tombs, shows that the orientations are largely dependent on tomb types. Generally, the knife-shaped and the earthen chamber tombs were south-facing. The predominant orientation of the catacomb tombs remained westward. However, the ratio of catacomb tombs facing south to those facing west rose towards the end of Pingcheng (Period II 7:22 [32%]; Period III 16:32 [50%]; Period IV 16:23 [70%]). The shift from west to south is even more noticeable in the group of brick tombs. During Periods IV and V, south-facing brick tombs (26 and 9) prevailed. The available data appear to support the re-

---

63 Datong daxue et al. 2006, 466–67. The support came from numerous leading scholars, see Lin Sheng-chih 2012: 8–9 and Ni Run'an 2018: 88–89, just to name two. For the discourse of the re-orientation of the imperial ritual of the Tuoba based on written sources, see Kang Le 1995.

orientation theory. Given the way the excavations were reported, this result should still be treated with caution. The orientation data in Fig. 7 are presumably valid only for the brick tombs. For most of the brick chamber tombs the basic information is available, while for other types (pit, catacomb and knife tombs) this is the case for only a few of the thousands of tombs. The dominance of south-facing tombs may be related to the influx of peoples from the Guan-Long region, as suggested by Ni Run'an (2018). During later periods, possible relocations of tribes using south-facing catacomb tombs may also be responsible for an increase in such tombs. Since the circumstances underlying the shift are to be clarified and the interactions between peoples are complex, Sinicization is only one possible explanation. Some of these interactions will be discussed below.

Burial customs

Single burials were generally the rule. Young adolescents and adults of all ages were interred in their own tombs. On only a few occasions was a child or newborn buried with its mother, or at least with a female person; an infant was occasionally interred in a large jar placed above the tomb chamber.[64]

In most cases, the deceased was laid in a stretched supine position inside the coffin. A prone or side position is rare. The head is usually pointed toward the entrance. From Period IV onward, head orientations varied greatly, particularly in earthen and brick-chambered tombs. If an individual was interred in a funerary house, he or she was laid out on a funerary bed against the back wall of the house. Another unusual feature is the interment of two bodies in one coffin.

Paired burials in a single coffin

Pit burials containing two or more bodies—possibly interred simultaneously—are known in Eurasia and North Africa from the Neolithic period. The Bronze and Iron Age kurgans on the steppe are rich in examples of paired or multiple burials. Paired burials in one single wooden coffin became more common over time. Several cases are documented between the second century BCE and the third or fourth century CE in Niya on the southern fringe of the Tarim Basin, and in the fourth and early fifth centuries CE paired burials were found in Guanzhong, southern Inner Mongolia, northern Hebei, and Manchuria.[65] Numerous double burials were unearthed in China, spanning from the Shang to the Western Jin periods, with each coffin containing only one body. In other words, a similar burial cult with two bodies in one single coffin was not evidenced in "Chinese" territory before the fifth century.[66] Pingcheng's paired burials were clearly introduced by migrants.

Quite a few tombs containing a coffin with two bodies have been unearthed in Pingcheng, but only 21 of them can be periodized. A paired burial in Pingcheng typically consists of an older male and a younger female, according to excavators, although latest excavations (all not published) indicate other possibilities. Table 3 shows that they appeared first in Period III and were observed primarily in catacomb tombs. Some brick-chambered tombs from Periods IV and V also housed single coffins that contained two bodies.

---

64 E.g., Yingbin dadao M54; Datong kaogu 2006c: 52. This tomb cannot be dated.
65 Song Xin 2023.
66 I am grateful to Professor Dr. Maria Khayutina for this information on Bronze Age China.

Table 3. Numbers of paired burials in one coffin in Pingcheng

Tomb types \ Period	II (398–435)	III (436–476)	IV (477–493)	V (post-494)	Total
Earthen pits	0	0	0	0	0
Catacomb tombs	0	DHCM13, DHCM50, DHCM81, DHCM102, DHCM126, HD2004M1, HD2004M6, YBDDM55	DHCM23, DHCM67, DHCM80, DHCM83, DHCM85, HD2004M6	0	14
Knife-shaped tombs	0	QLC2020M831	YBSYM7	0	2
Earthen-chambered tombs w/ a funerary house	0	[Yulongting III M8 at Shaling]		0	[1]
Brick tombs, single-chambered					
w/o a funerary house	0	0	HD2004M8, SLXCM1, XSJM1		3
w/ a funerary house			[Jia Bao, Song Shaozu, (both 477)]		[2]
Brick tombs, two or more chambered		HD1986M1		CZM1	2
Total	0	10 [+1]	10 [+2]	1	21 [+3]

[n]: number of the tombs with paired burials in a funerary house. For keys, see Appendix I.

The buried pairs in the catacomb tombs (with different orientations) of Period III were given animal offerings and adorned with personal decorative objects such as rings, earrings, and necklaces. Thus, their burial rites were not significantly different from those carried out for single interments in catacomb tombs. That is to say, paired interments in a single coffin were not "richer" or "poorer" than single burials.

There are also some burials with a young woman (most likely mother) and a child in one coffin. Yanbei shiyuan M7 (Period IV) is a special case, with a teenage girl (about 13 or 14 years old) and a child (6–8 years old; sex unknown) in one coffin. All grave goods, including ceramics and two crystal beads, were found near the girl, which indicates that she was the chief person in the coffin. The relationship between the girl and the child is unknown. Wei Zheng suggests that the burial could have been a posthumous marriage (*minghun* 冥婚).[67]

---

67 For the burial, see Liu Junxi 2008, 5–6, 218; Wei Zheng 2015: 461.

Figure 8 Paired burials in single coffins and funerary houses. 1. Biguiyuan M831 at Qilicun; 2. Dianhanchang M126; 3. Yulongting III M8 at Shaling.

After Zhang Quanchao et al. 2021: Fig. 3; Shanxi daxue et al. 2006, Plate 7.3; http://sx.people. com. cn/n2/2018/0420/c189130-31485018.html; retrieved April 23, 2018. With Permission of the Datong Archaeological Institute.

The bodies in the paired burials were laid in a stretched supine or side position (Fig. 8). Several instances show the bodies arranged in a demonstrably intimate manner, such as holding hands or embracing (Fig. 8.1). This was obviously intended to convey the impression that the interred pair had a close relationship. Only a few pairs display exactly the opposite arrangement (Fig. 8.2). To achieve the desired posture, the bodies must have been placed into the coffin while they were still manipulable. It can be assumed that both individuals died almost simultaneously. And the bodies must have been interred at the same time. This assumption can be substantiated by the observation that most tombs with a paired interment in one coffin do not exhibit signs of disturbance or re-opening. Only one case can be proven to be the secondary interment of a female, whose skeleton was laid *ex post* into the coffin of a male.[68] The well-preserved skeletons of M831 at Biguiyuan 碧桂園 near Qilicun 七里村, found in 2020, were identified as those of a 29 to 35-year-old male and a 35 to 40-year-old female, based on skeletal features and dentition. The arrangement of the bodies is of interest: although the young man was not much taller than the woman, she was intentionally positioned much lower so that her head could be laid on his shoulder (Fig. 8.1). While the male had severe and unhealed pre-mortem bone fractures on his right forearm and hand, which presumably have led to his early death, the female seemed to be healthy and thus died of unknown causes. The researchers postulate that she possibly "sacrificed herself for the demise of her husband."[69]

Based on the sparse records in the Book of Wei regarding forced suicide cases of wives after their husband's death, Chinese scholars proposed that these paired burials constitute archaeological evidence for a frequently discussed form of "killing of the widow," or *Totenfolge* ("following into death" or "accompanying in death").[70] They further state that the paired burial in one coffin, or the "2-in-1" burial, was a part of the mortuary culture of the Tuoba Xianbei.[71] Nevertheless, the paired burial in a single coffin is, as mentioned above, evidenced throughout Eurasia across time and space. Additionally, the written sources record only how the widow died, not how the couple was buried,[72] leaving the paired burials in a single coffin unexplained. By interpreting the deceased in these burials as "loving husband and wife," we may have imposed a relatively recent concept of romantic love on these archaeological findings. Since excavation reports often do not specify how sex was identified, it could also be problematic if the sex was judged simply by the posture in which the bodies were arranged. The two skeletons of the famous Tomb 16 in Modena (fourth–sixth century), Italy, excavated in 2009, were dubbed "the Lovers of Modena" for years since this "couple" was holding hands. An analysis in 2019, however, using proteins extracted from the dental enamels of both bodies proved that both were biological men.[73]

Bioarchaeologists found that the deceased in paired burials consumed a high proportion of animal proteins.[74] This result further supports the idea that this kind of burials in

---

68 Hudong 2004M8. Shanxi and Datong 2018: 63–64.
69 Zhang Quanchao et al. 2021. The article also offers a beautifully reconstructed scene of interment with both good-looking embracing "lovers," who were, however, depicted with the clothing style of the Luoyang period. A report of the excavation has not yet been published.
70 See the discussion in Shanxi daxue et al. 2006, 485–86. For a general discussion of the *Totenfolge* and its theoretical backgrounds, cf. Fisch 1998, 22–27.
71 Wei Zheng 2015; Wei Zheng and Cui Jiabao 2020: 129–30.
72 *Wei shu* 29.706, 34.799.
73 Lugli, Di Rocco and Vazzana et al. 2019.
74 Table 4 in Zhang Guowen et al. 2021: 11 shows variable but high $\delta^{15}N$ levels in all 15 sampled paired burials (although only two pairs were classified as "husband-and-wife") from several Pingcheng graveyards. This indicates that the individuals in a paired burial heavily relied on terrestrial animal proteins.

Pingcheng was indeed practiced by pastoralists. It is interesting to note that some later Pingcheng paired burials appeared in other tomb types, sometimes with other burial customs. The best example is Chenzhuang M1 (Period V), one of the largest tombs of the late Pingcheng period. The once lavishly furnished and painted brick tomb with double chambers was severely plundered. Among the few remaining artifacts are red and white carnelian stones for *Go* games. A single, large coffin (L. 2.8 m, W. 1.63–2.25 m) containing the skeletal remains of a man and a woman was found in the rear chamber. Whether this was an indication of a higher degree of "Sinicization" of the tomb occupants with pastoral roots (due to the *Go* stones) or the opposite (due to the paired burial) is a matter of perspective and speculation.

The placing of the bodies of a man and a woman within a funerary house (see next section) might be construed as another form of the "2-in-1" burial. The question is undoubtedly just how the deceased were deposited within such a sarcophagus. Funerary houses containing the bodies of a male and a female were found in at least three tombs. Yulongting 御龍庭 III M8 (Fig. 8.3) near Shaling was found intact, i.e., it had not been looted or reopened.[75] Since the entrance door of a funerary house is generally narrow, once the door and the tomb have been sealed, a later interment of an additional body is less likely. In other words, when two bodies are found in a funerary house, they must have been simultaneously put into the house. The same consideration can also be applied to the three Yanbei shiyuan tombs, each of which contains two or more coffins.[76] The one coffin was placed against the rear or one of the side walls of the chamber, while the other, slightly larger, coffin was positioned in the middle of the room. Usually, only one set of grave goods was present in the tomb, which was placed directly in front of the larger coffin. One cannot avoid the impression that both coffins were deposited in the chamber in a single action, since there was not much room for moving the coffins around. The interred individual in the smaller coffin, although buried in a coffin of his or her own, was possibly a "companion for the afterlife" for the other, who had died slightly earlier.[77]

Coffins, funerary houses, and funerary beds

Trapezoidal-shaped coffins, i.e., coffins with a front panel that was broader and higher than the rear panel, became commonly accepted. They were observed not only in all types of burials in the capital, Pingcheng, but also in all regions controlled by the Tuoba Xianbei. The styles, proportions, and finishes of the coffins may vary. But there is no evidence that other coffin shapes existed concurrently.

A sideboard of a Pingcheng coffin typically consisted of at least three well-gauged, long and tapering wooden planks connected with "dovetail" wooden tenons. The cover, built

---

75 The other two are the tombs of Jia Bao and Song Shaozu, both dated to 477, and both were severely looted.

76 Yanbei shiyuan M1, M2, M9. According to the report, the deceased in the smaller coffins in Yanbei shiyuan M2 and M9 were women. The larger coffin in M2 contained a pair of iron scissors. However, the relationship of the scissors to the female gender in Pingcheng is by no means clear, see below. A more careful examination of this tomb is necessary.

77 Certainly, one cannot rule out the possibility that the individual who died first was kept in a well-sealed coffin at home. And the interment would take place only after the second individual died. In any case, similar tombs with multiple coffins need to be examined with greater care.

using the same carpenter's technique, is sometimes arched in the cross-section. A well-manufactured coffin was lined with paper or with a thin, sometimes painted, layer of silk.[78] Coffin wood has rarely been examined botanically. The woods that have been studied all belonged to the *Pinus* spp., including those from large tombs such as Hudong M1 and the tomb at Chenzhuang. Duan Chengshi's 段成式 remark that the Northern Wei coffins were made of cypress wood may have referred to those from the Luoyang period (494–534).[79]

The majority of Pingcheng coffins were single ones (*guan* 棺). Only a few *guan*-coffins were nested inside an "outer coffin" (*guo* 槨), which probably belonged to the "luxury class." Several of these nested coffins were unearthed from catacomb tombs or earthen tombs with a square chamber, while the very large, two-chambered Chenzhuang tomb contained only a *guan* coffin, i.e., without a *guo* coffin. Coffins are typically between 1.8 and 2.2 m long and between 60 and 90 cm wide (at the head end). Some can be up to 1.6 m high, such as the one in the newly found Qilicun 2020M29 (see below), and the wooden planks can be as thick as 10 cm. Some of the nested coffins were wider than the dromos and the entrance corridor of the tomb. It is possible that the parts of an outer coffin were brought into the chamber individually and only assembled after the inner coffin had been placed in its correct location.

Two coffins in Pingcheng (from Dianhanchang M24, Period II, and Qilicun 2020M29, Period III) and two in Ih-Nur (from M2 and M3, Period III), Inner Mongolia, had a special construction: the interior of the coffins was divided into an upper and lower tier by a wooden board or litter. The body was laid on the board, while the grave goods, including ceramics, were placed on the lower tier.[80] The coffins of Qilicun 2020M29 and Ih-Nur M2 and M3 were richly furnished with valuable grave goods. The coffin of the old woman (50–55 years old) in the intact Dianhanchang M24, on the other hand, contained only three jars; otherwise, no grave gifts were deposited in the chamber. Dianhanchang M24, and Ih-Nur M2 and M3 are catacomb tombs, while Qilicun 2020M29 is a medium-sized brick tomb (3.12 m × 3.02 m, H. 2.82 m), the four walls of which are richly painted. As in Ih-Nur M3, additional grave goods were also deposited in the chamber of Qilicun 2020M29. The two-tiered coffins of Ih-Nur M2 and M3 were likely constructed to transport the corpse to a remote burial site after the funerary rituals had been completed at the place of departure. The well-crafted ceramics and coffins from both Ih-Nur tombs suggest that they were manufactured in a larger town, if not in Pingcheng, where skilled craftsmen were readily available. It appears, however, that the grave goods in the coffin of Qilicun M29 and the jars in the coffin of Dianhanchang M24 were all Pingcheng products, except for the fig

---

78 Several Pingcheng coffins were finished with this method, e.g., Dianhanchang M107, Dianhanchang M229, the Qijiapo tomb (Shanxi daxue 2006, 234, 316; Wang Yintian and Han Shengcun 1995: 14). For an image of the interior of the coffin from Ih-Nur M3, see, http://upload.northnews.cn/2014/0310/1394438017737.jpg, retrieved March 10, 2014. The surface of the coffin at Zhijiabao was leveled out with paper before it was painted; Liu and Gao 2004. Paper on coffins is attested to in several third to fourth century tombs in Yumen, Gansu. Gansu wenwu 2005; Deng Tianzhen et al. 2019.

79 *Youyang zazu* 13 (510: "It was customary for the Northern Wei people to pull out all the stops to organize opulent burials. They valued large and tall coffins, which were frequently constructed from cypress wood …" 後魏俗競厚葬，棺厚高大，多用柏木……), p. 123; Müller Sh. 2000, 210, note 92.

80 Shanxi daxue 2006, 159; Datong kaogu 2023: 36–37; Wang Dafang and Chen Heling 2015: 304. For Ih-Nr M2, see Neimenggu et al. 2016: 47; Ih-Nur M3, see Chen Yongzhi et al. 2016a; 2016b.

fruits in Qilicun M29. It is also worth noting that all tomb occupants except the one in Ih-Nur M2 wore chinstraps. Thus, one cannot exclude the possibility that the tiered coffins were associated with a specific funerary cult that we are unaware of.

Animal masks with rings in their muzzles made of lead, bronze, or gilded bronze appeared much more frequently on coffins and were more extravagant than they were in previous ages. Coffins decorated with animal masks were found in practically all types of tombs from Period II to Period IV, with the exception of knife-shaped tombs. Both the mask and the ring frequently feature novel elaborate ornaments, such as half-palmette scrolls and variations of the "lord of the animals" motifs.[81] The eyes of the masks were sometimes emphasized with painted eyeballs. The "rings" in muzzles were molded from thin ring-shaped metal sheets; the front side has the appearance of an iron coffin ring but is not robust enough to carry the weight of the coffin. Thus, animal masks with rings were primarily decorative. The rings used for transporting the coffin were of cast or forged iron and were fixed firmly to the coffin boards.

Animal masks in relief also decorate funerary houses, almost all funerary beds of stone, and the Yungang caves. In addition to the basic apotropaic function well-known in Han and Jin China, the popularity of this motif and during the Pingcheng period may be attributed to the introduction of Buddhist artworks from Central Asia or the Gupta Empire, where the motif was intensively applied. This also explains why Pingcheng's animal masks were preferably embellished with Central or West Asian motifs, such as the half-palmette scrolls or the Lord of the Animals mentioned above, and why most masks were closely associated with motifs of flowing water or pearl strings, as seen on the front of many funerary beds or the crowns of bodhisattvas.[82] According to the available information, the coffin from the 1986 Hudong M1 is the only one in Pingcheng that was both painted and decorated with gilded bronze animal masks and gilded studs of a lead-tin alloy (the coffin from Ih-Nur M3 is another example, but it was unearthed in Inner Mongolia). All other Pingcheng coffins with animal masks do not have figural paintings. 1986 Hudong M1 also yielded a silver-plated bronze plaque bearing a "birth by transformation" (*huasheng* 化生) motif, with a Buddha figure emerging from a lotus flower with the hands placed together in the Anjali mudra (hand gesture of greeting and paying respect). The plaque's original location in the tomb cannot be determined because of the severe looting; however, it is assumed that it previously decorated the coffin. The "transformation" motif symbolizes the entering of the soul of the deceased into the Western Paradise. In Pingcheng, eave-end tiles (*wadang*) with a "transformation" motif have been unearthed from numerous Buddhist sites and tombs; all depict a child amid a lotus flower. It is therefore intriguing why this specific plaque features a Buddha (indicating the thought of aupapādaka, "direct metamorphosis" of a bodhi-sattva?). Regardless, the prevalence of rebirth motifs in both temple and tomb sites from the 470s onwards reflects an increasing desire among the population in northern China to be reborn in Buddha's heaven or in the Pure Land of Buddha Amitabha.[83]

---

81 Wang Yintian 2019.
82 Zin 2003, 99–103; Müller Sh. 2019a, 403, note 67. The coffin painting from Hudong M1 features animal masks with pearl strings in their snouts; see Fig. 34 and the section "Pearl roundels" below.
83 Hou Xudong 1998, 173–90. For the archaeology of the reborn imagery in Pingcheng, see Okamura and Mukai 2007 119–107 (32–44); Wang Feifeng 2019.

Funerary beds and houses appear abruptly in Period III (Table 1) and are one of the most peculiar burial customs in Pingcheng. The earliest datable funerary house was unearthed from Lü Xu's tomb (456). As the constructional techniques employed in this stone house were already mature, it is probable that there were still earlier ones. A funerary bed was built in either a tomb chamber or a funerary house. For such an interment, the deceased was/were laid on a funerary bed, usually without a coffin. Water waves and animal masks were commonly used to decorate funerary beds, and they are occasionally complemented by floral scrolls or celestial musicians from Buddhist art similar to those found in the Yungang caves. In recent discussions, scholars tend to interpret the funerary beds and houses from the sixth century as a specific mortuary practice of the Sogdians in China. However, there is no indication that the deceased in Pingcheng were associated with the Sogdian culture. The ornamentation of funerary houses provides a far lesser indication of the religious beliefs of the interred individual than that of funerary beds. Some houses, such as those of Yuchi Dingzhou's wife and in Yunbolu M10, are even without any decorations. The house for Xing Hejiang 邢合姜 (469) is unique in that it was entirely painted with Buddhist images to emulate a cave chapel.[84] Archaeological data show that there were more females than males interred in stone houses in Pingcheng. Several tomb inscriptions explicitly state that the house was built for the wife or mother.[85]

We do not, as yet, have a clear picture of just who it was that was using this "furniture" and why they chose an interment on a funerary bed or in a funerary house. In some of the Tarim oases, the practice had been to place the deceased on wooden stretchers for their interment ever since the second millennium BCE. In third- or fourth-century Kucha, brick beds for corpses in tombs had already appeared. However, the interior furnishings of some of the Sichuan cliff tombs dated from the end of the Eastern Han period also remind us of those later funerary beds or houses.[86] In 2020, two funerary (brick) beds were found in the rear chamber of an elite tomb of the Sixteen Kingdom period in Zhongzhaocun 中兆村, Xi'an. This is the first indication that the highest-ranking individuals in the Guanzhong area were interred in this manner.[87] In the Tomb of the Great King 太王陵 in Ji'an 集安, Liaoning, a stone house was built in a stone chamber barely larger than the house itself. Two platforms, not funerary beds, were placed inside to accommodate the coffins. Besides, the entrance to the house of the Great King was located on the gable wall.[88] In contrast, the

---

84 Müller Sh. 2019a: 401–3, 409–12, 415, 428; Li Meitian and Zhang Zhizhong 2020.

85 Müller Sh. 2019a: 419–21. For inscriptions, see, for example, those for the wife of Yuchi Dingzhou, the wife of Xie Xing, Xing Hejiang and Zhang Zhilang, to name just a few. Datong kaogu 2011c; Chizhi and Liu Junxi 2014; Zhang Qingjie 2016; Ma Boyao 2021.

86 Müller Sh. 2019a: 414. Santai and Santai 2002; Sichuan sheng et al. 2007, 271–73, Color Pls. 297–301.

87 This tomb, Zhongzhaocun M100, has a total length of 80.74 m, and a depth of 11.86 m. Two 50–60 cm high brick beds were placed against the eastern and western walls of the rear chamber. The western bed, which held a trapezoidal coffin, was a simple, elevated platform common in the Liaoxi area (although of stone). The eastern bed is reported to have a short brick screen on each end of the frontal rim, leaving the middle section open. A pile of something on the bed appears to be the remains of the deceased, and there is no sign of a coffin. The fronts of the bases of both were painted with *humen* 壺門 decorations (for the term *humen*, see Jing and Liu 2010). For a short online description with some images see Xin Long et al. 2020.

88 This was possibly the tomb of the King Kwanggaet'o (r. 391–413), Jilin and Ji'an 2004, 236–53, 334. Four similar stone houses of the late Western Han period were recently discovered at Sangshuping 桑樹

doors to the Pingcheng stone houses were opened on the long side. While the afore-
mentioned examples could all have heralded the arrival of funerary houses and beds in
Pingcheng, we observe that five of the excavated houses exhibit features such as verandas
and octagonal columns that were typical in the northwestern region, spanning from the
Hexi corridor to Guanzhong, during the fourth–fifth centuries.[89] Indeed, according to the
inscriptions, four of the five Pingcheng stone house occupants or commissioners originated
from this region.[90] In light of the new findings at Sangshuping, it is still unclear whether the
funerary houses in Pingcheng originated from a Chinese or a foreign mortuary culture. It is
likely that this practice had several origins, all converging in Pingcheng. As for funerary
beds, Chinese culture offered only minor contributions, such as the shaping of the feet of a
funerary bed. The practice was absent in Chinese tombs.

The main difference between the mortuary furniture of Pingcheng and its forerunners,
such as the beds in the tomb at Zhongzhao Village and the house in the Koguryo tomb of
the Great King in Ji'an, is the social rank of the users. Earlier funerary houses and beds in
Pingcheng were apparently made for affluent residents, regardless of whether they were
commoners or officials. Later, individuals of high rank and aristocracy, such as Sima
Jinlong, or, more likely, his wife Qinwen jichen 欽文姬辰 (477), also opted for a stone bed.
There is, however, no evidence that the members of the Tuoba royal family ever used such
furniture. In the final years of Pingcheng, the number of finely crafted stone beds declined,
while more small brick tombs featured an economic brick bed as an integral part of a
chamber wall. This also meant a change in decoration: the carved water waves and animal
masks disappeared, and the fronts of the brick beds were now shaped in a way that was
understood as Mount Meru, the Buddhist cosmic mountain. A brick bed was even built in a
knife-shaped tomb, as mentioned above.[91]

Adornment for the deceased

Despite their scarcity, the very few excavated textiles from Pingcheng burials have the
potential to help understand the fabrics used in this region during the fifth century.
Unfortunately, none of these have been examined, with the only exception of the recently
excavated 2020M29 at Qilicun (the results of which have not yet been published). However,
through certain decorative objects ("jewelry") added to the buried bodies and certain
clothing accessories, we can make some guesses as to how the individuals were dressed at
that time and place, at least for their funerals.

坪 in northern Shaanxi (Xibei and Yulin 2022). As with the Great King's stone house in Ji'an, the doors
of these four were set on the gable wall. I appreciate Dr. Annette Kieser providing the Sangshuping
excavation report.

89 Müller Sh. 2019c, 410.

90 These are the houses of the wife of Yuchi Dingzhou (457), of Song Shaozu (477) of Dunhuang (Müller
Sh. 2019a, Table 3, nos. 1, 5, 9) as well as the stone house of Lü Xu (456) of Fufeng 扶風 and the
wooden house of Jia Bao (477) of Guzang, Zhang Zhizhong et al. 2021; Datong kaogu 2021a. The fifth
house with a veranda construction but without an inscription is Yulongting M8 at Shaling, Gu Shunfang
and Lü Xiaojing 2022.

91 E.g., Shaling M14; Datong kaogu 2014: 6. This tomb does not contain any grave goods and cannot be
attributed to a specific Pingcheng period. Since most of the brick beds emerged late, it is possible that
this tomb also belongs to Period IV or V; Müller Sh. 2017, 389 note 25. See also p. 35.

Table 4. Number of burials with body and clothing adornments

	Period	I (pre-398)					II (399–439)					III (440–476)					IV (477–493)				
		J	B	W	A	C	J	B	W	A	C	J	B	W	A	C	J	B	W	A	C
F	Pit											1		1			1				1
	Catacomb	1				1	7		2	1		7	2		4	4	3	1	2	4	
	Knife-shaped											1						2		2	
	Earthen chamber											1	1		2						
	Brick, single											1			1			1			
	Brick, multiple																1		1	1	
M	Pit																1				
	Catacomb						1		1	1					1			1			
	Knife-shaped											1	1								
	Earthen chamber												1								
	Brick, single											1			1	1					
	Brick, multiple												1								
N	Pit						1		1		1										
	Catacomb		1	1			1	4	1	2	2	12	4	2	4	3	6	3	2	4	1
	Knife-shaped								1			2			2		1				
	Earthen chamber																1				
	Brick, single.						2	1		1		3		1	4	1	3	1	5	5	
	Brick, multiple																1		1	1	

F: Female; M: Male; N: tomb occupants without sexing; J: Jewelry: B: belt buckles and belt fittings;
W: Weapons/tools; A: Accessories (mirrors, scissors, plaques for clothing, earpicks); C: chinstraps.

Earrings, finger rings and bangles of gold, silver, bronze, or even tin, as well as necklaces of semi-precious stones, were frequently found in Pingcheng tombs. Table 4 shows that, despite heavy looting, more than a third of the burials examined contain such adornments, along with belt buckles, belt fittings, pendants of various kinds, tools, and/or weapons. The highest frequency of these finds occurs in Period III, from the unification of the north to the beginning of the Taihe era. Jewelry was mainly discovered in catacomb tombs. Since most of the larger earthen-chambered and brick-chambered tombs were looted, it is likely that this result does not reflect the reality. On the other hand, in several intact middle-sized tombs containing numerous clay figurines, an expensive funerary house, or both, we do not find adornments or only a small amount of it.[92] The question of whether this was a personal

---

92 Of Period III, with a funerary house and figurines: Tombs of Lü Xu (456; with one belt buckle), Zhang Zhilang (460; without adornment). Of Period IV and without adornments: Yunbolu M10 (with a funerary house and figurines); Yuchang jiayuan M113 (a knife-shaped tomb with clay figurines).

choice, or the expression of a particular funerary custom cannot be answered here due to the small sample size. What is certain, however, is that most double-chambered tombs were indeed once the repositories of precious stones as well as gold and silver objects.

The results suggest that deceased females in Pingcheng were adorned with jewelry more often than deceased males,[93] which is consistent with data from the "northern zone" during the Xiongnu occupation (including Inner Mongolia, northern Shanxi, northern Shaanxi, and Ningxia).[94] In a double burial with two coffins, the main person (usually in a larger coffin) being buried appears to be the more richly adorned, regardless of whether they happen to be male or female. In paired burials in a single coffin, the female does not seem to be any less adorned than the male. But most of the deceased in such burials do not wear any jewelry. It should be noted that only a few of the excavated skeletons from Pingcheng burials were sex-identified. Qilangshan 七郎山 M20 in Inner Mongolia demonstrates that men also wore imposing gold earrings with heavy pendants of carnelian and glass beads.[95]

Two triangular openwork decorations on the forehead found in Dianhanchang M109 and a tomb from the Dongxin Square cemetery remind of the princely headgear in the Ajanta Cave 1 mural or that of some bodhisattvas in the Yungang Caves (Fig. 9).[96] Open-work metal pieces frequently adorned the headgear or clothing of the elite of the Yan king-doms in southern Manchuria and the Koguryo in the fourth and fifth centuries. Many of these pieces took up the motif of opposing birds (phoenixes),[97] which apparently came from the decorative repertoire of the Eastern Jin or even earlier. Two similar, but smaller triangular openwork ornaments with bird pairs in an opposite position have been found in the tomb of Feng Sufu 馮素弗 (415) in Beipiao, Liaoning,[98] who was the brother of the Northern Yan ruler Feng Ba 馮跋. In any case, there seems to have been an open boundary between secular and religious ornamentation, which mutually inspired one another.

The so-called jewelry sometimes consisted of a simple necklace with only one stone bead of carnelian, malachite, or crystal, or of an unimposing bracelet or ring made from bronze wire. But quite a few interred individuals wore necklaces with a number of colorful stone beads or pearls, and some had more than two bangles and rings.

Earrings of gold, silver and bronze were found in twenty-two tombs that can be periodized. Most of these are catacomb and knife-shaped tombs.[99] Nearly all earrings have

---

93 See Höllmann et al. 2016: 73–74. Similar practices can be observed in "Xiongnu" burials in Trans-baikalia, Dyrestui, and Ivolga as well. Yang Jianhua 2011, 244–46.

94 Shelach 2008.

95 Otani Ikue 2021: 327. Wu Songyan 2015 dates the tomb to the beginning of the fifth century.

96 If the date of Dianhanchang M109 (Period III, i.e., 440–476) is correct, all the images in the Yungang Caves, such as 5, 6, 11, and 16 were created later (c. beginning of 477 to c. 494). Only the mural paint-ings in Ajanta Cave 1 could have been contemporaneous.

97 Even engraved gold pectorals adopted this motif; Liaoning wenwu 2002, Pl. 38.12.

98 The original positions and contexts of these sheet ornaments in the tomb were lost through looting activities. The sheets illustrated here served originally as underlays for two openwork objects bearing the motif of a pair of opposing birds. They are about one-third smaller than the one found in M109. Originally, they were fastened onto a band or some such arrangement together with other ornaments.

99 Bronze earrings were found in eight, silver ones in six, and gold ones in eight tombs. In addition to the finds in Fig. 10, Qilicun M12, M37 and Yingbin dadao M19 also yielded gold earrings (Datong kaogu 2006a: Fig. 71; 2006c: Fig. 25) but cannot be treated in the present study for the lack of information.

Figure 9 Triangle "crown" ornament of bronze and gilded bronze with two opposing birds and flaming-rim motifs from (1) Dianhanchang M109; (2) a tomb at the Dongxin Square site (verso); (3) a bodhisattva figure in Yungang Cave 5.

(1) Photo by the author in the Datong Museum; (2) After http://www.360doc.com/content/19/ 0216/09/33885274_815277513.shtml, retrieved April 18, 2020; (3) After Zhang Zhuo (ed.), Yungang (Nanjing: Jiangsu meishu chubanshe, 2011), 62, Fig. 23. With permission of the Datong Museum and the Yungang Academy.

a crescent (or "C") shape, which, like many Gandharan earrings, has a thicker center and two tapered ends. Half of them were soldered with tiny rings for pendants. Both features (a thicker center and soldered-on tiny rings) distinguish the Pingcheng crescentic rings from similar rings in Parthian Iran and contemporary Koguryo and Silla. Although these crescent-shaped earrings sporadically appeared at Xianbei sites in Inner Mongolia, such as

Figure 10 Crescent-shaped earrings of the Pingcheng period. (1) Dianhanchang (DHC) M101, gold, with three soldered rings; (2) DHC M107, gold, the soldered attachment is broken; (3) DHC M128, gold; (4) DHC M129, gold, with a pin and a rotatable rosette of six granules at its end; (5) Yanbei shiyuan M12, silver; (6) Qilangshan M20, Inner Mongolia, bronze; (7) Ih-Nur M6, gold with three soldered rings and a crescent-moon cell with black enamel facing the front; (8) Heng'anjie M13, Datong, gold; (9) Hakutsuru Museum of Art, gold.

(1–4) After Shanxi daxue et al. 2006, Color Pls. 14.5–6, 16.4, 6; (5) After Liu Junxi 2008, Color pls. 4.2; (6) After Wei Jian 2004, Pl. 20.1; (7) After Chen Yongzhi et al. 2016b, 48; (8) Datong bowu 2018, 100, Cat.-No. 96; (9) After Otani 2012: Fig. 6-6. (1–4, 8) With permission of Professor Wang Yanqing; (5) With permission of the Datong Archaeological Institute; (6, 7, 9) Line-drawings by the author.

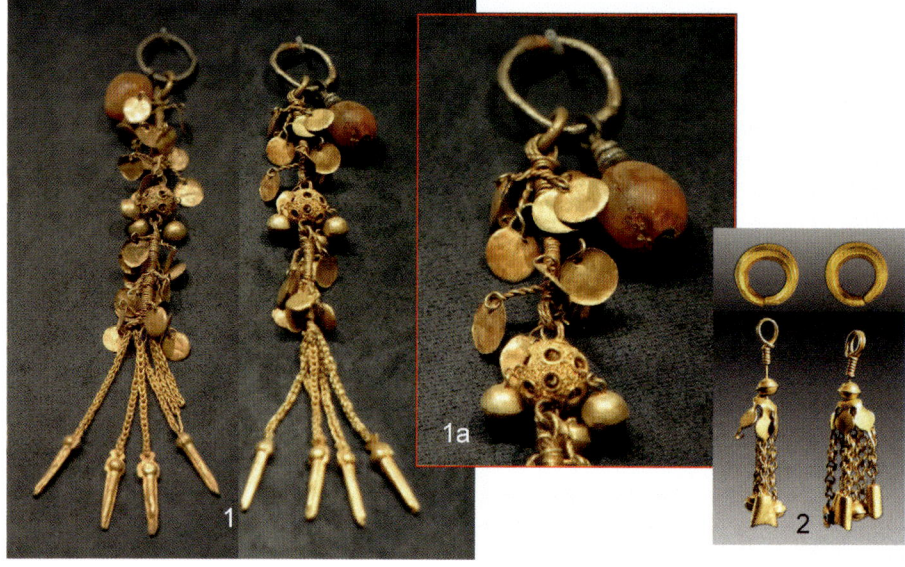

Figure 11 Gold pendants for earrings with hanging chains. From (1) a tomb at Jiaotongyuan excavated in 2004 (L. ca. 20 cm), (1a) Detail of the right pendant; (2) Dianhanchang M180 (L. ca. 3.85 cm; Period II); (3) a stone casket under a pagoda at Dingxian, Hebei, dated 481 (L. 9.2 cm; (3a) Detail of the right pendant.

(1, 3) Photos and drawings by the author ([3]: after Hebei sheng wenwu yanjiusuo [ed.], Hebei zhongyao kaogu faxian [1949–2009]. *Beijing: Kexue chubanshe, 2009, 247); (2) After Shanxi daxue et al. 2006, Color Pl. 17.2; with permission of Professor Wang Yanqing.*

Hulun Buir, Sandaowan, and Qilangshan, as early as the third to fourth centuries,[100] this observation is consistent with that of Otani Ikue (2012), who notes that the crescent-shaped earrings fundamentally differ from those early "Xianbei" earrings made from a twisted wire (*niusi* 扭絲) with or without leafy pendants from Manchuria, as well as those, also made from one single twisted wire, with a single-ring pendant (*danhuan* 單環), or those with a

---

100   Wei Jian 2004, 11, 28, 153, 162, 169. Some consider Qilangshan to be an early fifth-century site.

cast pendant with spiral motifs (*wowen* 渦紋) from the area west of the Xing'an Mountains. Not even the archaeological finds in the Three Yan and Koguryeo areas yield similar crescent-shaped earrings. Such earrings from the tombs of Pingcheng, to which small rings or pins were often soldered for hanging beads, pearls, or other kinds of pendants, obviously had a western origin, and, according to Otani, remained closely connected with Central Asians. A similar technique (e.g., Figs. 10.4, 10.7) was applied to craft the gold crescentic earring with a pearl pendant of Shijun (579).[101]

Only three pairs of earrings with gold pendants have been archaeologically excavated from Pingcheng tombs to date (Figs.10.8; 11.1–2). The pendants from the Jiaotongyuan 交通苑 site (Fig. 11.1) consist of two segments of straight wires that are tightly coiled up with additional gold wires and attached with dangling gold discs. A hollow, spherical gold bead with multiple eyelets and covered with fine granules (Fig. 11.1a) was set between the two segments. At the bottom of the lower segment, several loop-in-loop chains are attached, ending in elongated, pointed drops reminiscent of winged fruits (samaras). They could have been a variation of the "beechnut" motif that was extremely popular first in the Mediterranean and West Asian regions and then widespread on the Eurasian steppes since the first millennium BCE.[102] However, the distribution of "wing-fruit" drops are restricted only in Pingcheng and the adjacent sites in Inner Mongolia. A pair of golden earrings of the similar type, but with only one coiled-wire segment and five small plain spherical gold beads instead of a hollow one with granulation, were found in 1964 in a stone casket placed in the foundation of a pagoda in Dingxian 定縣, Hebei (Fig. 11.3).[103] The Dingxian earrings were among the devotional gifts donated by Empress Dowager Wenming and Emperor Xiaowen to the newly constructed pagoda in 481, indicating that they were brought from Pingcheng and highly valued. Based on the similar structure, Han Lisen et al. suggest that the donated Dingxian earrings may have been "tributes" from Koguyeo or Silla.[104] At least four additional pairs of earrings similar to those from Jiaotongyuan are found in museums or private collections.[105] Delacour notices that the hollow beads with eyelets were crafted in a separate goldsmith tradition than the segments and gold discs.[106] Since the Jiaotongyuan pendants have not been studied, this is not the place to discuss the goldsmithing techniques in detail. It is however worth noting that tassels made of loop-in-loop chains and segments of coiled wires with dangling discs stand out among the excavated jewelry from Koguryo and Silla, not a single earring from this region displays both features. In addition, the drop shapes from Pingcheng and Inner Mongolia pendants differ significantly from those from Koguryo and Silla. If these pendants arrived in Pingcheng as gifts or "tributes," they were probably modified to suit the current tastes of Pingcheng's elites. It is not even certain whether these pendants from Pingcheng and Inner Mongolian were used as earrings, as suggested in Fig. 11.2, or temple pendants, as the excavation data are not available.

---

101 Otani Ikue 2012, especially pp. 324–29.
102 Liu Yan et al. 2021: 268–73. The excavation of the Jiaotongyuan site is not yet published.
103 Hebei sheng 1966: 225. Otani Ikue 2012: 327; Han Lisen et al. 2013: 178.
104 Han Lisen et al. 2013, 296.
105 Two pairs are now in Japan, one pair in the Hohhot Museum (Otani Ikue 2022), and another pair in the Musée Guimet (Delacour 2002: 184–87), all without a clear provenance. The Guimet pair came, according to Delacour (2002: 184), from the Yikezhao Banner 伊克昭盟, modern Erdos City.
106 Delacour 2002: 185–87.

Figure 12 (1) Necklace of Han Farong from 11DHAM13 at the Heng'anjie site, Datong (Period IV); (2) Bodhisattva on the eastern window frame of Yungang Cave 13; (3–4) Figurine of a female dancer from Yanbei shiyuan (M52:23), and its back view.

(1, 2): after Datong kaogu 2015: 18, Fig. 13 and Zhang Zhuo (ed.), Yungang (Nanjing: Jiangsu meishu chubanshe, 2011), 151, Fig. 118. With permission of the Datong Archaeological Institute and the Yungang Academy; (3–4) Photos by the author (at the Datong Museum).

The pendants from Dianhanchang M180 (Period II) have very short, coiled-wire segments (Fig. 11.2) and were most likely made according to a steppe or Central Asian tradition. Their flat, bell-shaped drops find parallels in Sirkap, Taxila.[107]

---

[107] https://museumsofindia.gov.in/repository/record/nat_del-49-262-8-9800; accessed October 15, 2023.

The third Pingcheng earring pair with pendants comes from Han Farong's tomb (Period IV). The earrings are crescent-shaped and have two small soldered-on rings for hanging pendants (Fig. 10.8). Each earring bears a human image adorned with an urna and a wreath. And the image is flanked by two opposing "dragons," or Makaras, thus forming a master-of-animals motif.[108] The three rosettes on the front are set with red, green, and blue stones that depict a flower bud, an animal mask, and a parrot. The human image with an urna is reminiscent of the central figure on the earring pendants found in Tillya Tepe Tomb 2, first century BCE, although their hairstyles and headdresses are completely different. The most amazing features of the Heng'anjie earrings are, however, the hinged claps. A number of antique earrings of the Parthian period are known to have used this technique.[109] The motif combination and the hinged claps of the Heng'anjie earrings resemble an earring pair in the collection of the Hakutsuru Museum of Art 白鶴美術館 (Fig. 10.9) in Kobe, Japan, which has been dated to the Sui period based on inlay and granulation techniques.[110] Given that hinged clips are otherwise not evidenced in Pingcheng jewelry finds (except for a few chin-straps, see below), it is reasonable to assume that the Heng'anjie earrings were imported from a place where the influence of the Indian Buddhist arts and of the Hellenistic and West Asian jewelry techniques met. The region Bactria or Gandhara seems to be good candidates in this regard, since several earrings with similar hinged clips were found in Gandhara.[111] The long loop-in-loop chain of the right earring from Heng'anjie was broken, but the remaining chain is still attached to the uppermost small ring, indicating that the chain once formed a loop. A pair of earrings from the Late Hellenic period in the Metropolitan Museum of Art also has this unusual looping-chain structure, which may have served to hold the decorative front in place.[112]

In addition to the earring pair, the Heng'anjie tomb also yielded a necklace with more than 4200 beads of precious stones, glass, and gold. The reconstruction (Fig. 12.1) was based on the in-situ positions of the beads, and the result resembles the depictions found on numerous contemporary Bodhisattva statues in several Yungang caves and tomb figurines of female dancers from the same period (Figs. 12.2–3). Since similar necklaces mainly adorned bodhisattvas, they were undoubtedly a royal symbol. It is, however, debatable why dancers, as well as Han Farong, the woman buried in the Heng'anjie tomb, also wore such necklaces. Thus far, only a few female dancer figurines have been excavated. Only the two from Yanbei shiyuan M52 are decorated with such necklaces.[113] One specimen has the eye terminals of the necklace situated on its shoulders (Fig. 12.4), indicating that the necklace may have been fastened differently than the reconstructed one of Han Farong.

There are no deposits of chalcedony or agate in northern Shanxi. Rather, these stones were mined or collected from surface gravels in neighboring Inner Mongolia, northern

---

108 For high-resolution photos: https://m.weibo.cn/status/4793357161729189#&gid=1&pid=1; accessed October 16, 2023.
109 See, for example, Stöllner et al. 2004, vol. 2, Fig. 741.
110 Otani Ikue 2021, Fig. 6–6 and 328. The dating was made in the 1990s, when little fifth-century jewelry was available. New materials may help rethink the dating of the earrings in the Hakutsuru Museum.
111 Sengupta 2019, 48 Fig. 1.82, 50 Fig. 1.86, 94 Fig. 2.53, 192 Fig. 4.11, just to name a few.
112 For the function of the chains, see https://www.metmuseum.org/art/collection/search/256194; accessed October 17, 2023.
113 Liu Junxi 2008, 37, Fig. 26 (M52:23), Color Pl. 12.2 (M52:25),

Hebei, or even farther afield in southern Manchuria and Mongolia. It is therefore not sur-prising that the finds of carnelian, i.e., chalcedony in its red-orange hue, from the Chinese Bronze Age all lie along this distribution line.[114] These stones or beads were, consequently, either commercially imported or brought as personal belongings to Pingcheng. If they were imported, we do not know if they were already cut in their areas of origin or only on arrival in Pingcheng. Agate beads in Pingcheng tombs are not etched and are therefore different from those preferred in Central, South, or Southeast Asia.

Only a few amber beads are found in Pingcheng, chiefly in the tombs of Periods III and IV containing rich grave goods.[115] We have no knowledge of the sources of these ambers, nor do we know how they were imported. Two amber beads with ornaments typical for the Yungang Cave art indicate that they were carved in Pingcheng and may have been worn as amulets to ward off evil and ensure heavenly blessing.[116] Since the amber beads were high-ly valued by Xianbei aristocrats in the later Northern Dynasties, there were most likely more amber beads in Pingcheng, but they were not correctly identified.

"Body ornaments" of another kind are chinstraps. They were employed as a practical mortuary device to keep the lower jaw of the deceased from falling. The Pingcheng ones were mostly made of bronze, only a few were of silver or even gold.[117] When the bronze ones were covered with embroidered silk (Fig. 13.1a), they undoubtedly also belonged to luxurious goods and served to adorn the face of the deceased. Several chinstrap "designs" were found in Pingcheng, which indicates that various workshops were involved in the pro-duction. The most sophisticated ones have hinged joints between the bowl for the chin and the cheek band (Fig. 13.1), a metal technique otherwise not attested to in northern China. The simple chinstraps only have an oval bowl for the lower jaw, the two long bowl ends merge seamlessly into two individual, thin cheek strips.[118] Table 4 shows that chinstraps were mainly found in Period III, but decreased rapidly in Period IV and the material was also changed to lead. This downward trend accelerated after the move of the capital to Luo-yang. In the sixth century, the practice almost completely disappeared.[119] All chinstrap users, as far as their gender can be determined, were females, and most chinstraps were found in pit or catacomb burials. Only very few occupants in brick-chambered tombs used

---

114 Rawson 2010, 9; Kenoyer et al. 2022: 5–7.
115 Lin Hao 2020.
116 The Book of (Liu) Song tells that the Chinese considered amber a remedy for stab wounds caused by weapons (*Song shu* 3.60), probably because they had in mind a parallel to a pine tree, which heals its cuts by secreting resin, the basic substance of amber; see Schafer 1963, 248. But there is no indication that the idea was present in Pingcheng. Pingcheng's amber beads are decorated with lotus petals, floral scrolls, or dragon-tiger pairs. The one from the Qijiapo tomb bears an arrangement of all three motifs (Wang Yintian and Han Shengcun 1995), which resembles the depiction of heaven in Dunhuang Cave 249 (Western Wei). It is possible that the ornamentation on the bead alludes to a Buddhist heaven.
117 Several gold chinstraps were excavated in Datong in the past few years, but none were published. The term "bronze" is used here for convenience. The copper alloys were never examined. The metal sheets used to make the chin bowls are thin and must have been hammered. It is thus likely that the alloys differed from those of bronze to achieve a higher metal plasticity.
118 See, e.g., Shanxi daxue et al. 2006, Pl. 1.1 (Dianhanchang M53, Period IV); Müller Sh. 2003 [2006].
119 For the second half of the sixth century, only one chinstrap (of silver) has been discovered. That is the tomb of Han Zunian 韓祖念 (d. 568) of the Northern Qi dynasty, Taiyuan shi 2020, 8, 57.

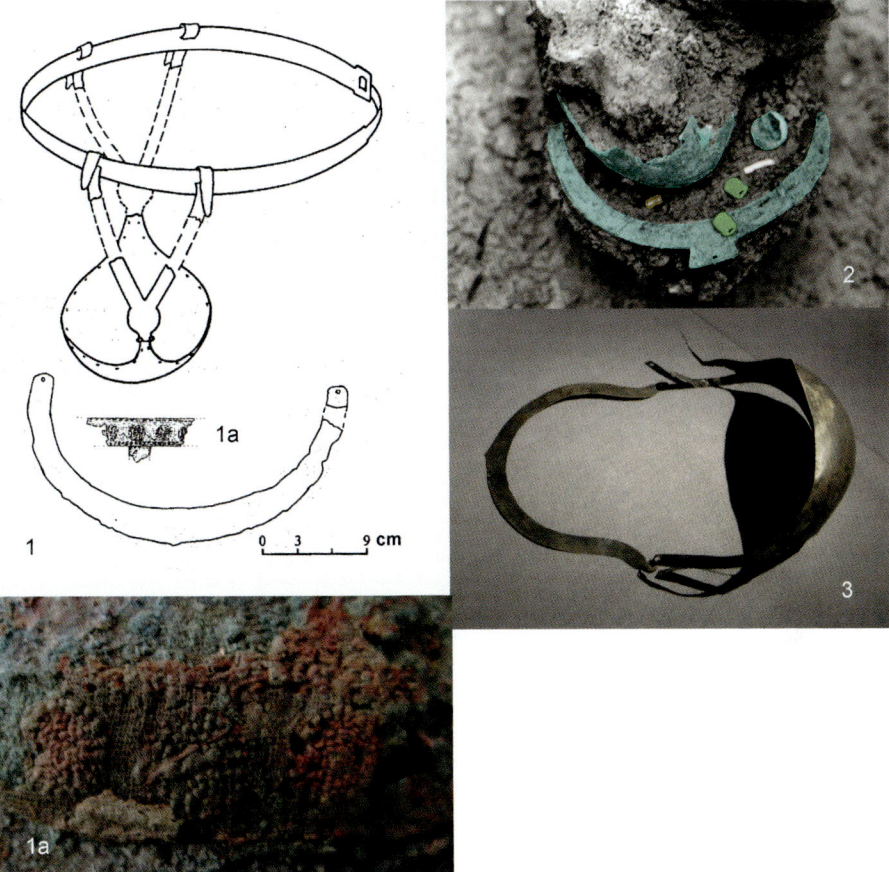

Figure 13 Chinstraps and crescent-shaped pectorals from (1) Dianhanchang (DHC) M107, (1a) embroidered textile on the bowl; (2) DHC M208 with stone (green), amber (yellow), and bone (white) beads; (3) from a looted tomb, of silver. The pectoral was falsely exhibited as the cheek strip.

(1–2) modified after Shanxi daxue et al. 2006, 233, Fig. 105G; Pl. 8. With permission of the Datong Archaeological Institute; (1a, 3) Photos by the author in the Datong Museum.

these devices. I have suggested elsewhere that the custom of using chinstraps may have been introduced from the Tarim Basin to Pingcheng.[120] Recent excavations in the Altai region indicate that some steppe members during the "Xianbei period" already incorporated the chin-binding practice into their funerary rite with a textile band.[121] Textile chinstraps were obviously widely used on the steppe in funerary rites, but it is difficult to find evi-

---

120 Müller Sh. 2003 [2006].
121 In Sheveet Khairkhan Tomb No. 4 (between first and third century CE). Otani Ikue 2021: 1–2 Fig. 2.

dence of them since textiles decompose easily. The Altai materials also give insight into the
reason why chinstraps were predominantly found among the catacomb tomb occupants in
Pingcheng and indicate that more deceased in Pingcheng might have used chinstraps, but of
textiles, which had decayed without leaving any traces. Lastly, the metal version may have
been an "upgrade" for some urbanized steppe peoples, alone the expensive material (bronze
was in shortage) would speak for the idea.

Crescent-shaped pectorals can be traced back to the Bronze Age on the steppe. Only
two are found in Pingcheng. Both tombs containing them were richly furnished, and both
deceased wore chinstraps. The co-existence is also evidenced in Ih-Nur, Inner Mongolia.
The relationship between the chinstrap and the pectoral is however unclear. The one from
Dianhanchang M107 resembles those of the Bodhisattvas and has an inconspicuous point-
ed-arch shape (Fig. 13.1, 12.2). The other one from Dianhanchang M208, is of the "steppe
type," i.e., it has, like that of Ih-Nur M6, a trapezoidal protrusion in the middle.[122] All these
four tombs belong to Period III. The occupant in M107 has been identified as a young female, while the skeletal remains in M208 are not sufficient for a sex determination. The
pectoral of the latter was painted blue and wrapped in silk, which may indicate that this
highly valued artifact was ritually deposited into the coffin.

It can be observed that the manner of decorating the corpses differs from older practices,
be they Chinese or Xianbei style. Jade, or nephrite, a stone highly valued by the Chinese, is
virtually non-existent in Pingcheng tombs.[123] Another tradition is also conspicuously absent
from Pingcheng: the tree-like ornament with dangling gold leaves as the headdress of the
Murong Xianbei elite. The only exception is a painted one on the coffin portraits from
Shaling M7, which appears to be a memory of the distant past, as discussed below. Perforated bronze sheets in the shape of drops or leaves were found in several tombs. However,
since their in-situ position in the tombs is unknown, we are not aware which part of the
body they were employed to decorate or how they were arranged to adorn the body. Only
from the Heng'anjie tomb do we know that such leaves were found gathered in front of the
forehead of the deceased woman.[124] They were most likely arranged in a specific way as a
headdress, perhaps in combination with mica flakes found next to them. Lastly, several
silver or bronze hairpins on top of skulls indicate that some individuals coiled tied their hair
in a topknot. Qilicun M29, excavated in 2020, indicates that the deceased wore a silver
hairpin under the Xianbei hat (see below). Likewise, the hair remains from Feng Shigong's
tomb in Guyuan indicate that many people did not braid their hair but tied it in buns.[125]

Personal belongings and weapons

Mirrors and scissors were found, though not in great numbers, in Pingcheng tombs of all
types in Periods III and IV. They were generally placed next to the head of the deceased,
but in some cases, a mirror was also found near the legs. Judging from the very few sex-
identified burials, more mirrors, or scissors, or both, are found in female burials. The male

---

122 Otani Ikue 2019: 131–34; Stark 2021, 71–76. For the finds, see Shanxi daxue et al. 2006, 233, 294.
123 Dien 2007a, 273; Müller Sh. 2019c, 392–93.
124 Datong kaogu 2015: 15, Fig. 4.
125 Datong kaogu 2023: 37. The hairpin was detected by an X-ray examination. For Feng Shigong's finds,
    see Ningxia Guyuan 1988a, without page number, last page of the black and white photos.

deceased were given a mirror in Wenyinglu M1 (Period III) and Yanbei shiyuan M2 (Period IV), and a pair of scissors in Dianhanchang M3 (Period III) and Yanbei shiyuan M2 (Period IV). As a result, it is not very clear whether both articles were indeed sex (or gender)-related, as they were throughout the Han and Jin periods.

The use of mirrors in funerary rites has a long tradition on the steppe. It is possible that the Pingcheng inhabitants followed their own steppe traditions in this regard. Unlike the sepulchral custom of breaking mirrors, known from Xiongnu burials during the Han period, the mirrors from Datong tombs remained intact.

Of the twenty-one reported mirrors, eighteen are made of iron and only three of bronze, and twelve were from catacomb graves. Their sizes range from 5 or 6 cm to 20 cm in diameter. One explanation for the very small number of bronze mirrors is the general shortage of copper after Han times, especially in northern China.[126] This is supported by the fact that bronze artifacts are rare in Pingcheng burials. The three bronze mirrors exhibit significant signs of wear, and their décor appears to be typical of Eastern Han or Western Jin times. Since no locally cast bronze mirrors from Pingcheng are known, they were probably heirlooms or dowries of the tomb occupants—one of them was a woman.[127] This is interesting because, unlike in the north, in the tombs of the Nanjing area during the Six Dynasties period, bronze mirrors were reserved exclusively for men.[128]

Iron mirrors in Pingcheng, corresponding to Dien's second stage of the development, were not bronze substitutes. Some placed on the lower legs, or the feet were apparently used for specific rituals. Many were regarded as valuable, as about one-third of the iron mirrors from Pingcheng were wrapped in silk fabrics. The one from the Qijiapo tomb was enclosed in an embroidered silk pouch. It is unclear whether they were inlaid with gold, such as the one from Feng Sufu's tomb, since the mirrors were not examined.[129]

Only twenty-five tombs, primarily of the catacomb type, contain belt buckles, strap ends, or ring fittings. They were laid near an arm, on the breast, or close to other parts of the body in six tombs. In the remaining tombs (of all Pingcheng periods), belt components were located near the waist of the deceased of both genders, indicating that they were part of the clothing and not simply grave gifts. Slightly more females than males were clad in garments fastened with belts. Women's use of belts (identified by belt buckles or fittings) suggests that their clothing was different from that of Xianbei women (without a belt; see below). This way of dressing the deceased was probably intended to preserve their own ethnic identity[130] despite the ongoing Xianbei-ization, at least in the coffin.

---

126 For the mirrors during the Six Dynasties see Dien 2007a, 261–66. He also indicates that iron mirrors were cast in northern China during the Three Kingdoms period due to the copper shortage.

127 Dianhanchang M54 (catacomb tomb), the only Period II tomb containing a mirror. It resembles the triangular-rimmed (三角緣) type common from the end of Eastern Han to the Sun Wu period. The second bronze mirror came from Dianhanchang M20 (catacomb tomb; Period IV). The skeleton decayed badly, and the gender cannot be determined. The motif "four beasts and four knobs" 四乳四 獸 is typical for the Jin mirrors; Shanxi daxue et al. 2006, 54 and 152. The third one is found in Ying-bin dadao M48, a knife-shaped tomb which cannot be periodized. Datong kaogu 2006c: 68, Fig. 55.

128 Kieser 2002, 102.

129 Wang Yintian and Han Shengcun 1995: 16; Dien 2007a, 266 for the second stage. For Feng Sufu's mirror and iron mirrors in general during the Sixteen Kingdoms period, Liaoning bowu 2015, 211–16.

130 Pearson 2001, 9: "(the vestments for the dead were) mourners' reading or representation of the dead person's former self-representation through dress,"

Belt parts were also found in individual square earthen and brick chamber tombs, such as the recently excavated tomb of Lü Xu (456) with a painted funerary stone house.[131]

Most of the belt fittings are of bronze or iron. Occasionally, gilded bronze belt buckles or silver ring fittings are found. Several types of buckles and ring fittings are found in Pingcheng. Together with other, often unavailable excavation data, they could provide clues as to the origin of the wearers.[132]

Very few long iron swords, composite bows (indicated by bone strengtheners), arrowheads, knives, and awls are found in Pingcheng. They were deposited in both male and female burials, usually aligned with one arm of the deceased individual or close to the waists. Most of the tombs containing them were of the catacomb type, but they were also found in some later brick-chambered tombs. Interestingly, more women's tombs than men's tombs contained knives or arrowheads, although mostly only one or two pieces. Flat-topped arrowheads, such as those from Dianhanchang M97 (Fig. 14, *above*, no. 2), the tomb of a young woman (20–25 years old), may have been made for hunting fur-bearing animals. Some coffin paintings also show hunters using similar arrowheads (Fig. 14, *below*). Therefore, arrowheads and small knives (all shorter than 20 cm) were most likely tools. The flat-topped arrowheads also indicate a northeastern origin of the deceased, since their distribution in the period between the first century BCE and the fifth century CE was limited to an area stretching from Jalainur 扎賚諾爾 and Hulun Buir 呼倫貝爾 to Jilin, Liaoning, and northern Korea.[133] None have been observed in the Trans-Baikal or Altai regions.

Only three long swords of the category of weapons were found in Pingcheng, all from catacomb burials: two are one-edged (*dao*) with a length of about 60 cm (Dianhanchang [DHC] M64, M227; Period unknown and II), the third, 120 cm long and double-edged (*jian*), is found in Yingbin dadao [YBDD] M65 (Period II). Those from DHC M64 and YBDD M65 each have a ring pommel that is typical of the Three Kingdoms and the Western Jin periods. While the Chinese of Han times valued combats with the long sword *jian*, in the following era it was gradually replaced by the chopping long *dao*, which proved more effective for mounted troops. Long swords *jian* were increasingly used in ceremonies or as personal accessories of the nobility.[134] Feng Shigong 馮始公 (489) in Guyuan was also interred with a long sword *jian* (L. c. 75 cm). Following this historical development of the double-edged long swords, both the sword in YBDD M65 and that of Feng Shigong seem to be heirlooms or highly prized ceremonial objects.

Lance heads and armor lamellae have not been found in Pingcheng burials to date, nor has horse gear, even though many Pingcheng inhabitants were supposedly pastoralists and possibly horse riders as well. Many mounted warrior figurines or rider figures in mural paintings also indicate that horse riding was omnipresent in Pingcheng. Two recent studies on bone fractures sampled from Dongxin Square and Jinmaoyuan sites suggest that certain injuries were caused by frequent horse riding.[135] It appears that horse gear, like agricultural

---

131 Zhang Zhizhong et al. 2021 mention a "belt ornament" 帶飾 without giving further details.
132 See the overview of the buckle finds in Pingcheng in Wang Yanqing 2017.
133 Zhongguo shehui 2018, 549, Fig. 9-19.
134 For the find of a long *dao* (L. 120 cm) with a ring pommel in Ulanqab, dated to Western Jin, see Huangfu 2007, 39. For the development of *jian*: Huangfu 2007, 37; Lorge 2011, 78, 80.
135 Li Pengzhen 2021: 31, 103; Wang Yu 2021: 40. For the close relationship between men and horses under the Tuoba rule, see Müller Sh. 2009.

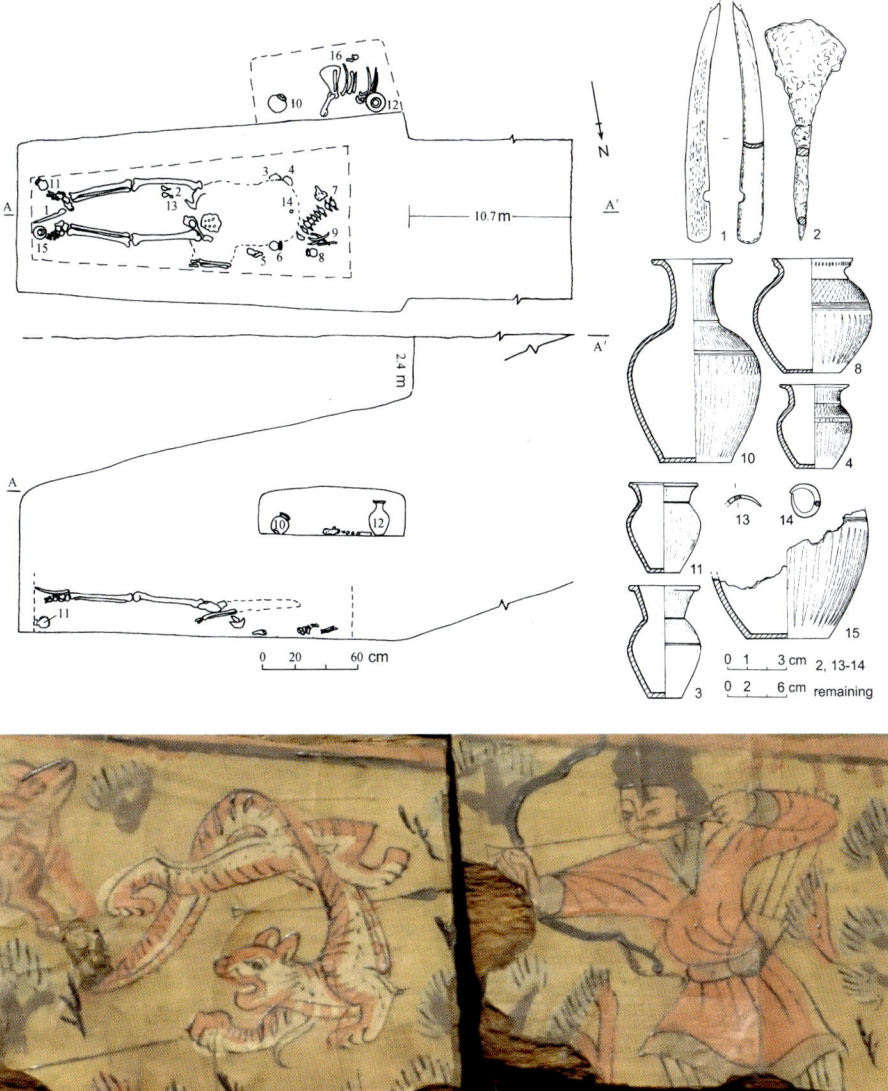

Figure 14 (*Above*) Weapons/tools from Dianhanchang M97 (Period II); 1 bone strengthener for bow, 2 iron arrowheads (3x), 3–4, 6, 8, 10–12, 15 ceramic vessels, 5, 7, 9, 16 animal bones, 13 bronze ring, 14 a silver earring; (*Below*) Coffin painting, possibly from Yingxian, fifth century.

Adapted after Shanxi daxue et al. 2006, 207–8, with permission of Professor Wang Yanqing; photo by the author in the Museum of Northern Dynasties Arts.

tools, was not considered appropriate for grave offerings in this city. Only a century ago, the more militant Murong and other northeastern groups celebrated the funerals of their deceased members by depositing horse-riding equipment (including saddles and iron stirrups), armor lamellae, and lethal weapons into the tombs, an act that emphasized the warrior status of the deceased. Only a few iron stirrups have been found in Pingcheng, but we only have the information that one came from the pillaged tomb of Sima Jinlong (dated 484), the third-largest tomb to date in the Pingcheng area. A pair of iron stirrups was found in the unlooted tomb of Feng Shigong in Guyuan, Ningxia. This tomb, like that of Sima Jinlong, did not yield any further horse equipment. Yuan Shu 元淑 (died 507), a Tuoba royal member of Shiyijian's lineage and military governor, was buried in Pingcheng without stirrups. Given that stirrups were found in the tombs of two individuals with distinguished military careers—both of whom most likely stood close to Empress Dowager Wenming, the de facto ruler until her death—it seems clear that stirrups were more a token of honor than a signifier of Tuoba or Xianbei identity.[136]

Animal offerings, food, and vessels

As mentioned above, another striking feature of many Pingcheng burials is the strong presence of animal offerings as meal for the dead. This differs significantly from the practices of the Xiongnu, who deposited animal skulls and extremities in tombs.[137] Only eight Pingcheng burials demonstrated a similar animal ritual: the heads and four hooves of horses, cattle, sheep/goats, or dogs were placed in the dromos, the entrance shaft, or near the entrance to the tomb chamber.[138] Animal sacrifices of this kind in Pingcheng were doubtlessly part of the tomb sealing procedure. The ritual, which has been practiced for centuries by numerous steppe peoples, can be traced back to the Bronze Age. The head and four extremities appear to have symbolized the whole animal and most likely represented the spiritual escort of the soul of the deceased into the afterlife, as well as the livestock property of the deceased.[139] Horse and cattle skulls were also found in some post-Pingcheng burials, such as those of Yao Qiji 姚齊姬 (dated 499) in present-day Baotou and of Gao Kun 高琨 (reburied in Pingcheng in 514), brother of the notorious chancellor Gao Zhao 高肇 of Korean descent.[140] According to the Book of the Northern Dynasties,[141] the inhabitants of the

---

136 Sima Jinlong stood close to Empress Dowager Wenming, while Feng Shigong and Wenming were presumably of the same clan. Song Xing 2002: 280–81; Luo Feng 2019, 142–45. For Yuan Shu's tomb, see Datong bowu 1989; Wang Yintian 1989.

137 Du Linyuan 2007. The southern Xiongnu still carried out the same practice, see Miller 2015, 175. But there were regional differences in animal deposition in Xiongnu tombs, Martin 2011.

138 Period II: Dianhanchang M63 (male, catacomb); Period III: Dianhanchang M50 (paired burial in one coffin; catacomb), Dianhanchang M57 (single burial, sex unknown, catacomb), Dianhanchang M66 (single burial, sex unknown, catacomb), Dianhanchang M107 (female, catacomb), the wife of Yuchi Dingzhou (457; brick chamber); Period IV: Dianhanchang M53 (female, pit); M101 (single burial, sex unknown, catacomb). Shanxi daxue et al. 2006, 11, 47, 57, 60, 63, 213, 224; Datong kaogu 2011c.

139 Martin 2011, 240; Liu Yuyang and Wang Hui 2017; Luo Feng 2018.

140 For Yao Qiji, see Zheng Long 1988, for Gao Kun, see Wang Yintian 1989, 68. For this tradition in the post-Pingcheng period, see Müller Sh. 2000, 183, 189–91.

141 *Bei shi* (49.1807) mentions "killing big horses" (大馬). This was most likely a corruption of "dogs and horses" (犬馬) due to the graphic similarity between *da* 大 and *quan* 犬. According to *Sanguo zhi* (30.832–33), a dog was sacrificed to escort the soul of the deceased to the Red Mountain, and the per-

Wuchuan Garrison 武川鎮, who defended the border against the invading Rouran tribe, continued sacrificing dogs and horses in funerary ceremonies until the final years of the Northern Wei, It appears that this steppe tradition was better preserved on the northern frontier than in Pingcheng, the capital.

Table 5. Animal sacrifices and animal offerings in Pingcheng burials

Period	Position in tomb	I (pre-398)	II (398-439)	III (440-476)	IV (477-494)	V (post-494)	Total
Pit	In filling	-	1	-	1	1	
	in front of coffin	-	2 [1]	-	-	-	2 [1]
	in coffin	-	1	-	1	-	2
Catacomb (with slope or shaft type of entrance)	In entrance	-	1 (shaft)	2 (shaft)	1 (shaft)	1 (slope)	
	in a wall niche	-	3 (slope)	4 (slope [2])	3 (slope, [1])	1 (slope)	11 (slope [3])
			1 (shaft)	5 (shaft)			6 (shaft)
	in front of the coffin	1 (slope [1])	5 (slope, [3])	9 (slope, [4])	7 (slope, [2])	1 (slope)	23 (slope [10])
			6 (shaft)	4 (shaft, [1])	3 (shaft [1])	1 (shaft, [1])	14 (shaft [3])
	in coffin		1 (slope) 4 (shaft)	3 (slope) 1 (shaft)	2 (slope)	-	6 (slope) 5 (shaft)
knife-shaped	in front of coffin	-	-	2 [1]	-	-	2 [1]
	in coffin			1			1
Earthen chamber w/ house	in front of funerary bed in the house	-	-	1 (on a ceramic tray)	-	-	1
	in chamber			1 [1]			1 [1]
Single-chambered brick tomb	in dromos	-	-	1	-	-	
	near entrance	-	-	-	2	-	2
	in chamber	-	2 [1]		3 [1]		5 [2]
	in front of a coffin/bed/house	-	-	1 (coffin)	4 [4]	1 [1]	6 [5]
	in coffin	-	1	-	-	-	1
double-chambered	in antechamber	-	1 [1]	-	-	-	1 [1]
Total (food)		1 [1]	27 [6]	32 [9]	25 [9]	4 [2]	89 [27]

[n]: number of tombs with animal offerings placed on a lacquer tray.

Gray-shaded rows indicate that the animals could have been used as sacrifices. These figures were not added to the total numbers.

---

sonal riding horse was sacrificed to accompany, or, to carry, the deceased into the afterlife; Schreiber 1947: 154. For the deposition of dogs and horses in tombs of "the forerunners of the Xianbei in Inner Mongolia, Müller Sh. 2000, 49–86. For the practice among other steppe groups, Martin 2011, 240.

The majority of the animals used for funerary meals are not zoologically identified. The few skeletons that were studied belonged to cattle, or sheep/goats. Horses have not been evidenced as food offerings in tombs so far, although horse meat was indeed consumed in daily life (see below). Fowls were served as offerings occasionally, dogs (as food) and pigs were found even less frequently. The food offerings in Dianhanchang M126 (Period III) are particularly intriguing, as a pig bone was found alongside the bones of sheep/goats, and the tomb was a paired burial in a single coffin, with a man and a woman interred with their backs against each other.[142] Additionally, the mural in the most recently excavated Qilicun 2020M29 (brick-chambered tomb) depicts, among other things, a female servant in Xianbei clothing feeding two pigs,[143] i.e., the animals were domesticated. At least this latter case indicates that a small percentage of Pingcheng's inhabitants came from sedentary populations who, unlike pastoralists, originally lived in humid ecological environments. It is unclear if the pig bones in the first case and a few additional tombs came from domestic pigs or wild boars. In any case, although wild boars were presumably among the game animals (see below; additionally, one coffin board from Inner Mongolia bears a scene with a Xianbei hunter shooting at a wild boar), pork did not seem to be much consumed.[144] It is also possible that part of the settled pastoralists accepted pigs as farm animals in the fifth century, and the report in the Book of Southern Qi about the pig raising in Pingcheng Palace was not entirely defamatory.[145]

Animal offerings were primarily found in catacomb tombs in all periods, but rarely in knife-shaped tombs. Individual earthen chamber tombs with funerary houses (of Period III) and few large, even painted, brick chamber tombs (of Periods III to V) also showed the same practice (Table 5). Some individuals of Chinese descent also adopted animal offerings. For example, a lacquer plate in front of the wooden funerary house of Jia Bao (477) of Guzang held sheep shoulders.[146]

There is no study of how offerings were prepared.[147] Usually, the rather meaty trunk, i.e., the entire ribcage and vertebrae with shoulders, as well as the forelegs of a sheep/goat or dog, or one or two limbs or shoulders of cattle, were served. They are commonly found in wall niches and occasionally in coffins as well. But most frequently, they were placed directly in front of the head panel of a coffin. Moreover, it appears that animal food offerings have been occurring more often in catacomb tombs with a long entrance slope in comparison to those with a vertical entrance shaft. This suggests that the people buried in the two subtypes of tombs performed their funerary rituals slightly differently. However, the current data are inadequate for a thorough study.

In addition to the indication of the tomb-type dependency of animal offerings, Tables 1 and 5 also seem to suggest that the total number of tombs containing animal offerings dropped slightly from 34% in Period III (32 out of 95 tombs) to 29% in Period IV (25 out

---

142 Shanxi daxue et al. 2006, 252. There are more cases in the unpublished Suibosi cemetery.
143 Datong kaogu 2023: 49, Fig. 31. Pigs are also depicted on the façade of the stone house for Xie Xing's wife (459).
144 Zhang Guowen et al. 2020, Figs. 2 and 5.
145 *Nan Qi shu* 57.984; Bray 2018, 128–31.
146 Datong kaogu 2021a: 28.
147 Studies on Pazyryk burials demonstrate that animal offerings were detached from already processed carcasses; cf. Simpson and Stepanova 2017, 159–60.

of 87 tombs). The number of animal offerings presented on the showy and costly lacquer plates dropped in catacomb tombs but increased in brick tombs from Periods III to IV (Table 5). Although the amount of data is insufficient for a serious study, my data collection shows that the quantity and animal parts for the funerary meal remained until the end of Pingcheng. We may cautiously assume that the effort required for animal offerings did not change much. However, some historical interludes may have had a short-term impact on the animal offerings in tombs, such as a ban on animal sacrifices in 472, imposed out of compassion for life by the "retired" Xianwendi 獻文帝, a devout follower of Buddhism, or the climatic catastrophes between 479 and 490, as well as a plague that ravaged cattle stocks in 487.[148]

The tomb of Yuchi Dingzhou's wife (457) contains the largest number of sacrificed animals known to date: sixteen animals (two horses, six oxen, four sheep/goats and four dogs) were killed for her funeral. Despite being economical in comparison to ancient burial practices involving animal sacrifices in the steppe, this form of animal consumption may have evoked disgust among individuals who grew up in an agrarian environment. The Confucian, or Ru, scholar Gao Yun 高允 (390–487) from Bohai 渤海 (present-day Hebei) submitted a well-known memorandum to Emperor Wencheng 文成帝 (r. 460–465), in which he complained about the excessive wedding and funeral celebrations of the Pingcheng populace.[149] One of the misdeeds committed, in his eyes, was the sacrifice of livestock. The complaint may be justified if he was thinking about funerals like the one for Yuchi Dingzhou's wife. However, given that most findings contain no more than two animals on average, regardless of whether the tomb was a small catacomb or a large double-chambered one, the number of animals killed appears moderate. However, we cannot rule out some funeral feasts, at which probably more animals had to give up their lives.

Recently, researchers have begun investigating food consumption in Pingcheng using isotopic stable carbon and nitrogen analysis. For this purpose, human and animal skeletons were sampled from large cemeteries at Dongxin Square, Yuchang jiayuan, and Huayu Square sites, which are assigned to the early (Dongxin), the mid- (Yuchang), and the mid- and late Pingcheng periods (Huayu) by archaeologists.[150] Their findings suggest that, in the early period, people primarily consumed the meat of wild or grazing animals (e.g., sheep, horses, or cattle, but few boars), i.e., the animals were hunted or herded. In the middle and late periods, meat consumption declined. Animal husbandry replaced hunting and herding, and meat came primarily from farmed animals, possibly including dogs. This is indicated by the finding that the animals for funerary meals from later tombs were fed the same plant diet as the one consumed by humans. If their conclusions are correct, numerous farms would be necessary to meet the food demand, since Pingcheng was densely populated. In this case, animal farms could only have been located in the suburbs or rural areas.[151]

The same researchers also emphasize the importance of cereals as staples. Cereal consumption increased when hunting and herding gave way to animal husbandry. They assert that some people in the late period even followed a vegetarian diet. Thus, they believe to be

---

148 *Wei shu* 108A.2740; Eisenberg 2008, Chapter 2 (retired emperorship); Hsu Sheng-I 2003: Table 3.
149 *Wei shu* 48.1073–75.
150 See Fig. 2, nos. 3, 8, 24 and p. 33, Note 35.
151 See p. 4, Note 20.

able to demonstrate the Tuoba Xianbei's transformation, or "Sinicization," from a nomadic pastoral society into a sedentary and agrarian one.[152] Since the archaeological data of the sampled tombs are not published—excepting Dianhanchang—and the sample sizes are small, the conclusions should be taken with caution. The interred persons at the Dianhanchang site, for example, had a high consumption of products of animals fed primarily with millet over the entire Pingcheng era.[153] Hence, the development of dietary habits was not a simple and linear process and the Sinicized foodways cannot be proven in all cemeteries. At present, we can only assume that each migrant group essentially followed its own dietary strategy. Naturally, it cannot be ruled out that people learned the cuisine from others.

The change in eating habits in northern China is also documented in writings such as the *Qimin yaoshu* 齊民要術 (Essential Techniques for the Common People / for the Qi [present-day Shandong] People) of Jia Sixie 賈思勰 (around the 540s). By the end of the Tuoba reign, northern China's culinary delights shifted away from grains and vegetables toward more dairy products and meat consumption.[154]

The main crops in Pingcheng were foxtail millet (*Setaria italica*) 粟 and broomcorn millet (*Panicum miliaceum*) 黍. Both were found at several sites. For example, the bottom of the lacquered coffin of Qilicun 2020M29 (Period III) was covered with a layer of broomcorn millet, and a jar filled with approximately 1.5 liter of millet of the same sort was deposited in the painted coffin of Dianhanchang M253 (Period IV). Large quantities of foxtail millet were also found in the remains of the imperial granary.[155] One walnut and fifteen almonds were found in Dianhanchang M107, and figs in Qilicun 2020M29. This walnut was identified as a cultivar from northern China. But at least almonds and figs were exotica and not yet grown in China. The figs are probably the earliest find in China.[156]

Vessels

Most ceramics from Pingcheng tombs are jars, jugs, crocks, or pans of gray-colored earthenware. The majority (c. 90%) of the grayware was fired between 750° and 950° C. Only a few (c. 6%) were fired at higher temperatures between 1000° and 1050° C.[157] Most of the jars and jugs are without handles. Cooking jars are sand-tempered. A number of mass-produced ceramic vessels from Dianhanchang cemetery for funerary use indicate the presence of local professional potters.[158] However, no kiln sites, except for Xicetian 西冊田, situated

---

152 Zhang Guowen et al. 2015: 704–5; Hou Liangliang and Gu Shunfang 2018a and 2018b.
153 Zhang Guowen et al. 2010.
154 Knechtges 1997: 236–37; Bray 2018; Knapp 2019.
155 Datong kaogu 2023: 37; Shanxi daxue et al. 2006, 587–89. Bray (2019, 364) points out that "while setaria millet was the main crop in the farming system described in the *Qimin yaoshu*, … Broomcorn millet (…) was needed to brew wines." It seems that the Pingcheng inhabitants consumed a great deal of alcoholic beverages. For the cellar find, see Shanxi and Datong 2016, For the botanical identification of the grain remains, see Liu Shan et al. 2022: 147.
156 Shanxi daxue et al. 2006, 581–87. The almonds from M107 came either from the Tarim Basin or from western Central Asia. The fig originated from southwest Asia and was first cultivated in China during the Tang dynasty. For the early walnut cultivation in China and Chinese encounters with figs, see Laufer 1919, 271–72, 410–14. For the spread of these fruits and nuts across Eurasia, see Spengler 2019, 219, 226–29.
157 Shanxi daxue et al. 2006, 544.
158 Shanxi daxue et al. 2006, 559.

on the Sanggan River and approximately 4.4 kilometers southeast to Datong, have been discovered in Pingcheng or its suburbs, and the works of pottery workshops are not mentioned in written sources.[159] Some ceramic vessels found in tombs had clearly seen actual use during the lifetime of the deceased, such as jars and bottles with signs of repair or cooking jars exhibiting soot on their outer surfaces. Jars and jugs were used for the storage of fluids and food. Jia Sixie of the sixth century described how to grease potteries to make them watertight. The method may have been applicable for the fifth century as well.[160]

The basic forms of jars and jugs and their decorations with vertically scraped strips retain steppe traditions.[161] From Period III on, gray pottery vessels bear rolled-on bands of half-palmette scrolls which resemble those depicted in the contemporaneous Yungang caves. On some rare specimens the scrolls were even delicately cold painted in red, white, and black colors (Fig. 15.1).[162] A limited number of small (H. < 12 cm), sand-mixed, and single-handled jugs are found only in catacomb and knife-shaped tombs of Periods III and IV (Fig. 15.3).[163] They represent a ceramic type that frequently appeared in regions west of Gansu since the Bronze Age, such as the Tarim Basin or further west, but not in the pre-dynastic Tuoba burials in Inner Mongolia, the Murong and Puyeo burials in southern Manchuria, or in northern China before the fifth century.

There are many ways of arranging vessels in burials. Quite often, a large bottle up to 40 or 50 cm in height was placed in front of the coffin. Sometimes, a lacquer tray holding several smaller jugs or jars, with or without animal offerings, was deposited in the same position. In knife-shaped tombs, the vessels and the offerings were set in front of the side plank of the coffin. Ceramic vessels were occasionally deposited just in coffins and not in chambers. Although assemblages of ceramics vary from tomb to tomb, the basic message that the deceased should be provided with all the necessities for the afterlife remains the same. Most ceramics for burials were ritually damaged, typically by breaking the mouth rim of a vessel or even its neck, which created a division between the worlds of the dead and the living.[164] This was initially only observed in grayware, but later also in glazed and celadon wares.

One of the most impressive earthenware assemblages was found in the Tiancun M1 (for location: Fig. 2.17), a Period III brick tomb probably with a double burial. In addition to the usual jars and jugs, it contains, twenty-eight small painted shallow bowls *zhan* 盞 (∅ 7.2 cm), twenty-three painted plates *pan* 盤 (∅ 10.3 cm), and seven large, painted eared cups

---

159 Wang Yintian et al. 2010. The Xicetian kiln fired primarily roof tiles and was probably an official workshop since its products were also found in the imperial caves in Yungang. A potters' quarter is first mentioned in sixth-century Luoyang, *Luoyag qielan ji* 5.249 and Jenner 1981, 47 and 113. Potters in Pingcheng were registered as *hu* 戶 (households) and were under state control. For the organization of craftsmen during the Northern Dynasties, see Pearce 1991.

160 *Qimin yaoshu* 63.357–58.

161 Müller Sh. 2019c, 384–85.

162 For example, the jugs from Jia Bao's tomb and Yanbei shiyuan M2.

163 These are: Dianhanchang (DHC) M150, M208, Qilicun M6, Yingbin dadao (YBDD) M87 (all of Period III); DHC M222, Qilicun M9, Hudong 2004M2, Yanbei shiyuan (YBSY) M18 (all of Period IV). Except for YBDD M87 and YBSY M18 (knife-shaped), all are catacomb tombs. See Appendix I, Nos. 2, 8, 11, 22 and 23 for references.

164 A parallel can be drawn from the European Bronze Age, see Brück and Fontijn 2013, 206.

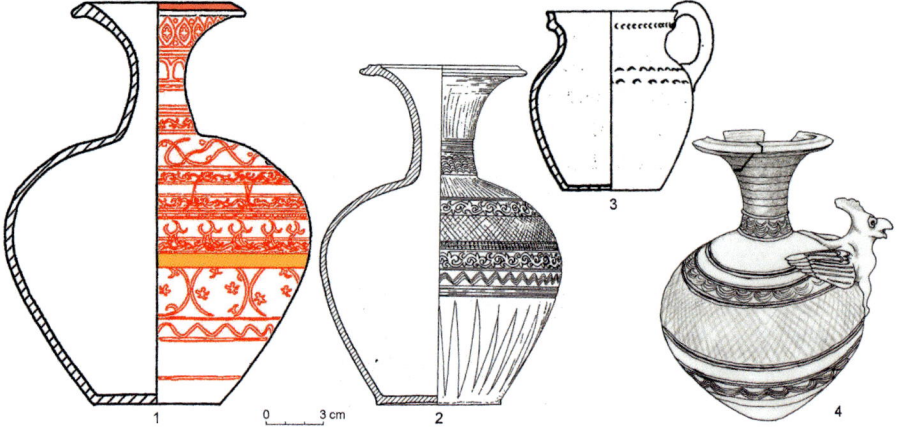

Figure 15 Graywares. (1) Jar with decoration in red and yellow painted on a white slip, from Jia Bao's tomb (477); (2) Jar with rolled-on bands bearing half-palmette scrolls and wave motifs, from Dianhanchang M14; (3); Handled jug from Dianhanchang M222; all from Period IV; (4) recently excavated "Chicken headed" ewer from Huatangcheng cemetery, measure and date unknown.

(1) Modified after Datong kaogu 2021a, 34, Fig. 27.2; (2–3) Shanxi daxue et al. 2006, 139, 307; with permission of the Datong Archaeological Institute and Professor Wang Yanqing. (4) Line-drawing by the author after http://cms.ahm.cn/hzgj/userfiles/2020/7/23/1595488871693/, accessed November 3, 2022.

erbei 耳杯 (16 cm × 9.5 cm), all in uniform sizes and shapes. Also included in this table set are five large pans *pen* 盆 in various sizes, all painted and bearing ornaments in relief, and a clay model of a wine cask with two ladles. All of them were apparently custom-made just for this funeral. The tableware in this tomb was set up for a large funerary banquet, something that had otherwise only been seen in mural paintings of certain tombs (see below).

Recent excavations at the Huatangcheng 華唐城 site (cf. Fig. 2.19) yielded a peculiar "chicken-headed ewer"-style jug (Fig. 15.4).[165] This ceramic type, though rare, was not entirely foreign to the local population, since two genuine Eastern Jin-styled chicken-headed ewers were also unearthed in Pingcheng,[166]. The jug in question has a bizarre composition. Although it resembles a chicken-headed ewer, it lacks a typical handle. Its form and painted or scraped grid pattern are common for the graywares of the later Pingcheng period. With its outspread wings and stout legs, both of which are absent from the chicken-headed spout on the Eastern Jin ewers, the bird is more reminiscent of a Garuda.

---

165 http://cms.ahm.cn/hzgj/userfiles/2020/7/23/1595488871693/, accessed November 3, 2022.

166 For the chicken-headed ewers of the Eastern Jin period, see Dien 2007a, 243–44. A chicken-headed ewer with dark brown glaze very typical of the Deqing kiln 德清窯 of the Eastern Jin period, for example, was discovered in Xiu Guangming's 宿光明 tomb (M14) at the Jinshu meichang site (Period IV); Han Shengcun et al. 1996: 67. Another one with green glaze was excavated at the Liuquan South Street 柳泉南街 site, Datong, in 2015, without any publication.

Figure 16 Glazed potteries with appliqué imitating granulated bezels. (1) Jar from Yingbin dadao M74 (Period V); (2) *zun* 尊-vessel from Qilicun M6 (Period III); (3) Lid from Sima Jinlong's tomb (484; Period IV); (4) Close-up of a "granulated bezel" of clay with a pale-colored filling.

(1, 3) After Datong kaogu 2006c: 67, Fig. 48; 2 and Nanjing bowu 2018, 163. With permission of the Datong Archaeological Institute and the Datong Museum. (2) Photo by the author in the Datong Museum.

The large number of glazed ceramics from Pingcheng of different shapes, sizes, and decorations discovered in the past few years contradict the earlier opinion that the tradition of glazed ceramics ceased to exist after the fall of the Western Jin dynasty.[167] During the final decades of the fifth century, potters began to "paint" products with various colored glazes. The soldier and horse figurines from Sima Jinlong's (484) tomb best illustrate this new trend. The popularity of this handicraft remained strong in the new capital Luoyang, where potters employed polychrome glazes on earthenware bowls to imitate Sasanian glass.

Several late Pingcheng glazed ceramics display yet another innovation: they bear appliquéd clay reliefs imitating granulated bezels known from metalworks (Fig. 16.1–3). Each "bezel" is possibly filled with pale-colored powered glass (without analysis; Fig. 16.4), which, by firing, forms enamel. While the Luoyang and later Northern Qi periods saw further development of the polychrome glaze technique, the enameling technique vanished abruptly in northern China after the fifth century. This specific knowledge was possibly brought to Pingcheng in the second half of the fifth century by certain foreign

---

167　For a recent study of the glazed ceramics of Pingcheng, see Lu Bin and Wang Aiguo 2016.

1   2   3

Figure 17 Celadon stoneware vessels. (1) Jar from Dianhanchang M22 (Period III); (2) Spittoon from Sima Jinlong's tomb (484; Period IV); (3) Bowl from Yanbei shiyuan M1 (Period IV).

(1–2) Photos by the author in the Datong Museum; (3) After Liu Junxi 2008, Color pl. 6.1, with permission of the Datong Archaeological Institute.

craftsmen. It appears that these people did not move with the court to Luoyang to uphold their handicraft tradition in China. The enamel technique was, as is well known, reintroduced to China first during the late imperial period. On the other hand, the potters' efforts to imitate metalwork remained influential in northern China's ceramic production.[168] The skeuomorphism in Pingcheng followed the material hierarchy,[169] with one notable exception: the famous blue glass bottle in blown technique from Yingbin dadao M16, which, in fact, mimics the form of Pingcheng grayware.[170] The reason for this imitation in reverse hierarchy direction is not clear. The fact that grayware continued to be buried in tombs even after more valuable celadon and white ware were developed and prevailed among the funerary ceramics during the later Northern Dynasties may indicate that Xianbei grayware possessed certain high ritual values of which we are not aware.

Early celadon stoneware in the north was supplied by the south.[171] In the fifth century, northerners were still unable to fire such a glaze. Only a few celadon wares were unearthed in Pingcheng, and they clearly came from the south. The jar from Dianhanchang M22 with a lid and four shoulder lugs (Period III) is typical for the southern Zhejiang and Fujian

---

168 For the polychrome shards in Luoyang, see An Jiayao 2004, 61; Kobayashi Hitoshi 2012; for ceramic developments in the north, Müller Sh. 2019c, 389–90. The ornamental influence came mainly from Central Asia, Rawson 1991.

169 Vickers 1999, particularly p. 13.

170 Müller, Sh. 2019, 395 and the references given there.

171 Geng Shuo 2015.

kilns.[172] The only spittoon found in Pingcheng celadon is that of Sima Jinlong (484) (Fig. 17),[173] indicating that the associated table manner (as table waste bins) or hygiene behavior was not present there. All the celadon wares from Pingcheng were not part of the ceramic assemblages for funerary rituals but instead valued artifacts or heirlooms of the deceased.

Table 6.1 Number of Pingcheng burials containing lacquer vessels

Period / Tomb types	I (pre-398)	II (398-439)	III (440-476)	IV (477-493)	V (post-493)	Total
Earthen pit	-	1	1	-	-	2
Catacomb tomb	1	9	20	11	3	44
Knife-shaped tomb	-	-	2	3	-	5
Earthen chamber tomb w/ a funerary house	-	-	3	-	1	4
Brick tombs	-	3	3	14	3	23
Total	1	13	29	28	7	78

Table 6.2 Types and number of lacquer vessels in Pingcheng burials

Period / vessels	I (pre-398)	II (398–439)	III (440–476)	IV (477–493)	V (post-493)	Total
Round platter/tray	1	4	13	14	3	35
Rectangular platter	-	1	2	2	1	6
Plate	-	1	12	9	-	22
Dish	-	-	2	2	-	4
Eared cup	-	7	16	17	2	42
Beaker	-	-	1	1	-	2
Bowl	-	3	11	15	-	29
Fruit box *ke*	-	1	1 rd.	1	-	3
Round box	-	-	-	2	-	2
Jar	-	-	-	1	-	1
Wine cast	-	-	-	1	-	1
Unknown shape	1	5	3	4	4	17
Total	2	22	61	69	10	164

platter: ⌀ > 30 cm; plate: ⌀ < 30 cm; rd.: round, the remaining fruit boxes are rectangular in shape.

---

172 Shanxi daxue et al. 2006, 152–55. Because of this jar, Li Shuyun (2008) surmises that the occupant of Dianhanchang M22 was Chinese. The offerings of sheep limbs and ribs on a large lacquer platter, on the other hand, suggest a steppe-style burial ritual. If Li's hypothesis is true, it would imply that the deceased and his or her family abandoned the Chinese identity and burial practices in favor of a steppe way of mourning.

173 The largest and finest example of any Six-Dynasties spittoon excavated to date is that of Sima Jinlong. It has an excellent glaze and was probably fired in a Western-Jin or Liu-Song imperial kiln; cf. Song Xin 2002: 286.

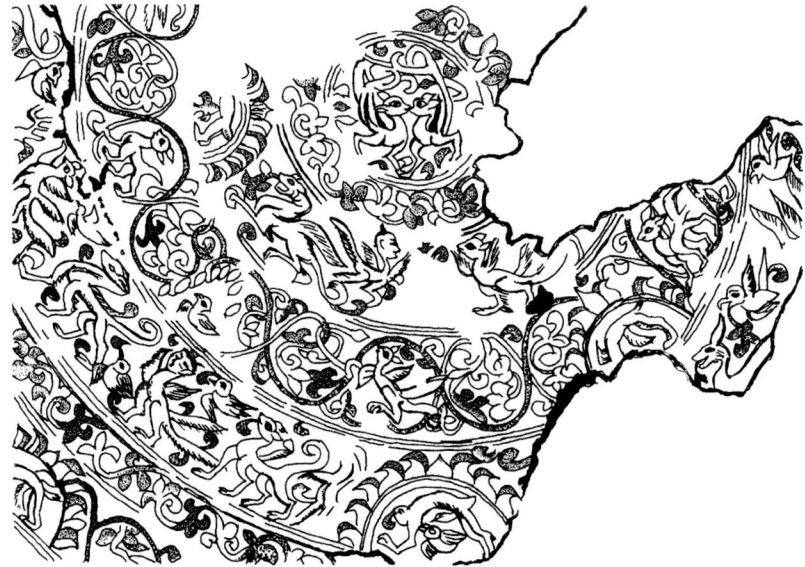

Figure 18 A large lacquer platter from a Pingcheng tomb at the Nanhuan Road, Datong. The surface is partitioned into concentric rings, each filled with half-palmette scrolls and animal figures.
Line-drawing by the author based on a photo kindly provided by Professor Wang Yanqing.

The wealth of lacquer artifacts found in Pingcheng tombs is unanticipated, as lacquerware has largely vanished from contemporary southern tombs.[174] A possible explanation is that it was a steppe heritage. Steppe peoples regarded Chinese lacquerwares as prestige objects. Animal offerings were sometimes presented on lacquer plates in burials from the Xiongnu period in Mongolia.[175] In Pingcheng, lacquer vessels were also employed for the presentation of food offerings. Table 6.1 shows that catacomb tombs yielded more lacquer vessels than tombs of other types during Period III, but during Period IV, slightly more lacquerware was found in brick tombs. Lacquer vessels come in a variety of shapes, but the most common ones are round plates or trays. Only six platters have a rectangular form, all used for animal offerings. (Table 6.2). Three characteristic Chinese lacquer artifacts, the compartmentalized boxes (*ke* 㮮), were also discovered in Pingcheng tombs. Two rectangular ones from Dianhanchang M180 (Period II) and Sima Jilong's tomb (Period IV) were probably heirlooms, as this form had long since disappeared in southern China.[176] The one from Qilicun M29 has a round shape and could have been an import from the contemporary south. But this assumption would have to be confirmed by chemical and technical analyses.

---

174 Kieser 2018; For a brief survey of lacquerwares of the Pingcheng period, Müller Sh. 2019b. Pingcheng tombs contained more lacquer artifacts than have hitherto been reported (personal communication with the excavators in September 2019). Many of them were in advanced states of deterioration by the time of the excavation and could not be collected (and some were not recorded).

175 Ernenebaatar et al. 2011, 306.

176 Müller Sh. 2019b: 48–49; 2019c, Fig. 18.2, No. 14; Kieser 2019, 435.

The demand for larger and more colorful lacquer platters grew over time. They were preferably placed near the tomb entrance, often in front of the coffin, or a prominent place where mourners and guests could easily see them. Large sizes were probably also practical because they were able to hold half a sheep, half a dog, or a lower limb of cattle. The largest round platter of Period III has a diameter of 58 cm. This attains a diameter of 83 cm for Periods IV and V. The rectangular one from the final period (V) measures 80 cm by 38 cm. Not only are the large sizes something new, but the decorations on lacquer vessels also reflect the Pingcheng art of the day (Fig. 18). Some exquisitely painted lacquer trays and bowls were probably locally manufactured in Pingcheng with imported lacquer sap, although evidence of this is currently unavailable.[177] On the other hand, vessels with traditional Chinese shapes, such as eared cups, were evidently still highly valued as ritual vessels, whereas they were at this time already fading into oblivion in the south.[178]

Table 7. Occurrence of cauldrons in Pingcheng burials

Period　　　　　Tomb types	II (398-439)	III (440-476)	IV (477-493)
Catacomb tombs		Dianhancheng M116 (II-Fe)	
Knife-shaped tombs			Yingbin dadao M76 (II-Fe)
Earthen chamber tombs w/ a funerary house	-	Zhijiabao 1997 tomb (II-Fe);	
Brick tombs (single chambered)	Shaling M7 (XN-Fe) Tongjiawan M7 (I-Br) Erdianchang M37 (I-Br)	Tiancun M1 (II-C)	Yanbei shiyuan M52 (II-C)
Brick tombs (double chambered)			Sima Jinlong tomb (II-Fe)

Br: bronze; C: clay; Fe: iron; I: Type I; II: Type II; XN: Xiongnu Type

Metal steppe cauldrons with openwork pedestals found in Pingcheng can be divided into two types: a lidded bucket with an arched handle (Type I; Figs. 19.2–3), and a lidless vessel with a pair of small round handles attached to the upper rim of the main body (Type II; Figs. 19.5–8). The latter has several subgroups. The forerunners of Type II can generally be traced back to the first century CE in the Hulun Buir region. Similar cauldrons appear later in southern Manchuria, especially at the Lamadong 喇嘛洞 site, Liaoning, in the fourth century.[179] The bucket-shaped cauldrons are confined to the territory of the Northern

---

177 Müller Sh. 2019b: 50–51 and Fig. 1.
178 Pirazzoli-t'Serstevens 2002.
179 Guo Wu 2007: 66–67.

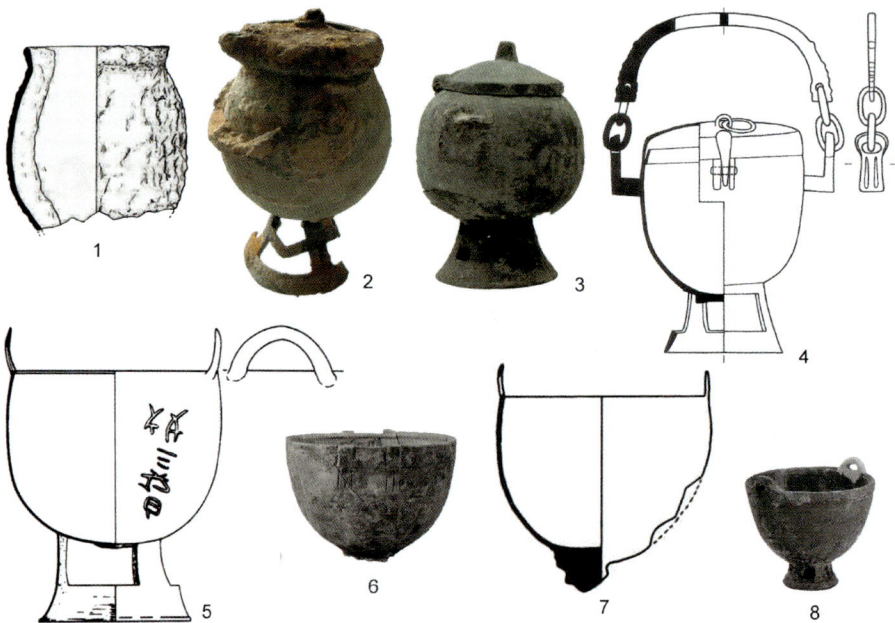

Figure 19 Cauldrons of Pingcheng from (1) Shaling M7, iron; (2) Tongjiawan M7, bronze on an iron ring pedestal; (3) Erdianchang M37, bronze; (4) Feng Sufu's tomb (died 415), bronze; (5) 1997 Zhijiabao tomb with a funerary house, bronze; (6) Tiancun M1, clay; (7) Yingbin dadao M76, iron; (8) Yanbei shiyuan M52, clay. (1–2): Period II; (3–6): Period III; (7–8): Period IV.

After Datong kaogu 2006b: 8 Fig. 4.1 (1); Datong kaogu 2006c: 69, Fig. 38.8 (7); Datong kaogu 2010; 14, Fig. 38 (6); Liu Junxi 2008, 33, Plate 6.1 (8); Liaoning bowu 2015, 25, Fig. 16.1 (4); Wang Yintian and Liu Junxi 2001: 41, Fig. 4 (5). (2–3) Photos by the author.

Yan kingdom (409–436) (Fig.19.4).[180] The iron cauldron of Shaling M7 (Fig. 19.1) with a retracted short neck belongs to neither type and is comparable to only one other find of an iron cauldron in a Southern Xiongnu burial at Budonggou 補洞溝 (second century CE) in the Ordos region.[181] Cauldrons were found in different tomb types in Pingcheng, but, interestingly, chiefly in brick-chambered tombs (Table 7).[182] This clearly associates the origin of their occupants with the steppe and indicates the high status of the deceased. The cauldron from the Zhijiabao tomb (Fig. 19.5) is the only one that bears an inscription. Four Chinese characters *bai bing san nu* 白兵三奴 were cast upside down into the outer wall. But the

---

180 Guo Wu 2007: 77; Pan Ling 2015, 8, 10, 12–13.
181 Pan Ling and He Yumeng 2015, 449 Fig. 1, no. 13.
182 Possibly due to the heavy looting of the many richly furnished catacomb burials, Dianhanchang M116 is the only tomb of this type that yielded a cauldron. It housed a large coffin decorated with gilded bronze animal masks and many gilded bronze studs, which distinguished the burial from the "average" ones. Shanxi daxue et al. 2006, 245.

meaning of this inscription is unknown.[183] Ceramic imitations first appeared in Period III (Figs. 19.6, 19.8). One could speculate that the ceramic ones in the richly furnished Tiancun M1 and Yanbei shiyuan M52 represented a minimum of effort to maintain the great steppe tradition. While metal cauldrons still existed in border regions, reflecting a strong steppe tradition persisting among some garrison soldiers, they disappeared entirely later in Luoyang. This legacy was taken up again only in the era of the Northern Qi and the Zhou, but the cauldrons appearing in the second half of the sixth century were, in most cases, only miniatures. [184]

An iron "pot" 鐵鍋 was found in Sima Jinlong's tomb. The mere mention of a 9 cm high pedestal of this "pot" suffices to identify the "pot" as a cauldron (Table 7). Although Jinlong's mother was a Tuoba princess, he most likely inherited the royal Jin tradition from his father. I therefore suggest that the cauldron was a gift from Jinlong's father-in-law He Douba 賀豆跋 (or He 賀 of Tufa 禿髮), alias Yuan He 源賀 in a Sinicized version, to his daughter Qinwen Jichen for her funeral in 474. He Douba was the Defender-in-Chief 太尉 of the early Northern Wei state until his death in 479. When Jinlong died in 484, the body of Jichen and probably much of her grave goods were transferred to the new tomb.[185]

Lamps

Lamps of various shapes and materials were unearthed in large Xiongnu tombs in Mongolia, in tombs found on the Korean peninsula, in Western regions, and in Southern Xiongnu tombs in Ordos.[186] In contrast, the early fifth-century Tuoba tombs in Inner Mongolia rarely contained lamps. This changed again in Pingcheng, as fifty-two Pingcheng tombs of all types (except for pits) spanning from Period II to V contained lamps (Fig. 20). In catacomb tombs, lamps were placed in front or on the corner of a coffin, or in the wall niche. In knife-shaped tombs, lamps stood in front of a side plank of a coffin. In earthen or brick chamber tombs, they were frequently placed near the entrance, on one of the front corners of the chamber, or in its middle. If a tomb contains a funerary house or bed, the lamp will stand directly in front of them. These positions show that lamps were not only integrated into the burial rituals of many inhabitants but also played a central role in funerals. Some single burials even possessed two lamps of different styles. Since some small bowls that may have been used as oil lamps (Fig. 20.2) were not recognized as such, we can assume that more tombs were equipped with lamps. The relatively strong presence of lamps in the tombs of Pingcheng may have been the result of cultural interactions in this city.[187]

Lamps from Pingcheng tombs were primarily made of clay and stone, with only a few made of iron. The most common type has an oil dish and a high pedestal in the shape of a column (Fig. 20.7).[188] This type first appeared in the Central Plains during the Eastern Han dynasty and soon spread to the Hexi and Ordos regions during the Cao Wei and Western

183 Wang Yintian and Liu Junxi 2001: 41–42.
184 Pan Ling 2015, 92–109; Müller Sh. 2019c, 397.
185 Song Xin 2002: 279–80. The cauldron was only mentioned in passing in the report. No detail is given.
186 This is explained as the adoption of Chinese customs. For the finds in Ordos, see Du Linyuan 2007.
187 Dien 2014; Jinno Megumi 2021. Jinno contends that the East Asian method of lighting a soft wick on the rim of an oil dish was influenced by West Asian lamps, ibid, 42.
188 Dien 2014: 296–303.

Figure 20 (1) Ceramic lamp with high openwork pedestals from Yingbin dadao M56 (H/ø: 13.4/12.7 cm); (2) Ceramic lamp bowl containing carbonized fibrous material from Qilicun M26 (H/ø: 4.8/10.8 cm); (3) Ceramic lamp emulating iron-rod lamps, such as (4), from Tiancun tomb (H/ø: 10.9/11.8 cm); (4) Iron lamp on a rack of short rods from Jinshu meichang M14 (H/ø: 10/12 cm); (5) Ceramic multi-armed lamp from Yanbei shiyuan M2 (H: 41 cm); (6) Iron lamp on a slender stem from Yingbin dadao M19 (H/ø: 78.2/10 cm); (7) Stone lamp on a column-shaped stem and a plinth from Sima Jinlong's tomb (484; H/ø: 37.5/25.5 cm). All except for (6) are on a similar scale.

(1–4, 6) After Datong kaogu 2006c: 57, Fig. 16; Datong kaogu 2006a: 48, Fig. 70; Datong kaogu 2010, front cover; Han Shengcun et al. 1996: inside front cover; Datong kaogu 2006c: 57 Fig. 16. With permission of the Datong Archaeological Institute. (5, 7) Photos by the author in the Datong Museum.

periods. Peoples from these regions most likely brought the column-type of lamps to Ping-cheng. Quite a few stone lamps of this type evolved into works of art with intricate sculp-tures of animals and human figures. However, they all came from looted tombs.

Pingcheng III saw the emergence of multi-armed lamps (Fig. 20.5), along with clay fig-urines. Before that, similar lamps, apparently vestiges of the magnificent Eastern Han multi-armed lamps, were found only in a few large Chang'an tombs of the Sixteen King-doms period. Most of the Chang'an lamps have nine small oil dishes, eight are held by thin arms protruding from the central stem, and the ninth stands on top of the stem. The ap-pliquéd Buddha figures on the central stems of two recently excavated ones from Xi'an indicate that such multi-armed lamps were associated with certain Buddhist or Daoist funerary rituals in that region.[189] The side oil dishes of the multi-armed lamps in Pingcheng were slanted so strongly that they could not hold oil, hence they were probably nonfunc-tional. Even so, such lamps still occupied a prominent place in burials. The Tiancun lamp, for example, stood in the center of the chamber, directly in front of the funerary bed, while a smaller lamp imitating an iron lamp (Fig. 20.3) was placed in the southeastern corner. The multi-armed lamp from Yunbolu M10 stood directly at the entrance of the stone house. Once the capital was moved to Luoyang, the multi-armed lamps vanished.

A unique type found only in Pingcheng are iron lamps with bases made of short rods welded together (Fig. 20.4). They apparently inspired some lamps made of stone and clay (Fig. 20.3). The iron lamps of this type were usually found in brick-chambered tombs. A stone lamp imitating the type was found in a catacomb burial with a painted coffin. The iron lamp found in Ih-Nur M1 in Inner Mongolia, featuring two kneeling "Atlas" figures supporting the oil dish, may represent a flamboyant variant of this type.[190]

Only a few iron lamps from Pingcheng have an openwork base and a tall and slender stem holding a fuel dish. They are remotely reminiscent of Roman candelabra in their basic construction (Fig. 20.6). The iron lamp from the catacomb tomb Yingbin dadao M19 (H. 78.2 cm) bears striking similarities to an iron lamp discovered at Lamadong. Both appear to have been lit with solid fuel, since they both have a pricket in the dish.[191] Another tall iron lamp, located in the southeastern corner of the chamber of 2020M29 at Qilicun, lacks a pricket, but has some soot on the rim of the dish,[192] indicating that it was lit with a soft wick, a novel lighting method for the fifth century, discussed above. These tall iron lamps from Pingcheng, though sharing a similar shape, were most likely of different ages.

The only fuel analysis was conducted on the residues found in four iron lamps from Ih-Nur M3, which reveals that the fuel was ram tallow admixed with a small amount of beeswax. While ram tallow was already in use in Western Han times, as was evidenced in Liu Sheng's tomb at Mancheng, beeswax had to be imported from the southern or north-western regions. The analysis consequently indicates the high status of the deceased in Ih-Nur M3, which enabled him/her to get access to this foreign product.[193]

---

189 Liu Daiyun et al. 2010, 125.
190 For the stone lamp in DHCM253: Shanxi daxue et al. 2006: 332; For Ih-Nur lamp: Chen Yongzhi et al. 2016b: 52.
191 Datong kaogu 2006c: 59; Liaoning wenwu et al. 2004: 277, Fig. 19.3, Pl. 17.3.
192 Datong kaogu 2023: 56 (H. 52.5 cm).
193 Han Huarui et al. 2019. No further information of the lamp is available. The excavation report is not yet published. For other fuel analyses, see Dien 2014, 288 and idem. 2007b.

Table 8. Burial goods at Dianhanchang (DHC) and Ih-Nur, Inner Mongolia, sites

Tomb no. / Orientation / Occupant	Adornment	Belt fittings	Grave goods	Lacquers	Animals
DHC M107 / E / young girl	Bronze chinstrap and pectoral		1 gilded silver bowl, 1 Sasan. glass bowl, 1 silver jar	(instead: a bronze platter with 1 wooden plate, 1 eared cup and 1 spoon)	Horse mandible
DHC M109 / E / female (20–25)	Bronze triangl. "crown" and chinstrap		1 gilded silver-stemmed bowl, 1 silver bowl	lacquer platter	Animal ribs and vertebrae
Ih-Nur M1 / N / female	Gold chinstrap		1 silver bowl, 1 gilded silver tripod bronze platter, 1 blue glass bowl	1 lacquer plate with 2 painted lacquer bowls	?
Ih-Nur M3 / N / female (?)	Gold chinstrap and pectoral	with carnelian inlays		1 lacquer plate with 3 lacquer bowls, 2 eared cups and 1 spoon. 1 elephant-shaped lacquer vessel	Animal shoulder blades and limbs
Ih-Nur M6 / S / male(25-30)	Gold pectoral	ditto		1 lacquer platter (?)	?

Burial clusters in cemeteries

Based on the proximity of tombs to one another, their uniform orientation, and the similarity of tomb constructions and burial rites, it was proposed that there were several "family groups" in the Dianhanchang cemetery.[194] But only two appear plausible. They include the east-facing catacomb tombs (M107, 109, 116, 102, 103, 106, and 126) and the south-facing knife-shaped tombs (M129, 153, 113, 114, and 79) (Fig. 21, the magenta and green group; both of Period III). However, only the east-facing tombs provide sufficient information to demonstrate rather homogeneous burial practices. In particular, a stone lamp was intentionally broken in two and deposited in M102 and M116, indicating their inherent relationship to each other. The famous M107 between them yielded a stone lamp of the same type. Its occupant, a teenage girl, wore a bronze chinstrap and a crescent-shaped pectoral. A similar pectoral adorned the young woman in M109 nearby, who additionally wore a diadem with a triangular bronze openwork ornament (see above). With the neighboring, less richly furnished M103, M106, and M126, they most likely formed a culturally cohesive group. Notably, similar funerary accoutrements with chinstraps and pectorals are also observed in the catacomb burials in Ih-Nur, Inner Mongolia (Table 8).[195]

---

194 Shanxi daxue 2006 et al., 486–87; Wei Zheng 2011: 84.
195 Thus far, only the materials of Ih-Nur M1 are published, Zhongguo renmin et al. 2017. The information of M3 and M6 are taken from Chen Yongzhi et al. 2016a, 2016b.

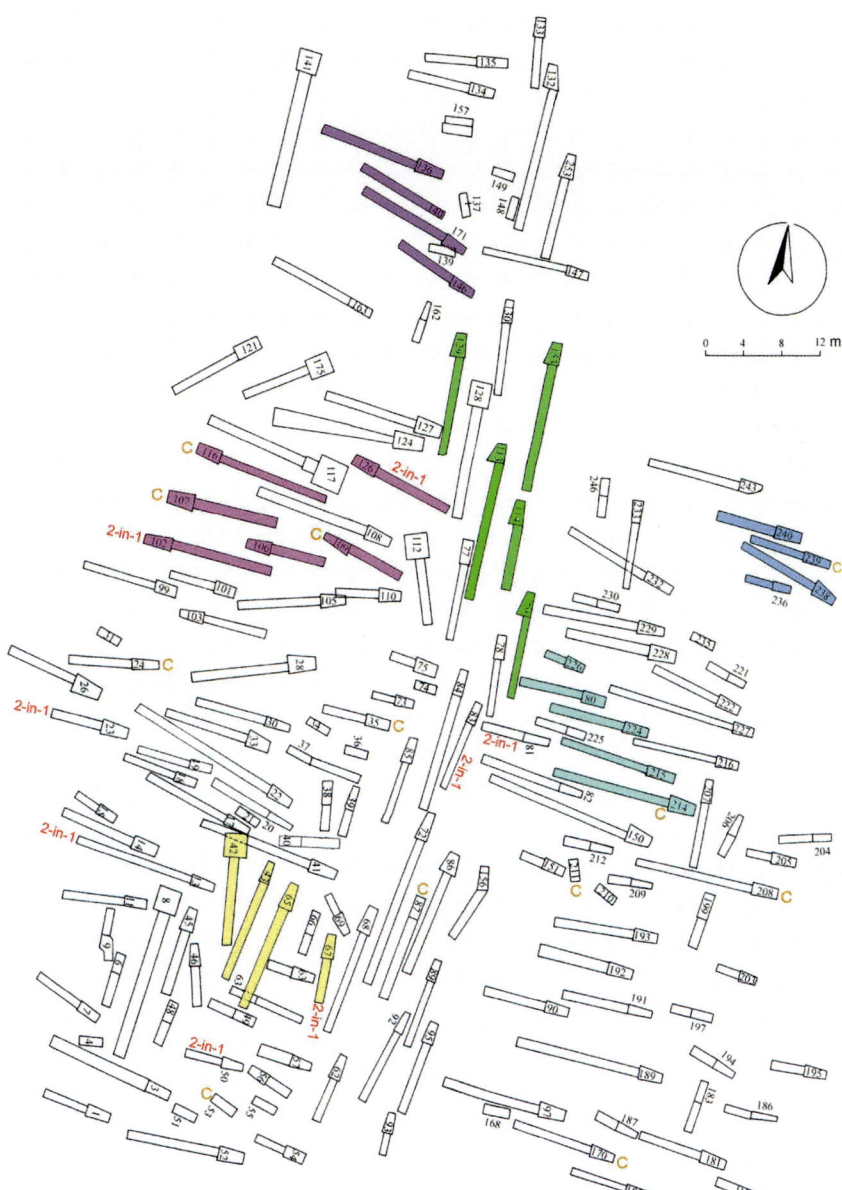

Figure 21 Burial clusters in Dianhanchang Cemetery as suggested by the excavators. Only the six east-facing catacomb tombs (magenta) seem to possess some intrinsic ritual factors that mark them as a group. 2-in-1: paired burials in one single coffin; C: occurrence of chinstraps.

Modified after Shanxi daxue et al. 2006, Fig. 2.

Although the five Ih-Nur tombs are all oriented differently, something that could have been determined by the local topography, the tomb construction, luxury goods, and the presence of animal sacrifices and offerings (although we have no information on Ih-Nur M1 and M6) are comparable to those of the Dianhanchang group. Another common feature of both groups is the use of the partially gilded silver bowls of Kushano-Bactrian origin found in DHC M107 and Ih-Nur M1 (Table 8). Both were not placed in the coffins but in the wall niche of DHC M107 or, serving as the lid of a jar, near the coffin of Ih-Nur M1. This indicates that despite their high values, both were not simply treated as treasures but were actually employed in the burial ceremonies.

The connection of this Dianhanchang group to Central Asia or the steppe is further suggested by the paired burials in a single coffin found in DHC M102 and M126 (Fig. 21). However, the deceased in both tombs were arranged in a unique back-to-back position (Fig. 8.2) not seen anywhere else, confirming their close relationship.[196]

Short summary

The large bulk of Pingcheng's population is composed of peoples interred in catacomb tombs. Animals are often found as offerings, sometimes also as sacrifices in them. In a relatively large percentage of these tombs, the male and female occupants were buried with belt fittings or jewelry. Since all these features were frequently evidenced in burials on the steppe, we may assume that many of them were tribal members who joined the Tuoba lords and came as the first inhabitants to Pingcheng. There were certainly many subgroups, but it is not possible to go into them in more detail within the scope of this study. Another early group were the individuals buried in brick chamber tombs. The limited data show that they had burial customs similar to those interred in catacomb tombs, but some of them had painted chambers, while catacomb tomb owners "only" had painted coffins. Nevertheless, the topics and motifs of the paintings from both types of burials were similar (see below). The parallels existed from Periods II to III. One cannot help but get the impression that the tomb occupants in early brick tombs were also steppe dwellers. However, it is unclear which factors were decisive for the choice of a catacomb or a brick chamber tomb.

Peoples with other burial customs came later. Archaeology can indeed demonstrate that the new populations arrived in waves, as recorded in written sources. Square earthen-chambered and most of the knife-shaped tombs, for example, appear first in Period III. From then on, not only did new features come with the immigrants, but local innovations also appeared. New customs such as paired burials in a single coffin, the use of funerary houses and beds, chinstraps and, above all, tomb figurines suddenly appeared in Pingcheng, although we are still not sure of their places of origin, except for the figurines. Some of these new traditions strongly influenced later burial customs in the cities of the Northern Dynasties (e.g., tomb figurines, funerary houses, and, particularly, stone beds), while others penetrated into rural areas or military regions (e.g., earthen funerary beds and paired burials in a single coffin). Local imitations and variations were also created in Pingcheng, for example, funerary beds lined with bricks or even glazed tiles, an idiosyncratic version of chicken-headed ewers, clay-and-glaze imitation of metal bezels filled with enamel, or a blown glassware in the shape of a typical Xianbei grayware jug.

---

196 Shanxi daxue et al. 2006, 214–15, 251–52.

Memories and identities

Recent studies suggest that issues related to "identity," "cultural memory," and "ethnicity" can be explored using archaeologically excavated material remains, despite their inherently complex expressions and varying weightings. The practices that lay behind the excavated artifacts, in particular, may be instructive if properly read.[197] A group of individuals established a collective sense of their living environment and perceived a common picture of their past through their "communicative memories," i.e., everyday communications such as the recurrent use of everyday objects or telling jokes or reciting a myth, among other things, about a common "origin."[198] Additionally, by adopting "strategies of distinction," and by demonstrating group solidarity, such as wearing specific clothing, using certain utensils and/or consuming certain food in a particular manner, a group of people can draw (imaginary) boundaries between itself, i.e., "us," and "others," who do not act in the same way.[199] The practices observed in the archaeological remains can be understood as signals of "communicative memories" and/or "group solidarity," which are essential to the acknowledgement of group identity. Clothing and adornment for bodies, among other factors, are effective material signals and the most visible approach for presenting a "group," or "ethnic," identity.[200] The term "ethnic group" is indeed not related to human physical or biological traits, but rather a concept that was constructed by people who conducted similar social practices. An "ethnic" group constantly "reactivates" its common cultural memory of the past through ritualized actions or ceremonies. In archaeology, these practices, or "ethnic markers," can therefore be rituals, religions, appreciation of stylistic features, or human-material (object) entanglement.[201]

Pingcheng was a city of migrants. It can be assumed that the material remains found in tombs bear traces of the memories of the past of the interred individuals as well as the new identities gained in Pingcheng. Notwithstanding the insufficient documentation of many of the Pingcheng tomb findings, the available details of tomb paintings, sculptures, and grave good assemblages allow for an examination of identity of tomb occupants to some extent.

In addition to safeguarding the identities of the past, material remains also reflect how the relocated individuals, who were without the support of their familiar environment and quotidian artifacts, adapted to the new living conditions. This may account for the vital innovations observed in Pingcheng within its short one-hundred-year history.[202]

Tomb paintings and tomb figurines

As previously mentioned, clay figurines and inscriptions did not attract much interest of the early steppe inhabitants. Paintings, on the other hand, emerged early in elite "Xiongnu"

---

197 Díaz-Andreu and Lucy 2005; Pohl 2010; Kleemann 2010; Stockhammer 2012; Smith 2013.
198 Assmann 1995; idem. 1997 (2018).
199 Lucy 2005; Pohl 2010; Smith 2013.
200 Pearson 2001, 9.
201 Fisher and Loren 2003, 225.
202 Robin Fleming (2021) discusses the economic, political, and material dislocation in Roman Britain during the fifth century CE and the subsequent restructuring of a new material culture. Although the situation in Pingcheng was different, the description "fundamental changes in the structure of everyday life" (ibid., 6) can be equally applied to the forced migrants in Pingcheng.

tombs in Mongolia. Selected Chinese ornamental repertoires (e.g., textile patterns) and techniques (e.g., lacquer paintings), adapted to fit their own visual expressions and symbolism, were applied to the coffins of the Xiongnu elites to display status and prestige.[203] Third- and fourth-century paintings on tomb chamber walls and coffins are found in southern Manchuria (the territory of the Murong Xianbei and the Koguryo people), in Qinghai (that of the Tuyuhun) and in Hexi (mixed ethnicities). Coffins with figural lacquer paintings seem to be limited to southern Manchuria, while the Qinghai and Hexi finds were all using water-based paints. Noteworthily, very few fourth-century tomb and coffin paintings are found in Inner Mongolia so far,[204] but this changed soon.

Paintings occurred in twenty-seven Pingcheng burials (excluding the tombs built with bricks with impressed ornaments) (Table 2.1). Another ten Pingcheng Period tombs with murals or painted coffins are located on the southern fringe of the Sanggan Valley in Shanxi, as well as in Inner Mongolia, Hebei, and Ningxia.[205] The number of paintings exceeds all expectations and attests to an artistic vigor that no art historian would have attributed to these "barbarians" only some twenty years ago.

The demand for expensive colors, skilled painters, and the high degree of organization required to work in tombs explain why tomb murals were only affordable to the rich and powerful in Pingcheng. Lacquer-painted coffins, which were found in brick-chambered tombs such as Shaling M7 and Erdianchang M37 (both Period II) as well as Hudong M1 (Period III), belonged to the same "luxury" category.[206] Only the tomb of Poduoluo (= Shaling M7) contains both murals and a lacquer-painted coffin, as will be discussed below. Since Pingcheng had to import lacquer sap and there were only a limited number of lacquer painters available,[207] it is reasonable to assume that the interred individuals or their families

203 See those tombs found in Noyon Uul, Gol Mod and Duulga Uul, Brosseder 2015: 254, notes 134–35.
204 For southern Manchuria, Liaoning bowu et al. 1984; Xu Ji 1985; Liaoning wenwu 1997; Liaoning bowu 2015, 12–15, Fig. 8. For Hexi, Wu Hong 2008. For Qinghai, Xu Xinguo 2011. Only two painted coffins of the pre-Pingcheng era are counted by Lin Sheng-chih 2012: 10 in southern Inner Mongolia.
205 These are: a lacquer-painted coffin allegedly from Yingxian 應縣, Shanxi (now in the Museum for Northern Dynasties Arts in Datong), the lacquer-painted coffin of Ih-Nur M3 (Chen Yongzhi et al. 2016b: 46), three red and white painted coffins at Qilangshan site (Wei Jian 2004, 146, 155, 166), two wooden coffins painted with water soluble pigments from Siziwangqi 四子王旗 in Ulanqab (now in the Inner Mongolia Museum in Hohhot), and a painted tomb from Jimingyi 雞鳴驛, Holingol (Liu Rui'e and Zhu Jialong 1999), all in Inner Mongolia. Except for the coffin from Ih-Nur M3, all were known through looting activities or purchased from receivers of stolen goods. The Siziwangqi coffins can be dated to the Pingcheng period based on their shapes and painting styles. The topics and styles of the Jimingyi tomb mural suggest that the tomb was probably constructed in the Sixteen Kingdoms period or in early Northern Wei times. Additionally, there is one painted tomb in Lincheng 臨城 (Hebei and Lincheng 2001, and Ni Run'an 2004), and, lastly, a lacquer-painted coffin (489) was found at Guyuan, Ningxia (Ningxia Guyuan 1988a and Luo Feng 2019).
206 Two additional lacquer-painted coffins were found near Datong, one from M9 at the Da-Zhun Railway 大準鐵路, one from a tomb at Hudong Railroad Classification Yard 湖東編組站 site, and another one from Anliuzhuang 安留莊 M8; see Wang Yanqing and Gao Feng 2016 and Gao Feng 2008: 318. These excavations were not reported, and clear photos are unavailable. The photo of Da-Zhun Railway M9 was taken on site, which shows brick walls in the background. At least in this case, it is certain that the two lacquered coffins were found in a brick-chambered tomb.
207 In addition to lacquer paintings, lacquerware was found mainly in southern Manchuria and northern Korea in the fourth century. It can be assumed that well-trained lacquer painters of the early Pingcheng era came from that area, Müller Sh. 2019b: 53–54.

were more than affluent to commission such works. More coffins adopted water-based paints than lacquer. The coffins painted with water-soluble pigments all come from cata-comb tombs, and the paintings all have a yellow background. The special mixture of inor-ganic and organic pigments for green with orpiment and indigo identified on the Zhijiabao coffin indicates that knowledge of painting was indeed transmitted from Hexi and the west-ern regions to Pingcheng (see above),[208] although the motifs and compositions were com-pletely different. These coffin paintings were colorful and elaborate, the coffin surfaces well treated and often covered with a layer of very thin silk tabby. The fact that all such catacomb tombs were massively looted suggests that large amounts of wealth were once hoarded in the coffins. These are clues for the high rank and status of the interred persons in the painted coffins from catacomb tombs.

The funerary paintings in Pingcheng exhibit a new and standardized scheme: the portrait of the deceased (on the wall opposite the tomb entrance or on the head panel of a coffin), a military procession or, more frequently, a large-scale hunting and an open-air feast (on both side walls or the side planks of a coffin), while the entrances are guarded by supernatural images (something not generally seen in coffin paintings). This scheme is however not necessarily followed by the paintings on funerary houses, which are explored further below.

Xianbei clothing

Before discussing the tomb paintings, it is necessary to point out that, with only very few exceptions, human figures in Pingcheng and other regions occupied by the Tuoba Xianbei were depicted as "Xianbei," or more precisely, as wearing the so-called Xianbei clothing 鮮卑服, a modern term not mentioned in written sources. Paintings, sculptures, or textiles are the only sources of this attire (Fig. 22). Both men and women were depicted wearing tall hats and knee-length caftans or tunics, but only men wore belts; women did not. Below, the men wore wide trousers while the women wore long skirts that were either pleated or made by stitching together six pieces of fabric (Figs. 22.1, 22.3). The hat was sewn from four pieces of felt or fabric and had a flap on the back (Fig. 22.4). From the 430s onwards, sepulchral and religious artworks from Pingcheng show people across ethnic boundaries in this attire, whether they were commoners or members of royal families. It appears that the attire served to convey a sense of belonging to a larger social group, the Xianbei.[209]

While the men's clothing was widespread on the steppe, the most salient feature of this clothing was the dome-shaped hat. Mid-fourth century paintings from southern Manchuria and Hexi depict laborers and peasants wearing similar clothing, with the flap of the hat fre-quently flying upward.[210] The Chinese in those regions were thus familiar with the hat and wore it as well. They, however, only referred to the hat by describing it without associating it with a specific name.[211] Clay figurines from the fourth-century Guanzhong, such as those

---

208 Guo et al. 2023.

209 Fisher and Loren 2003, 225, argues that "by means of dress, ornamentation, body modification, pos-ture, gesture, and representation, an individual has the ability to 'put on a social skin', allowing self-identification as a member of a larger or different social or interest group".

210 Song Xin 2006, 96–100.

211 Such a textile hat was found in the tomb of a Chinese woman Sun Gounü 孫狗女 (d. 377) in Yumen 玉門, Gansu. The inventory lists the piece as touyi 頭衣, lit., "head-dress." Zhao Feng et al. 2008,

Figure 22 Xianbei hat and garments. (1) Figurines of male and female attendants from Sima Jinlong's tomb (484); (2) Portraits of Tuoba Jia, the Prince of Guangyang, and his wife (left) on an embroidered Buddhist banner (dated to 486) excavated at Dunhuang, Gansu; (3) Figurine of a female dancer from Yanbei shiyuan M2 (Period IV); (4) Back view of a Xianbei hat; (5) Portrait of the deceased from Yunbolilu M1. 5. 1, 2, 4:

(1, 5) Line drawings by the author after photos from the Datong Museum and Datong kaogu 2011a: 17 Fig. 9; (3, 5) colored based on the published photos; (2) After Dunhuang 1972: 57; (4) After Liu Junxi 2008, Color pl. 20.2. With permission of the Datong Archaeological Institute.

soldiers from the Caochangpo 草廠坡 tomb near Xi'an, were similarly depicted with such upturned flaps. Consequently, both paintings and sculptures demonstrate a certain degree of consistency in the depiction of the hat for the "service staff" in these northern regions.

In contrast, men of high rank in southern Manchuria of the same period were generally portrayed in tombs as local dignitaries ("portraits of rank") wearing flat hats as well as robes in Chinese style. Their elite status was further underlined by attributes such as a deer-tail whisk or fan and an armrest.[212] Judging from the few available images, high-class ladies in Manchuria dressed themselves up according to the clothing and makeup fashionable in Chang'an style in Jin times: A short jacket was worn over a blouse with loose sleeves and a long skirt sewn with strips of two alternating colors. "Beauty spots" were adhered to the forehead and cheeks. Strands of hair were elaborately coiled up to form several loops and plugged with decorative hairpins, combs, or jewelry.

Indeed, visual evidence derived from paintings or other images cannot always be taken literally and must be carefully differentiated. Noteworthily, it was in Pingcheng that high-

---

108–9. Tuyuhun's headgear, for example, was called "big hat with a long skirt [flap]" (*datou changqun mao* 大頭長裙帽) by the southern Chinese; *Liang shu* 54.810.

212 Laursen 2011, Figs. 5.38–41. For "portraits of rank," see Spiro 1990, 38–44. High-ranking deceased in the early Koguryo period were apparently portrayed according to the same scheme, Perrin 2016. For headdresses of men in southern Manchuria, see Kong Sŏk-ku 2018 (1998). For a general discussion, see also Dien 2007a, 302–5.

ranking individuals began to adopt a Xianbei-style appearance by wearing Xianbei clothing. The earliest instance was found in Shaling M7, dated 435 or earlier (see below). Toward the end of the Pingcheng period, we find that the Jakata of Śyāma (睒子 / 睒摩迦) near the entrance to Yungang Cave 9 (Fig. 23) was illustrated with Xianbei figures. The same phe-

Figure 23 The scene with the king's shooting at the filial Śyāma from the Śyāma jataka. Stone relief next to the entrance of Yungang Cave 9.
Photo by the author.

nomenon can be perceived elsewhere in the Tuoba territory: On the coffin of Feng Shigong (489) in Guyuan, for example, appear the filial Shun and his family, as well as King Father of the East and Queen Mother of the West in Xianbei clothing (see below). In Chang'an (Xi'an), a Buddhist stele of 471 depicts Buddha in his early lives as an individual in Xianbei clothing. Spiro referred to the Buddha images of 471 as being "naturalized." I believe it was more. It appears that the world of the Tuoba Wei was at this time interpreted by its people through the lens of the Xianbei. The result was, as Mark Edward Lewis puts it, "inventing a Chinese history and cosmos in which everyone was Xianbei, or a Xianbei world that embodied Chinese history and values."[213] It is conceivable that, during the

---

213 Spiro 2001; Lewis 2009, 168.

Northern Dynasties, murals, coffin paintings, or even painted stone houses could be viewed by the mourners.[214] Thus, the Xianbei depictions were "public" imagery and conveyed a "national" identity. Some people went so far as to have themselves buried in this attire, such as the deceased in Qilicun 2020M29.[215] The above-mentioned finds of clothing accessories in some catacomb tombs that do not correspond to those of the Xianbei clothing provide indications in the mortuary archaeology that regional or ethnic identities persisted. After death, people were apparently dressed according to their own cultural tradition and thus preserved their own identity that no one except the family could see.

The Xianbei clothing also saw modifications over time. From Period III onwards, a specific *kandys* cloak become part of the outfit. It has ornate pendant sleeves and is worn over the shoulders. Xie Xing on the rear wall of the stone house for his wife was portraited with the cloak (Fig. 35.2), as were the couple in the mural of Yunbolilu M1 (Fig. 22.5).[216] Early on, during the Sixteen Kingdoms period, clay figurines of high military officers were clad with this type of cloaks in the Guanzhong region.[217] Figurines of military officers with similar accoutrement appeared somewhat later in Pingcheng of Period IV. A *kandys* was originally an overcoat worn by Median dignitaries.[218] Due to the high prestige associated with it, the *kandys* was embraced by the Persian nobility and thereafter imitated by steppe leaders.[219] It appears that some elite inhabitants in Pingcheng adopted this sign of distinction from the steppe, although we have very little information about the latter.

Notably, the Central Asians are only the major group that visually differ from the Xianbei, primarily in their physiognomy and clothing. They wore belted caftans and caps with a short flap of a different style as that of the Xianbei, or conical hats, which will be discussed in more detail below.

Interestingly, images of "Chinese" in the styles of the Han and Jin dynasties are almost not present in Pingcheng. The lacquer-painted screen from Sima Jinlong's tomb is the only exception, which may indicate that the screen came from another era and place.[220]

Portraits of the deceased

Early in the Chinese world, a space was created in the burial chamber for the honoring of the deceased, which Wu Hung designates as the "spirit seat" (*lingwei* 靈位).[221] In the Eastern Han tombs, the space was occupied by portraits of the deceased in a funerary banquet setting. However, the focus was on the man, as can be read by his frontal sitting posture and his self-presentation as a Chinese official (the aforementioned "portrait of ranks"). The wife was often portraited in profile, if at all, and her portrait was less prominently positioned.

---

214 Zheng Yan 2012:50.
215 At least a textile Xianbei hat was discovered in this tomb; Datong kaogu 2023: 37 and Fig. 13.
216 The image of the tomb occupant's wife was broken away, but her right empty sleeve is still visible.
217 See the excavation documentation for the Zhongzhaocun tomb, Xi'an, discovered in 2019: http://wwj.xa.gov.cn/xwzx/gzdt/5ff4145df8fd1c596659b2cc.html; accessed February 23, 2021.
218 For example, on the reliefs of Apadana in Persepolis (sixth/fifth century BCE), Dien 2007a, 317–19.
219 According to Gervers-Molnár 1973, 5–18, the *kandys* probably evolved from a herdsman's coat to accommodate sudden weather changes. It has enjoyed great popularity among Persian and Parthian aristocrats, on the Eurasian steppe and in Central Asia, even until today. See also Lingley 2014.
220 Wu Hung 2009.
221 Song Xin 2002: 287.

Before the fifth century, the funerary portraits were painted on a side wall of the antecham-ber or middle chamber, according to Tseng Chin-Yin and Wei Zheng. Both also point out that Shaling M7 was the first instance for a central positioning of the funerary portraits on the wall facing the entrance in the coffin chamber of a tomb.[222] The same positioning oc-curred, however, earlier in frontier regions, for example, in two Eastern Han tombs in Jing-bian 靖邊 and Dingbian 定邊 (northern Shaanxi), [223] where numerous pastoralists dwelled. The same is attested to in an Eastern Jin tomb (end of the fourth century) in Zhaotong 昭通, Yunnan.[224] The new positioning of the "portrait of ranks" was probably created by local governors to emphasize their centrality in the world they lived. The idea was then adopted by some of the non-Chinese population. The centrally located portraits in Shaling M7 is therefore a continuation of the older tradition. Nevertheless, the funerary portraits on the head panel of the coffin from this tomb indeed represent a novel development. Only five fifth-century coffins show portrait paintings in this position. The coffin from Shaling M7 is probably the only case for Pingcheng. Two more coffins were purchased from looted tombs, thus are without provenance. The fourth was the coffin of Ih-Nur M3,[225] and the last "coffin portrait" was that of Feng Shigong.

Funerary portraits appeared in all tomb murals of Periods II and III as well as in two funerary houses, [226] but vanished completely from tombs of Pingcheng thereafter. The subject (and format) was not taken up in the north until the second half of the sixth century, when the Xianbei tradition was restored, but it only lasted for a short time.

The portraits of a couple in a tomb do not necessarily indicate a double burial. The fu-nerary house of Xie Xing's wife bears Xie Xing and her portraits, although according to the inscription, it was dedicated to her alone. In contrast, Liang Bahu was portraited alone in the mural, while two coffins (probably for him and his wife) were found in the chamber.

A portrait of the deceased in Pingcheng was always accompanied by other scenes (see below). An exception is the painting on Ih-Nur M3's coffin, which, as mentioned, was pro-bably manufactured in Pingcheng or another large city. It only contains the portrait of a nobleman in Xianbei garb. The side planks of the coffin were adorned with numerous animal masks and studs, but no further paintings. The excavators suggest that the deceased was a family member of a local tribal leader who belonged to the Gaoju on the eastern steppe. We have too little information about the mortuary art on the steppe after the great Xiongnu age. However, funerary portraits did not seem to be a usual commemorative practice in that region prior to the rise of the Turks. Gaoju or not, the Ih-Nur's portrait was an adoption of a funerary rite for the elites in Pingcheng.[227]

---

222 Tseng 2013, 78–89 and Wei Zheng 2018: 74.
223 At Yangqiaopan 楊橋畔 and Haotan 郝灘. The tombs were formerly considered "Chinese." Recent discussions tend to attribute them as tombs of the local Xiongnu population. Wallace 2019: 211–12.
224 The tomb of Huo Chengsi 霍承嗣. Dien 2007a, 153. Based on the inscription, Li Ming 2019 argues that the tomb was constructed to accommodate not the body but the soul of Huo, who died elsewhere. The ramp and entrance were, according to Li, too narrow for a coffin to pass through.
225 The looted ones are now in the Inner Mongolia Museum (Hohhot) and the Museum of the Northern Dynasties Arts (Datong). For Ih-Nur M3, see Chen Zhiyong et al. 2016, 46 and Color Plate IV.
226 The funerary houses from the 1997 Zhijiabao tomb and of Xie Xing's wife; Appendix I, Nos. 25, 28.
227 The excavators claim that the interred individual was a woman, although to my knowledge the mortal remains have not been examined; Chen Yongzhi et al. 2016b: 55–56.

Banquet and "Arrival of a Lady" scenes

In addition to the traditional funerary banquet (*Totenmahl*), which honored the dead and was painted directly in front of the portrait(s) of the deceased,[228] several tomb murals and coffin paintings from Periods II and III show a composition that, to the best of my knowledge, only occurs in Pingcheng. It contains a large-scale scene of an outdoor banquet combined with another scene with a noblewoman and her female entourage.[229] In my view, the latter, which I tentatively call the "Arrival of a Lady," gives the outdoor banquet a different meaning from that of the conventional *Totenmahl*. The earliest depiction is found on the western half of the southern wall of Shaling M7 (Period II) (Fig. 24). It illustrates a lady sitting in a white square tent,[230] with her ladies-in-waiting in front of her. Three further square tents were erected behind her tent, possibly for her female attendants. There are several parked vehicles in the background, and in the foreground, an open-air kitchen. Two large fabric partitions separated the "parking lot" and the kitchen from the banquet area, and it appears that the ladies would be escorted to the banquet area. The meaning of the scene has not been widely discussed. I have proposed elsewhere that this scene may represent the genesis of the Tuoba, i.e., the mythical liaison of Jiefen 詰汾, father of the Tuoba progenitor Liwei 力微 (174–277), with the daughter of Sky 天女.[231] If this is true, the scene would be a pictorial reconstruction of a cultural memory that is otherwise only transmitted orally. Not all tomb paintings from Pingcheng have this scene.[232] However, all coffin paintings using water-based paints (all Period III) contain the "Arrival" scene (Fig. 25),[233] which always locates on the right plank. Note that the excavated coffins come from west-oriented catacomb tombs, the scene in question is thus always facing the north. Since the same topic was painted on the southern wall of the chamber in Shaling M7, the scene also faces north. Whether this orientation has a significance is unclear. It presumably has a cosmic meaning. The "Arrival" scenes on coffin paintings vary. Some only show square tents placed on vehicles (tent carts), others show tents placed on the ground. None of them

---

228 For "funerary banquets" in early China and their pictorial representations, see Nylan 2016.

229 For example, Shaling M7 (Period II), Huayu II tomb, the coffin of Zhijiabao (both Period III), and several painted coffins without provenance in the Museum of the Northern Dynasties Arts.

230 Square tents images from Pingcheng were all associated with women, they should not be mixed with the so-called yurts, see Müller Sh. 2017.

231 Müller Sh. 2017, 192 and note 51. For the myth, *Wei shu* 1.2–3, Holmgren 1982, 53 and Duthie 2015: 74–75. Holmgren (p. 22) considers that Liwei's supernatural birth, which explains his long life, indicates a power struggle between a side-line with Jiefen-lineage on the route of the forced southward migration. Since Liwei won, this myth may have been used to assert his god-given leadership of the Tuoba; cf. Pearce 2023, Chap. 5.

232 According to Lü Pengzhen (2013, 10–11), for example, the mural in Yingbin dadao M16 does not contain this scene. This tomb cannot be treated in this paper since its excavation results are not published. The coffin painting from Hudong M1, does not bear the scene with tents, either. Additionally, none of the painted funerary houses is decorated with the "Arrival" scene.

233 Dianhanchang M185 (Period II) and M253 (Fig. 25.1), and the coffin from Zhijiabao (Fig. 25.2), both belonging to Period III. A square tent on a vehicle in the coffin painting of Dianhanchang M185 is, despite damage, recognizable; Shanxi daxue et al. 2006, Color Plate 2.2. Additionally, a wooden coffin painted with water-based pigments, a painted stone coffin (possibly Period II), and a lacquer-painted coffin, all without a provenance and all in the Museum for Northern Dynasties Arts in Datong, display the same subject matter.

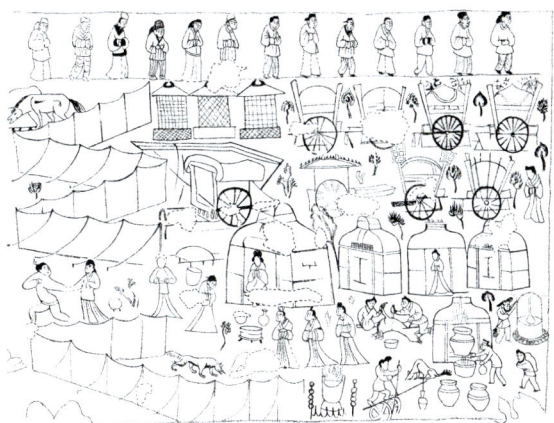

Figure 24 *Above*: The banquet and the "Arrival of a Lady" on the southern wall of Shaling M7. *Below*: Line-drawing of the "Arrival" scene.

After Datong kaogu 2006b: Fig. 41; with permission of the Datong Archaeological Institute. Line-drawing by the author.

depict a person in a Chinese-style building (Fig. 24 *above*, left). Nevertheless, in all these coffin paintings, the host is engaged in a drinking ceremony with guests in the banquet area, which is separated from the "parking lot" by large fabric partitions. Despite the variations, the theme is ostentatious and recognizable. It seems that the scene was intentionally recited at these funerals (including that for the deceased in Shaling M7), allowing the family of the buried to recall and reaffirm their ties with the Tuoba rulers.

The tomb mural of Liang Bahu 梁拔胡 (died 461) (= Tongjiawan M9) best illustrates how this subject was treated with less care over time. Its "Arrival" scene was depicted in a much-abridged manner and partially incorrectly. The arriving ladies, now in Xianbei clothing, are shown marching to the kitchen instead of being fetched for the banquet. The outdoor banquet disappeared, and only the funerary feast for the deceased remained.[234] The

---

234 Shanxi and Datong 2015, Fig. 37. For more details, see Müller Sh. 2017, 192.

host, i.e., Liang Bahu, is shown here no longer expecting the lady but rather, as in previous ages, celebrating his own feast. Furthermore, Liang's tomb faced to the south; the "Arrival" scene was now on the western wall, losing its original orientation.

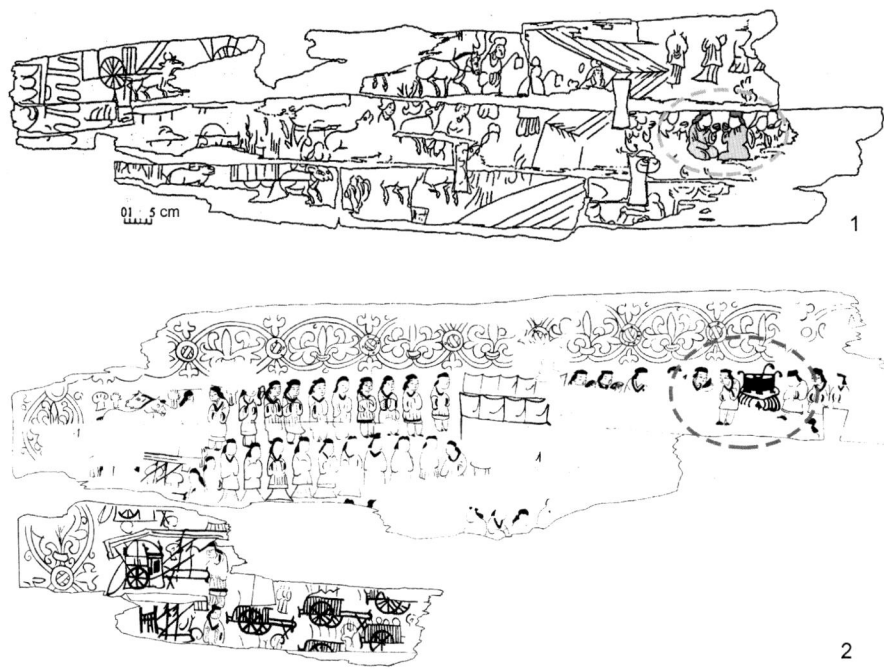

Figure 25 "Arrival" (*left*) and "banquet" scenes (*right;* with highlights) on side planks of painted coffins from (1) Dianhanchang M253 and (2) Zhijiabao tomb, both Period III.
After Shanxi daxue et al. 2006, Fig. 140c, and Liu Junxi and Gao Feng 2004, Figs. 5–6; with permission of the Datong Archaeological Institute.

The later "Arrival" narrative was expressed by means of figurines and models. The square tents of Yanbei shiyuan M2, for example, stood in front of several carts. Dancers, musicians and acrobats were grouped around a wine cask on a table, representing a banquet. All were placed in front of the main coffin (Fig. 26).[235] Yunbolu M10, as Qiao Liping and Zhang Zhizhong (2017) rightly point out, also has a similar setting.[236]

---

235 Müller Sh. 2017, 191–93.

236 Its stone house was flanked by two tent models. Accordingly, one may even speculate that the house was intended to allude to the main square "tent" in which the arriving lady stayed (the deceased was identified as a woman). This may explain the unusual window openings of the house, which remind of those of a square tent and are otherwise not evidenced in any other funerary houses.

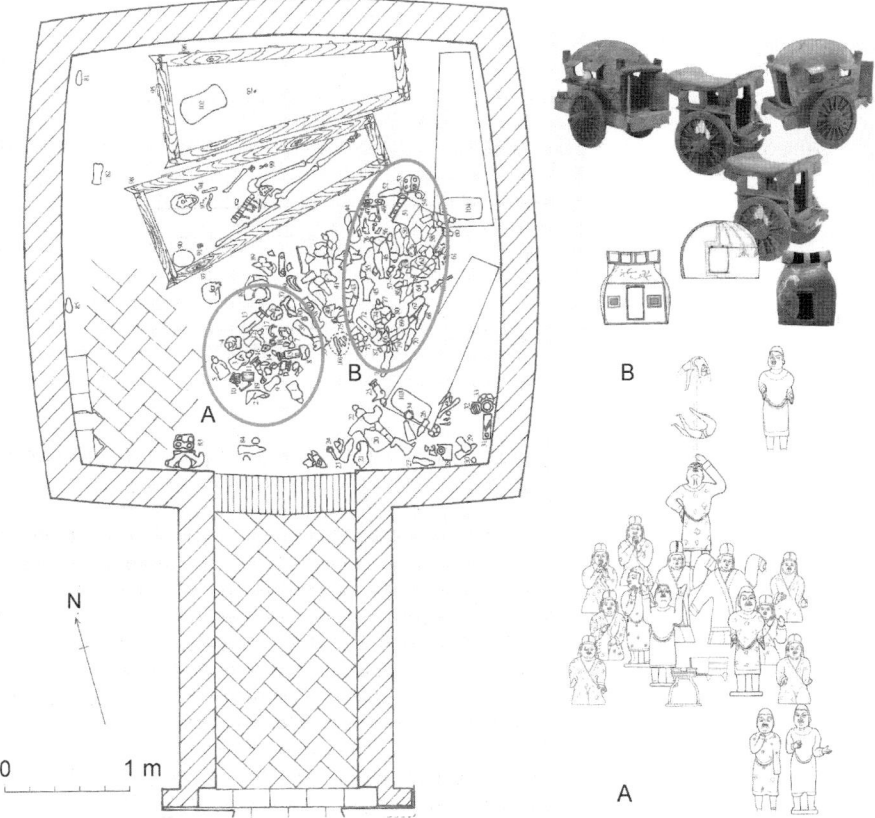

Figure 26 "Arrival" scene represented by figurine assemblage in Yanbei shiyuan M2 (Period IV).
Figurines and models arranged in two groups: (A) Music and acrobatic troupes as well as a dining
table and a wine cask for the banquet; (B) "Arrival" of the guests with tents and vehicles.

(Right) Based on Liu Junxi 2008, 42–69. With permission of the Datong Archaeological Institute.
(A, B) Arrangements of the figurines and models by the author based on the floor plan.

Entertainments and Central Asians

Although Central Asians were depicted as musicians, dancers in the western regions, such
as in Zhangye (Gansu) and Loulan (Xinjiang), in the third and fourth centuries, they also
appeared in tomb murals from the same region as rich merchants or celebrating nobles.[237]

237 See Digengpo 地埂坡 M4 in Zhangye, Gansu. la Vaissière 2011: 138 identifies two of its images as
the earliest portrayals of Sogdian traders found in the territory of modern China, whereas those of the
musicians and dancers (one of them is baring his genitals) were possibly people from Chāch. The

In the tomb art of Pingcheng, on the other hand, depictions of Central Asians were primarily associated with musicians and acrobats in banquet and procession scenes (Figs. 27.2–3). Thus, in the visual art, they were subjectively perceived as members of lower social strata, although there was the ample evidence in written sources of the success and great wealth of some Central Asian inhabitants in Pingcheng.[238]

As already mentioned, the images of the Central Asians are the only group from Pingcheng that can be visually distinguished from the Xianbei by their physiognomy and clothing. Both criteria, which show similarities to Buddhist sculptures from certain Tarim oases such as Kucha or Miran, or from areas further west, ensure that they can indeed be identified as "Central Asians." They were however portrayed in a generic manner, without clear iconographic references to their individual places of origin. Only images of men were present in Pingcheng, not of women. Men's belted caftans typically feature a round collar and side seam slits, which are not observed in Xianbei tunics. Their headgear is either a small hat lacking a brim but with a short flap made of a soft fabric, with or without a pointed or knotted "Phrygian" tip, or a conical hat made of some hard materials (Fig. 28). Besides, most of them are depicted in tall boots, whereas the majority of the figures in Xianbei clothing wore only shoes.

Central Asians emerged in tomb paintings or as tomb figurines in Pingcheng around the mid-fifth century, approximately one decade after the conquest of the Hexi area, including Guzang, by the Northern Wei in 439 and the subsequent deportation of the local population. Many Central Asians, including Sogdians, were among the forced immigrants.[239] James C. Y. Watt points out that the entertainer figurines of Central Asian appearance in Pingcheng were of a novel type.[240] Images of vague "foreigners," or *Hu*, appeared in the Han iconography, but such figures were less related to scenes of acrobatics or music and dance than with their roles as warriors or door guardians.[241] And their occurrence concentrated in Shandong and northern Jiangsu. After the Han state fell, in the region of the lower Yangzi River, images of Central Asian musicians with pointed hats, large eyes and high noses appeared on "soul jars."[242] They soon vanished after. The tombs from the third- and fourth-century Chang'an and the surrounding regions, where ethnically very mixed groups once lived, did not contain images of Central Asian acrobats or musicians, even though figurines of Central Asian warriors were prominently present.[243] Following the Han tradition, the

---

report is not published. For good photos, see Xu Guangji 2012, Vol. 9, Pls. 29–38. For the Loulan Painted Tomb (fourth century) discovered in 2003, see Xu Guangji 2012, Vol. 9, 199–207. Based on the distinctive belt form, Chen Xiaolu 2012 argues that the depicted persons were of Kushan origin.

238 The *Xu gaosengzhuan* 續高僧傳 (j. 16, 435) of Dao Xuan 道宣 of Tang times mentioned a devout Buddhist millionaire in Pingcheng named Kang (a Sogdian?) who constructed a cloister in the city for an Indian *dyana* master during the last quarter of the fifth century. For a good review of the images of western monks in Yungang, see Wang Yanqing 2012.

239 *Wei shu* 102.2270; *Bei shi* 97.3221; la Vaissière and Trombert 2004, 944; la Vaissière 2005, 61–70.

240 Watt 2004, 17. Pirazzoli-t'Serstevens 2008, 10–12 explains that people with "foreign" physiognomies were believed to be endowed with supernatural powers and to belong to the celestial realm.

241 Hsing I-t'ien 2000.

242 Dien 2001, 516–17; 2007, 350; Wu Hung 2015: 291–95.

243 The Yuezhi and the Sute (Sogdians) were among the major tribal groups in the Guanzhong area during the fourth century, many were engaged as mercenaries in the local armies; Ma Changshou 1985, 20–

Figure 27 Acrobatic scenes in murals from (1) Shaling M7, northern wall; (2ab) Liang Bahu's tomb, northern wall; (3) Yanbei shiyuan M2.

(2ab, 3) After Shanxi and Datong 2015: 18, Fig. 33 (detail), Datong bowu 2019a, 22 and Liu Junxi 2008, Color Pl. 23. (1) Line-drawing by the author based on the reconstruction of Professor Wang Yanqing; with permission of the Datong Archaeological Institute and Datong Museum.

"foreigners" or *Hu* appeared primarily as soldiers or guardians of tomb entrances. Thus, the Central Asians in Pingcheng indeed represent a new type of image, not only in terms of their artistic function, but also in terms of the shaping of their physical appearance. Unlike their "foreigner" predecessors of Han and Jin times with expressionless faces and hollow eyes, the Pingcheng figurines of Central Asians were endowed with emotions and life. We may even assume that that they were probably painted or modeled by craftsmen from a completely different art tradition.

The earliest acrobatic scene in Pingcheng is evidenced in the Shaling M7 mural (435 or earlier) (Fig. 27.1).[244] In the tomb art of Pingcheng, pole-climbing became synonymous with acrobatic art. The "bottom man" was typically a strong Central Asian who held the perch pole on his forehead, and the performance was always accompanied by a music band consisting of several Central Asians (Figs. 27.2–3).[245] The ethnicities of the figures on the pole are uncertain. Most of them were half-naked or barely clothed, while the bottom man and the musicians were always fully dressed.

The figures on the pole are rather small; this was possibly intended to suggest their young ages or the dizzying heights of the poles. It seems that by the mid-fifth century, pole-climbing had become both spectacular and vulgar (Figs. 27.2–3),[246] which echoes Gao

---

22, 35–38. Figurines depicting Central Asian warriors were found, e.g., in a fourth-century tomb at Xinjing; Ningxia Guyuan 1988b.

244 For another rather early painted tomb with an acrobatic scene, see Datong kaogu 2023: Fig. 35.

245 Leidy 2004a.

246 Climbers were covered only with loincloths, if any. Some figures have curved lines on their chest, possibly implying naked female breasts.

Figure 28 Dancers with snapping fingers. (1) Mural fragment from a looted tomb; (2) Reliefs on an inkstone/stand from Zhouchengchang, Datong; (3) Stone lamp from Jia Bao's tomb (477) and detail of a dancer.

(1) Photo by the author in the Museum for Northern Dynasties Arts; (3) After Wang Yanqig 2012, 570, Fig. 7 and Datong kaogu 2021a: 29 Fig. 10; with permission of Professor Wang Yanqing and the Datong Archaeological Institute; line-drawing by the author.

Yun's complaint regarding the celebration orgies for weddings and funerals. Interestingly, acrobatic depictions largely disappeared from tombs after the Pingcheng period and recurred only once again in early Tang times.[247]

A small group of Central Asian dancers was depicted leaping and raising their fingers over their heads to make a sharp and rapid sound known as a "Persian snap." The dancer images are found in one tomb mural, in the reliefs of two stone lamps (one in Jia Bao's tomb, dated to 477), and an "inkstone" (or a stand) (Fig. 28).[248] This novel style of dance,

---

247 It appears that some people in Tang times still found vulgarity appealing and amusing. This is indicated by a group of figurines from the Tang tomb M31 in the southern suburb of Xi'an. It shows a pyramid of boys piled up on the head of a burly Central Asian "bottom man." The topmost boy is depicted with his trouser crotch open, as if he were about to pee. Xi'an shi 2004: 57 Fig. 62.

248 The object is interpreted by Leidy (2004b, 164) as a "stand" for ritual use, for example "for offerings in funerary or seasonal observances." Like most Chinese researchers, Zhang Fan (2022) classifies the object as an "inkstone" because its dimensions match those of some excavated pieces from the same

Figure 29 Chain dance. (*Left*) Procession scene of Shaling M7, northern wall; (*Right*) Banquet scene of Liang Bahu's tomb (461); northern wall).

Courtesy of Professor Wang Yanqing and after Shanxi and Datong 2015: 18, Fig. 33 (detail); with permission of the Datong Archaeological Institute.

which was previously unknown in northern China, differs from the chain dance observed in Shaling M7 and the tomb of Liang Bahu (Fig. 29).[249] It is possible that the iconography of the "Persian snap" dancer was first introduced to Hexi together with certain themes from Gandharan art, in which such dancers were part of a procession or festival and served as an expression of celebration.[250] From Hexi, the motif was further transmitted to Pingcheng and integrated into the local Buddhist art. The south side of the truncated ceiling in the ante-chamber of Yungang Cave 12 (dated to the period between the 470s and 490s) was deco-rated with five 1.35-meter-high clay figures of four musicians and a Persian-snap dancer. It was probably no coincidence that the dance appeared in Jia Bao's tomb, since he was a man of Guzang. The close interaction between Buddhist and funerary rites in Pingcheng may explain why this dance image was incorporated into the mortuary art. It represented not only a funerary celebration, but possibly also an entry into Buddhist heaven. The Persian snap dance was not evidenced in Luoyang but reappeared on the Sino-Sogdian stone funerary beds or houses of the second half of the sixth and the seventh centuries. These images were then understood as the so-called "Sogdian leap" or "Sogdian whirl" dances.[251]

---

era. Due to the strong Buddhist symbolism of the ornamentation executed on this object, including eight lotus flowers in relief on its underside (Datong bowu 2018, 140–41), I am more inclined to accept Leidy's interpretation. For the "Persian snap," see Muzio 2019. The second lamp was found in the Xinggangcheng 星港城 cemetery in Datong and is not yet reported.

249 For the literary and archaeological evidence of chain dances in China, see Wang Yanqing 2019. The dancers on both tomb murals all wear feathered headgear. They leaped and stepped on the ground in rhythm, linking their arms. Similar headgear occurred in Koguryo murals, but not the dance itself. The motif entirely disappeared from tomb art after the 460s. *Nan shi* 63.1536, *Bei shi* 48.1762, and *Sui shu* 22.639 describe the dancers crossing their arms or held hands (*lian bi* 連臂 or *lian shou* 連手) while kicking or leaping (*ta* 踏/躢) rhythmically to a Huibo melody 迴波樂. The accounts must therefore have referred to certain types of chain dances, which all took place in farewell scenes. Therefore, the chain dances on Pingcheng tomb murals can possibly be interpreted in the same context.

250 Muzio 2019, 73–80. To my knowledge, only a single image of a "Persian snap" dancer appeared earlier and was found in Dahuting M2 in Mixian of the Eastern Han dynasty (Henan sheng 1993, 239, Fig. 188), which indicates the very early but sporadic influences of Buddhist art.

251 For Sogdian dances, see Zhang Qingjie 2005.

Figure 30 Camel groom. Front of the brick bed in Wenyinglu M1. *After Datong kaogu 2011b: front cover, inner page; with permission of the Datong Archaeological Institute.*

Figure 31 Guardians on the doors of the stone house of Zhang Zhilang (460; *left*) and the walls of the entrance corridor to the tomb chamber of the Prince of Danyang (end of fifth century; *right*).

   Line-drawings after Xu Guangji 2012, Vol. 2, Pl. 29 (right) and "Museum Photograph of the Datong Museum" (https://www.facebook.com/407143410046793/photos/pcb.415347849226349/ 415347685893032/?type=3&theater; accessed November 28, 2023; left) by Monika Zin (right) and author (left). Courtesy of Professor Monika Zin.

Central Asians were also depicted as attendants in the coffin paintings of Hudong 1986M1 or as camel grooms (Fig. 30) in several tombs, but never as horse grooms, which was a role generally reserved for the Xianbei. It seems that by the fifth century, tomb guardians with a "foreign" physiognomy of the Western Jin began to forfeit the supernatural power that had been ascribed to them. In Pingcheng, the guarding of tomb entrances was taken over by warriors with fangs or demonic faces, or by Vajrapani- or Yaksha-like deities (Fig. 31),[252] who may have been introduced from various oases of the Tarim Basin. Their iconography and origins need to be further studied.

Hunting and/or military procession

Hunting was highly developed and structured throughout Eurasia and was used both as a military exercise and a recreational activity for the nobility. Thomas T. Allsen points out that, while hunters displayed their skills, they also asserted their prestige and high social status.[253] Entries in the history of the Northern Wei confirm that hunting was much valued in Pingcheng society.[254] However, this theme was not addressed in all tomb paintings there. No stone house ever featured a hunting scene, nor were hunting scenes or hunters ever represented by figurines. Six Pingcheng tombs that contained a hunting scene all belonged to Period III or earlier.[255] None of the tomb occupants, except for Liang Bahu (460), can be unidentified.

Tomb paintings during the fourth century in Hexi, Manchuria and northern Korea did include hunting scenes. Examples are the murals in the Yuantaizi 袁台子 tomb in Chaoyang of the Former Yan period (337–370) and the Koguryo tomb at Tokhung-ri, dated to 408.[256] The topic can even be traced further back to Han mortuary art. It was particularly popular in the border regions between the Chinese and the Xiongnu of Han times.[257] The hunting scenes in Pingcheng differ from those of the previous ages. They generally occupy the entire surface of a wall or a coffin sideboard and do not portray the heroic or cosmic killings of fierce animals, such as boars or tigers, or supernatural creatures by a single hunter.[258] Instead, hunters on horseback or on foot are shown chasing the fleeing animals in

---

252 See, for example, the tombs at Wenyinglu and of Prince of Danyang (Period III and IV), as well as on the funerary houses of Lü Xu (456), Zhang Zhilang (460), and Xing Hejiang (469).

253 Allsen 2006.

254 Tseng 2013, 29–37. Tseng has however treated only the kingly hunting activities. Entries in the *Wei shu* show that hunting was also a favorite hobby among high officials, including those of Chinese origin. The high position of hunting was maintained until the end of the Northern Wei dynasty; Liu Meiyun and Wei Haiqing 2014, 426.

255 The mural in Yingbin dadao M16 (possibly Period II), the painted coffins from Dianhanchang M229 and 1997 Zhijiabao tomb, the murals in Yunbolilu 09DYM1, in 2019 Huayu II tomb, and Liang Bahu's tomb (all Period III; cf. Appendix I, Nos. 2, 17, 23, 26, 28). More hunting scenes on coffin paintings are known in Inner Mongolia and Yingxian, Shanxi (cf. Fig. 14 and Note 205). The last hunting scene of the Pingcheng period appears on the coffin painting of Feng Shigong (489) at Guyuan.

256 Liaoning bowu et al. 1984; Xu Guangji 2012, vol. 9, Pl. 40. Smith 1998, 296–98. Some other Koguryo painted tombs (in Jilin and in P'yong'an) contain such scenes as well.

257 Wallace 2010. Her analyses are based on the tomb reliefs in Shaanxi and Shanxi during Han times, which partially reflected the lives and beliefs of the pastoralists, such as the Xiongnu, of the region.

258 For example, in the Yuantaizi tomb of Former Yan times, or in the Koguryo tomb at Yaksu-ri 藥水里 古墳 (fifth century); Kim Wŏn-yong 1983, Fig. 7. The tomb occupants can be discerned by their exceptional clothing, large statures, and richly decorated mounts. The identification of the figure on

groups in a forest landscape intersected by winding mountain chains and rivers, which was typical of the Pingcheng landscape art, but not observed in earlier paintings in China's interior. In three cases, a hunting scene was painted opposite the banquet scene (the other tomb paintings are not completely preserved); the hunt may thus allude to enjoyment in a celestial realm.[259] Although the mural in Yunbolilu M1 is an exception, as it depicts in the center of the composition a hunter under a large tree, which may indicate his role as tomb owner, it also implies the same enjoyment idea: The hunter was sitting in a posture reminiscent of the pensive Bodhisattva Maitreya, who is to be reborn into the human world as Buddha.[260]

Another large-scale painting composition in Pingcheng concerns the military procession of the tomb occupant that typically consists of warriors, weapons and standard bearers, military bands, both mounted and on foot, female attendants, and acrobats. Such scenes of military processions are found early in northern Chinese tombs and then disseminated to Gansu, Sichuan and Hunan. Their occurrence culminated in the fourth century in southern Manchuria in the form of mural paintings and, in the Guan-Long area (a region stretching from the present-day Xi'an basin to eastern Gansu), in the form of clay figurines.

Several Pingcheng tomb paintings include such a scene, for example, from Shaling M7 (both the mural and the coffin), on the coffin from Zhijiabao and the lacquer-painted coffin in the Museum of Northern Dynasties Arts, as well as Zhang Zhilang's funerary house.[261] The occupant of Shaling M7, and Zhang Zhilang, or their families, opted for this scene in lieu of the more popular hunting one. The two coffin paintings, however, include both scenes. In the center of the procession scene in Shaling M7, there is a Chinese-style quadriga (*luche* 輅車),[262] while a *tongxian* 通幰 vehicle (an ox cart with a long sun shield) occupies the same position in the coffin painting from the Zhijiabao tomb. The figures on

---

the western wall of the Yaksu-ri tomb as the tomb occupant is further supported by his shooting at a tiger with a whistling arrow, which suggests his status as commander.

259 Wallace 2010, Chapter 5. She argues that the hunting scenes in Shaanxi and Shanxi tombs of Eastern Han times represented an act of combating wild animals and malignant spirits that blocked the soul's entry to Heaven, where Xiwangmu presides. In the Former Yan and Koguryo tombs, the hunting was depicted either above the Animals of the Four Directions or on the ceiling. This positioning suggests that the hunt belonged to the celestial world.

260 Lin Sheng-chih 2019: 86-92. In this case, the figure might have represented the tomb occupant.

261 For a brief account of the lacquer painted coffin, see Müller Sh. 2019b, 54–55. Some archaeologists assumed that the looted coffin came from the tomb of Yifu Mogui 乙弗莫瓌 (458) or his son Yifu Qiangui 乾歸 (485). On these two persons, see the contribution by Zhang Qingjie in this volume. The Yifu resided in what is now Qinghai before they were subdued by the Northern Wei. A report of the funerary house of Zhang Zhilang is not published, cf. Gu Shunfang and Lü Xiaojing 2022 for a brief description. For the painted Zhijiabao coffin, Liu Junxi and Gao Feng 2004.

262 For the *luche* identification, see Wu Jiao 2021: 62–63. The *luche* was a prerogative of the emperor and highly privileged nobles. The presence of a staff with seven textile streamers at the back of the vehicle leads Wu Jiao to conclude that the Shaling M7 vehicle was painted according to Western Jin ritual regulations. Similar chariots were depicted in the Song copy of the *Nymph of the Luo River* attributed to Gu Kaizhi 顧愷之 (c. 344–c. 406) and on the northern and southern slopes of the ceiling of Dunhuang Cave 249 (Western Wei). Further examples are found in Tang times (ibid., 62). The chariot in Dunhuang 249 allude to a ride ascending to the Trayastrimsa Heaven (*Daoli tian* 忉利天) on the peak of Sumeru, while the chariot in the departing scene of the *Nymph of the Luo River* scroll demonstrates the high status of the passenger.

the carriages in both cases are larger than the surrounding soldiers, and the one in the Zhi-jiabao painting is dressed in a *kandys* coat. We may conclude that these two figures represent tomb masters.[263] Clay figurines were employed to depict the military procession after they had been introduced to Pingcheng. However, the tombs of Song Shaozu (477) and Sima Jinlong and his wife (474 and 484) are the only ones that have such a formation.

Military bands in processions, referred to as *guchui* 鼓吹 (drums and winds on foot) and *qichui* 騎吹 (mounted winds), served to display the extraordinary military ranks of certain personages in the Han dynasty. In fourth-century Guanzhong, however, a new type of band appeared in large processions: the *hengchui* 橫吹 with drums and long horns (*hujiao* 胡角 "barbarian horns").[264] The "barbarian horns" are mentioned in a fifth-century passage preserved in the *Taiping yulan* 太平御覽, which describes that the troops of the western Rong 西戎 and Qiang 羌 tribesmen (in the Guanzhong and eastern Gansu areas) employed long bronze music instruments in the shape of bull horns to intimidate Chinese army horses.[265] The Book of [Liu] Song documents a gradual decline of the *guchui* band from a military honor to a personal demonstration of pomp and circumstance by court members. However, the *hengchui* band remained strictly reserved for high-ranking military officers commanding forces of ten thousand soldiers or more.[266] This was certainly also true in northern states. Large fourth- and fifth-century tombs in Guanzhong contain figurine formations with similar horns, with the figurines both mounted and on foot.[267] Horns of the same type were also portrayed in some Koguryo tomb murals. However, the horn blowers were not part of a large military procession but constituted together with drummers and/or other musicians small music troupes that were separate from the military marches.[268] Consequently, the Koguryan composition could not have served as a model for the Pingcheng depictions.

---

263 Appendix I, No. 13, 28. A clay figurine leading a small procession from Yuchang jiayuan M113 (Appendix I, No. 24), a late knife-shaped tomb, may have also represented the tomb master (see below).

264 For a list of Northern Dynasties tombs containing the figurines of military bands (up to 2004) and a new study of the typology of figurines from the Guanzhong area during the Sixteen Kingdoms period (but without counts of each figurine type), see Yue Qi and Liu Weipeng 2004 and Lin Zeyang 2021. For the *guchui* and *hengchui* bands, see Dien 2004, idem. 2007a, 350–51 and Yishui 1981.

265 The text in the *Taiping yulan* 136.85 is quoted from a lost passage in the Treatise on Music 樂志 of the Book of Song (*Song shu*). The present-day version of the Treatise is shorter but provides different information: "Some say (the horn) comes from the Wu 吳 and Yue 越 region." (*Song shu* 19.559) However, far more long-horn images are found in the north than the south during the fourth century. For an overview, see Yue Qi and Liu Weipeng 2004: 47–52. Similar horns are carved on the northern gate of Sanchi I, first century BCE. Further west, the Nordic lure or the Celtic carnyx, both long bronze trumpets, were also deployed in battles to intimidate enemies. See Kaufmann 1981, 64.

266 *Song shu* 19.559; Dien 2004, 92; Yishui 1981: 87.

267 Dien 2004. No less than four Sixteen Kingdoms period tombs in Xi'an contain horn blowing figurines. The largest troupe of them with seven mounted horn blowers is found in the Zhongzhaocun tomb in Xianyang, see Notes 87 and 217. The best known are those in the Caochangpo and the Xinji 新集 tomb; Shaanxi sheng 1959; Ningxia Guyuan 1988b. The Caochangpo tomb has been re-dated to the pre-Northern Wei period, Müller Sh. 2000, 100–17, Zhongguo shehui 2018, 122.

268 E.g., the mural in Anak Tomb 3, of Dong Shou (357); see the excellent reconstruction by the Northeast Asian History Foundation: http://contents.nahf.or.kr/goguryeo/anak3/an_html_en/int2_1.html; August 9, 2020. See also the depiction on the eastern wall in the Susan-ri tomb, dated to the second half of the fifth century; http://contents.nahf.or.kr/goguryeo/susanri/wall.html; accessed June 11, 2019.

Figure 32 Drummers and long-horn blowers in Shaling M7, northern wall.
(Left) Detail from the mural reconstruction; courtesy of Professor Wang Yanqing; (right) line-drawing by the author.

The mural in Shaling M7 (435 or earlier) in Pingcheng clearly portrays a *hengchui* band with six mounted long-horn blowers following six mounted drummers (Fig. 32), which is discussed in detail below. Similar assemblages found in Song Shaozu's (477), and Sima Jinlong's (484) tombs contain only two mounted long-horn blowers each. Song Shaozu was, according to the tomb inscription, a regional inspector (*cishi* 刺史) of Youzhou 幽州 ,[269] which belonged to a "superior (or large) region" (*shangzhou* 上州, *dazhou* 大州) during the Northern Wei period (rank 3). The rank of an inspector in one of the "superior regions" was equivalent to that of a garrison commander 鎮將/鎮都大將, as a superior region had its own armies over which the inspector took command.[270] Song's career appears to have been high enough to warrant a symbolic military procession with a *hengchui* band at his burial.[271] The same interpretation can be applied to the military processions found in the tomb of Sima Jinlong, who was the garrison commander of Yunzhong 雲中 (present-day southern Inner Mongolia).[272] In contrast, the absence of a procession scene in the murals of Liang Bahu (461), who was Director of the Ministry of Personnel 選部尚書, clearly shows

---

269 For Song Shaozu's life, see Tseng 2013, 91–92.

270 Kubozoe Yoshifumi 2015, 138–49.

271 My interpretation differs fundamentally from that of Tseng 2013, 91–97, who argues that the paintings on Song's funerary house reflected his *habitus* and were intended to serve his personal enjoyment in the afterlife, while the procession of Xianbei figurines expressed his desire to "fit in" the steppe-zone culture. According to Tseng, Song's military rank was too low to allow him to deploy this emblem of honor, and the array of parade figurines was therefore an appropriation of an imaginary status.

272 The number of horn-blowing figurines from this tomb is not clear, since the findings are not completely reported. Yunzhong was the heartland of the Tuoba core group and the burial ground for distinguished ministers and military officers, princes, and all emperors before Xiaowendi. It was also a defense zone for protecting Pingcheng against the invading Rouran. Persons appointed to safeguard Yunzhong were invested with high prestige. There were two sets of military processions in the tomb of Sima Jinlong due to the different clays and glazes used for the figurines. The excavators presume that one set could have been given to Jinlong's wife (died 474), who was also of high nobility, see Shanxi and Shanxi 1972; Song Xin 2002: 277–78.

Figure 33 "Cock's comb" and trident hats. (1) Rearguard from Shaling M7, northern wall; (2) Warrior (M5:100) from Song Shaozu's tomb (477); (3) Long-horn blower (horn lost) in Sima Jinlong's tomb (484); (4) Gold plaque (detail) from Yanchi, Ningxia; (5) Hat from Noin Ula Tomb No. 6; (6) Painted coffin (detail) from Guolimu 郭里木 tomb, Qinghai; (7) Figurine, originally mounted, from Heba Chang's tomb (553) in Taiyuan, Shanxi.

(1, 3) Curtesy of Professor Wang Yanqing; (2) After Liu Junxi 2008, Pl. 80.4; (4) Curtesy of Professor Ma Qiang of the Ningxia archaeological Institute; (5, 6) After Rudenko 1978, Pl. 16; 3 2 and Tong Tao and Wertmann 2010, Fig. 11. (2, 6) With permission of the Datong Archaeological Institute and Professor Tong Tao; (3, 7) line-drawings and photo (in the Shanxi Museum) by the author.

that his civil post and relatively low rank did not entitle him to military honors at his funeral. These examples indicate that Pingcheng's elite residents, despite their various origins and cultural backgrounds, formed a well-defined hierarchy of status and rank early on, and that an alleged appropriation of a higher distinction beyond one's own standing, at least in Song Shaozu's and Sima Jinlong's cases, did not take place.[273]

In Pingcheng's procession scenes, one image group stands out. The figures are characterized by hats with a triangular, but turned-up, brim and a top protrusion; from a side view, the hat resembles a trident. In Shaling M7's mural, the images appear as members of the *hengchui* band and the rearguard behind the chariot (Figs. 32, 33.1).[274] The so-called "cock's comb" hats worn by the figurines of mounted warriors and long-horn blowers in the tombs of Song Shaozu and Sima Jinlong bear similar details: Their hats are painted or incised with triangle lines on both sides and the front (Figs. 33.2–3), suggesting that the two very broad side brims are folded up and fixed to the top protrusion. Thus, the "cock's comb" and "trident" hats may have referred to the same headgear but were differently expressed in artworks. Similar hats ("cock's comb" and "trident") can be traced back to the Guanzhong area of the fourth and the early fifth century, for example, in the Caochangpo tomb in Xi'an.[275] A gold plaque (dated to 418; Fig. 33.4) discovered in Gufengzhuang 古峰莊 in Yanchi 鹽池, Ningxia, provides further support for the close relationship between the trident-hat wearing images and the Guan-Long region during the Sixteen Kingdoms period. Three human images wearing such hats and being referred to as "wise kings" 明明 by the inscription incised on the back side are portrayed as heroic horsemen hunting mythical animals.[276]

After the Northern Wei, the image reappeared in the second half of the sixth century, however, only in two regions: in Jinyang 晉陽 (present-day Taiyuan), for example, in the Northern Qi tomb of Heba Chang 賀跋昌 (died 552) (Fig. 33.7) in the north, and in the contact zone between the north and the south such as in Xiangyang 襄陽, Hubei, in Dengxian 鄧縣 and Xichuan 淅川, Henan, and in Ankang 安康, Shaanxi. Afterwords, the same hat was sighted in the region more to the west, such as in coffin paintings found in Qinghai (seventh century) as well as in Mu Tai's 穆泰 tomb (730) in Qingcheng 慶城, Gansu. Due to its wide distribution, the hat was identified as a clothing item typical of Xianbei, of Chinese officials, of Tubo-Tibetans, or Tuyuhun (Fig. 33.6).[277] As was common

---

273 See for example Tseng 2013, 95–96, idem. 2019, and Zhang 2018.
274 The same trident hats are also observed in the procession scenes on the lacquer painted coffin in the Museum of Northern Dynasties Arts and in the murals of Zhang Zhilang's funerary house.
275 Shaanxi sheng 1959, Fig. 3.6; Akiyama et al. 1968, Figs 339–40.
276 Bai Shuli 2007; Ni Yuzhan and Wang Wenguang 2016. The plague was found in 2006. An inscription incised on the verso gives information about the date and descriptions of the iconography.
277 The hat has been ascribed to different "ethnic groups." For a Xianbei identification, Huo Wei 2007, 269–71. Juliano (1980, 51 and Fig. 43–44) identifies it as *jiahuaguan* (*chien-hua-kuan*) 建華冠 of the Han Dynasty based on Harada 1967. The assumption, however, was made at a time when archaeological evidence was sparse. For a Tubo identification, see Tong Tao and Wertmann 2010, Fig. 11, Fig. 20, 208, Heller 2016, 168 note 29 suggests naming it "A zha" hat since the finding was embedded in the context of the Tuyuhun culture. For finds in Xiangyang, Xichuan, Ankang, and tombs of Heba Chang, and in Mu Tai, see Xiangyang shi 2019: 40, Fig. 6; Nanyang and Xichuan 1996: 28 Fig. 5; Li Qiliang and Xu Xinyin 1986, Fig. 3.5, Pl. III.1; Taiyuan shi 2003: 18 Fig. 16; Qingyang and Qingcheng 2008: 36 Fig. 10. The originally mounted figurine in Heba Chang's tomb is

with their predecessors in the Guan-Long area and Pingcheng, the "trident"-hat wearers of these later periods were part of a military music band, warriors, or hunters. Furthermore, in the seventh century, some high-ranking women in present-day Qinghai were also depicted with such hats, which appeared to form part of a group-identifying wardrobe.[278]

Early depictions of the hat during the fourth and fifth centuries relate it with a horse-riding culture. In the mural of Shaling M7, riders wearing such hats are shown escorting the quadriga of the tomb occupant. They also appear at the vanguard of the procession and are also guarding it from behind. The positioning of such riders reflects the trust and the appreciation placed in them. But who are the "trident" or "cock's comb" hat wearers? Recalling the Noin Ula find of the Xiongnu, a wool hat sewn from two halves was found in Kurgan No. 6 (Fig. 33.5). Rudenko considers this type of hat to have been typical for ancient stock-breeders in the Eurasian steppes.[279] This style of hat was not known for the Xianbei prior to the foundation of the dynasty due to the lack of pictorial material. Nevertheless, it is conceivable that the images of the "trident" or "cock's comb"-hat wearers symbolized, as Ni Yuzhan and Wang Wenguang have suggested,[280] members of some Xiongnu groups in the Guan-Long area during the late fourth and the early fifth century, since these latter settled in a large number along the Wei River 渭河 valley.[281] Some recently discovered petro-glyphs of the first century CE in Wujiachuan, Gansu, with images of horsemen wearing "three-horned" headdresses may further support the idea due to the proximity of the afore-mentioned geographical distribution.[282] The hat epitomized, so to speak, the fearless warriors and hunters that the Xiongnu aspired to be. The image was apparently brought by migrants from the Guan-Long region to Pingcheng, where it was kept alive among the military members. In the second half of the sixth century, the association of the hat with the military band was preserved in the north only in the stronghold of the "Men of Dai" 代人 in Jinyang. However, there was another disseminating route: despite a paucity of archaeological evidence in the Guanzhong region after the Tuoba invasion, the image possibly survived locally. When Xiangyang regained importance, the image spread with emigrants from Guanzhong to the contact zone between the north and the south, where the images with a trident hat were employed in tomb art to depict honorary escorts.[283] The high regard once associated with the hat persisted in the farther western areas controlled by the Tuyuhun and the Tibetans, and it became a sign of identity for certain peoples, mentioned above.

Pearl-roundel painting imitating a textile pattern
This category of paintings can only be seen on three lacquer-painted coffins, from Dazhun tielu 大准鐵路 M9, Erdianchang M37 (Period II), and Hudong M1 (Period III), according

---

designated as an acrobat. An acrobat however never appears as a rider in the Northern Dynasties. The raised right hand suggests that the figurine depicted a drummer.

278 Heller 2016, Fig. 3 (a woman), 5, 12 (both "envoys").
279 Rudenko 1969, 38.
280 Ni Yuzhan and Wang Wenguang 2016: 83.
281 Liu Shufen 2002: 4–5.
282 Varenov and Kudinova 2020. They also indicate that the anthropomorphic boulders from Khudyakov burial site in Altai during the Turkic period continued to use the "three-horned" headdress wearing images. They, however, believe that these images represent ancient deities or shamans.
283 Li Meitian 2016: 91–93. For Xiangyang, see Chittick 2010.

to the survey of Wang Yanqing and Gao Feng.[284] The paintings on the remaining parts of these coffins all contain large pearl roundels filled with half-naked deity and animal figures. However, only the report on Hudong M1 provides clear enough photos for an examination. Judging by the painting composition on the less than half of the left plank that remained, its side planks were probably entirely painted with pearl roundels against a black ground. The foot panel bore a Han motif of a "half-open door," but with two attendant images dressed in Central Asian garb, as previously mentioned. Bonnie Cheng, along with Wang Yanqing and Gao Feng, suggest that the Hudong painting featuring interlacing pearl roundels was intended to emulate a silk covering for the coffin that was well evidenced in the Chinese funerary tradition.[285] The later coffin of Feng Shigong from Guyuan, dated to 489, was similarly painted with repeated pearl roundels but overlapped by hexagons. Like those on the Hudong coffin, its roundels contain figures of deities and supernatural creatures in pairs (but not as mirror images),[286] although they are less intricate. Feng Shigong's coffin painting incorporated additional elements: The upper and lower borders of the side planks were painted with stories of filial sons, a topic from the Spring and Autumn of Master Yan *Yanzi chunqiu* (see below), and images of hunting Xianbei riders. The juxtaposition of narrative and decorative themes apparently indicates that Feng Shigong's coffin painting, rather than an attempt to replicate cloth, was a decoration in its own right. The other two above-mentioned Pingcheng coffin paintings, as per the descriptions provided by Wang Yanqing and Gao Feng, similarly incorporated diverse themes, making them more closely related to the concept of Feng Shigong's coffin art than Hudong's. The painting on side planks of the Hudong coffin, which clearly aims to replicate a textile pattern, is therefore unique.

The pearl roundels in Hudong M1's coffin painting are large (∅ approximately 30 cm) and run in both vertical and horizontal directions. The interstices are filled with vegetal ornaments or human figures. This composition recalls a pattern repeat of the pearl-roundel weaves of the sixth and seventh centuries. Cheng, as well as Wang and Gao, are cautious when comparing the painting to a weave. The former speaks specifically of the emulation of an embroidered fabric, for the obvious reason that the technique required to weave large-sized polychrome pattern repeats in East Asia had not yet been developed. It is notable that none of the Hudong roundels, being individually painted and not multiplied by repeating mechanical procedures, are identical to the others (Fig. 34). On the other hand, the tangential points of the Hudong roundels, as well as the roundels on the coffin from Erdianchang M37,[287] were decorated with the Pingcheng-typical animal masks in the horizontal and (Persian?) beaded rings (or lotus flowers?) in the vertical direction. This feature is observed to recur in certain pearl-roundel weaves of the late sixth or seventh century,[288] indicating

284 Wang Yanqing and Gao Feng 2016: 189–91 and 199 Fig. 11.2, as well as Datong kaogu 2019: 22–24 and Datong kaogu 2004b. The Dazhun tielu tomb is not reported. The Hudong coffin no longer exists.
285 Cheng 2014, 131–32; 140–42. Wang Yanqing and Gao Feng 2016: 200.
286 *Wei shu* 61.1361 mentions a damask weave with "immortal" motifs 仙人文綾 in Pingcheng during the reign of Wenming and Xiaowen (late 470s–490s), cited in Wang Yanqing and Gao Feng 2016: 198. Both authors propose that the woven *xianren* may have resembled those on the painted coffins.
287 Datong kaogu 2019: 22. There is no complete illustration available.
288 Zhao Feng and Qi Dongfang 2011, 88–89, 91 Fig. 3 (Northern Dynasties), and 99 Fig. 1 (Tang). In all these weave fragments, the animal masks appear in the weft direction and the beaded rings (referred to

Figure 34 Pearl roundels on the left plank of the coffin from Hudong M1.
Drawing by the author based on Datong kaogu 2004b: 30 Fig. 8.

that Hudong's pattern had a significant impact on the future weave design vocabulary. Since this decorative method of connecting pearl roundels did not occur earlier, I tentatively refer to it as "Pingcheng framework."

Pearl roundels also adorn eave-end tiles *wadang*, but only a few of them have been discovered so far. The roundel frequently frames a lotus flower or a reborn soul emerging from a lotus flower. Such tiles were unearthed from a palace and several Buddhist sites, including the Yungang Caves, in Pingcheng and its suburbs, as well as from sites in the then Yunzhong commandery (present-day Togtoh 托克托, Inner Mongolia).[289] It is, however, unclear when such tiles first appeared or, more importantly, how they were arranged on the eaves. As they were all single finds, they were possibly interspersed among other decorative eave tiles and did not build a continuous string of roundels. Pearl roundels were also occasionally adopted to embellish the crowns of bodhisattvas in Yungang, either alone or together with other circular ornaments, while they were absent from the contemporaneous Dunhuang caves.[290]

It appears that the isolated pearl roundels thus far found in Pingcheng and vicinities were imbedded primarily in Buddhist art. Carol Bromberg, Matteo Compareti, and Joel Walker all note that single circles aligned with pearl borders are documented in early Indian

---

as "flowers") in the warp direction. But the description for Fig. 1 on page 99 does not correctly recognize this composition. The reconstruction of the pattern repeat in Fig. 3 is thus erroneous.

289 Wang Feifeng 2019.

290 Cheng 2014, 134; 136. In addition to the one in Cave 18 mentioned by Cheng, Cave 9 (one of the Buddha's attendant bodhisattvas wearing a crown with a pearl roundel on each side) and Caves 11 and 17 (Bodhisattvas Maitreya with crowns with Buddha Shakyamuni in a pearl roundel). Caves 17 and 18 were constructed between the 460s and 470s, while Caves 9 and 11 are dated to the mid- and late Yungang periods (480s–490s). For a brief survey of crown types found in Yungang, see Li Ye 2018.

art dating back to the first century BCE, either in architecture or jewelry. And Walker further indicates that the pearl-roundel motif was possibly developed in northern India.[291] Pearl roundels first appeared as repeating patterns on the garments of Sasanian rulers and their entourage in the seventh century, as evidenced by the rock reliefs at Tag-e Bustan.[292] Taking this development into account, it is plausible that early Indian examples with single pearl roundels may have inspired craftsmen in Pingcheng to embellish Buddhist structures and palace buildings with pearl-roundel-bearing eave tiles. However, as mentioned, this did not seem to have been common due to the small number of finds.[293]

The pearl roundels that were aligned and gave off the impression of two-dimensional repeating patterns, as in the Hudong and Erdianchang coffin paintings, underwent a different process. As mentioned above, both paintings presumably imitated embroidery. But they predate all known specimens with pattern repeats of pearl roundels. The earliest datable textile fragment came from a tomb in Astana dated to 551, suggesting that the fabric was woven slightly earlier. The earliest written record of pearl roundels, or simply aligned beads, is a "gauze with (the motifs of) peacocks and pearl strings" 連珠孔雀羅, mentioned in conjunction with a party organized by the infamous Zu Ting 祖珽, the then regional inspector *cishi* of Binzhou (Taiyuan), in the 540s.[294] During the Northern Qi period, as is well known, the "Central Asian" funerary beds from Anyang and Taiyuan and the mural from Xu Xianxiu's tomb (571) in Taiyuan all show garments with such roundels.

The mature arrangement of Erdianchang's and Hudong's pearl-roundel patterns indicates that they had forerunners. Bonnie Cheng proposed that the fourth-century bronze metalwork from southern Manchuria inspired the creation of ornamental hexagons in Pingcheng.[295] But a model for the repeating pearl roundels remains obscure, and their origin cannot be clarified here.

At any rate, the attendants in "Central Asian" clothing on the foot panel of the Hudong coffin also suggest that the occupant was connected in some way to the Iranian world. It is even possible that he originated from a state in Central Asia. Notably, the Hudong roundels were filled with figures drawn from the repertoire of Buddhist and sepulchral art of Pingcheng, rather than Persian mythic creatures. Therefore, the painted "shroud" on Hudong M1's coffin was effectively Buddhist in nature. Moreover, the presence of animal offerings indicates that his funerary ritual followed, at least in part, that of the steppe people.

Paintings on funerary houses

To date, funerary houses have not been discovered in other regions under Tuoba rule. In Pingcheng, funerary houses were only found during Period III and the first years of Period

---

291 Bromberg 1983, Compareti 2009; 2014: 42–44; Walker 2018, 265. However, Walker (ibid.) empha-
     sizes that the high prestige associated with pearls in Sasanian culture and society made pearl roundels
     "a central feature of the iconographic vocabulary of the Persian world, widely deployed both within
     and beyond the empire."

292 Compareti 2016, 87–88; and see more references there.

293 Compareti 2020: 29, whose argument is based on the Hudong M1 find.

294 Meister 1970: Fig. 10 and 20; Shang Gang 2011, 22–23, citing *Bei Qi shu* 39.514. It is however uncer-
     tain as to the appearance of the "pearl strings."

295 Cheng 2014, 134.

Figure 35 Portraits of the deceased in (1) the stone house from the Zhijiabao tomb and (2) the stone house for Xie Xing's wife (459).

(1) After Wang Yintian and Liu Junxi 2001; with permission of the Datong Archaeological Institute; (2) Courtesy of Professor Zhang Qingjie.

IV (those of Song Shaozu and Jia Bao, both dated to 477). Six out of the eleven known funerary houses are adorned with paintings, and five of the six houses also bear an inscription for personal identification. Paintings are spread principally on the inner walls and the façades. Not all paintings in funerary houses are published, but the available materials indicate that the painting subjects and motifs, unlike murals in tomb chambers, tend to pertain to private interests.

Only two funerary houses contain portraits of the tomb occupants: the one from Zhijiabao found in 1997 and that for Xie Xing's wife (Fig. 35). These images—with Xianbei headdresses and long, loose attire, like those in Shaling M7's mural—were placed in the middle of the rear walls. Other funerary houses bear varying painting topics. The stone house of Lü Xu 呂續 (456) at Zhijiabao, excavated in 2020, is both carved and painted with two sets of the Four Directional Animals, i.e., the Dark Warrior of the North, the Green Dragon of the East, the Vermillion Bird of the South and the White Tiger of the West, along with other hybrid human-animal deities on the inner walls. Moreover, a Buddha in relief was carved on the western outer wall, and two servants in Xianbei attire were painted on the inner southern wall.[296] The door panel of Zhang Zhilang's 張智朗 house (460), the only component of this richly decorated stone house that has been published thus far, is painted on both sides with slightly modified Chinese motifs:[297] the front with a pair of feathered deities standing on two peacocks, a symbol of the south, or an incarnation of the Buddha, and the reverse with a figure wearing a robe and an official cap similar to those worn during Jin times. Both feathered deities are holding an incense burner in one hand, and a pole with three tassels on top in another.[298] A recent publication mentions briefly that the inner walls were painted with figures clad in Xianbei clothing marching in a procession, as well as with a caparisoned horse and a *Tongxian* cart.[299] The stone house of Xing He-jiang 邢合姜 (469) found near Tongjiawan was painted with apsaras, worshipers in Xianbei clothing, and the Seven Buddhas. The rear wall was painted with Buddhas Shakyamuni and Prabhutaratna, whose iconography was derived from the Lotus Sutra 妙法蓮華經 (*Sad-dharma Pundarika Sutra*) and symbolized Shakyamuni's final teaching.[300] Lastly, Song Shaozu's funerary house is decorated with motifs reminiscent of the Han iconography. One may have been a contemporary interpretation of the story of "Killing Three Warriors with Two Peaches" (二桃殺三士) (Fig. 36) preserved in the *Yanzi Chunqiu* 晏子春秋 (the

---

296 Zhang Zhizhong et al. 2021; Wei Zheng 2022.

297 Chizhi and Liu Junxi 2014. The inscription carved on the façade states that Zhang, a native of Tai-yuan, was the wife of General Mao Dezu 毛德祖 (356–429) from Xingyang 榮陽 (near present-day Xingyang). According to *Jin shu* 81.2129 and *Song shu* 95.2329, Mao served the Liu Song dynasty but defected to the Northern Wei, possibly in 423, and died there. Notably, Zhang's inscription records only Mao's titles that he received from the Northern Wei court, which show that Mao was highly respected there. Zhang married Mao at the age of thirty-one, far beyond the average age of marriage for women, which lay between sixteen and twenty (Hinsch 2018, 8). Zhang may have been "awarded" (as a captive?) to Mao by the imperial court. Nothing else is known of her. The surname Zhang does not guarantee a Chinese descent. The animal offerings in her funerary house show that she was commemorated with a steppe custom. She may have been a member of those Zhangs related to the Wuhuan or Xiongnu, Yao Weiyuan 1962, 254, 278, 358.

298 Peacocks were designated as "Birds of Viet" during the Tang era; Schafer 1963, 96–99. The earliest image of a feathered deity carrying an insignia reminiscent of the standard of a Roman Legion is found in the tomb painting of Bu Qianqiu 卜千秋 (ca. 9 CE) in Luoyang. Symbolizing an envoy of "Heaven" 天帝, the image guides Bu Qianqiu's soul to the realm of Xiwangmu. According to Sun Yan (2006: 70), the image spread to other sites in Henan, to northern Shaanxi, and northern Jiangsu during Eastern Han times. After the Han dynasty, it vanished from the Central Plains but reappeared in south China, primarily in the metropolitan area of the capital Jianye 建業 of the Sun Wu kingdom in modern Nanjing and vicinity, as well as in the Koguryo state. For a recent find of a feathered image of Sun Wu times from Datu in Anhui, see Ye Runqing 2016: 15.

299 Gu Shunfang and Lü Xiaojing 2022: 61.

300 Li Meitian and Zhang Zhizhong 2020; Datong kaogu 2022. For the Seven Buddhas and the Lotus Sutra, see Ch'en 1964, 174, 378–82.

Figure 36 (1) Line drawing of the painting in Song Shaozu's funerary house; (2) Stone relief "Killing Three Warriors with Two Peaches" from Wu Liang shrine at Jiaxiang, Shandong, Eastern Han.
(1) Liu Junxi 2008, 129 Fig. 133, with permission of the Datong Archaeological Institute; (2) Chavannes 1909, Pl. LXIII (detail).

Spring and Autumn of Master Yan).[301] Only some minimal paintings on Jia Bao's wooden house are preserved, they seem to be ornamental scrolls with half palmettes. No figure paintings are otherwise found in this house.

The paintings summarized above appear to express personal wishes for a blissful after-life, with the deceased either being safeguarded by the Daoist and Buddhist deities (Lü Xu and Zhang Zhilang) or being absolved of their sins and reborn in the Buddhist paradise (Xing Hejiang). Since the "Two Peaches" story about loyalty and moral valor had gradually faded into oblivion after Han times, its depiction in Song's funerary house could have reflected his family tradition from Dunhuang, where the Confucian teachings were still well

---

301 Müller Sh., "Reappraising the paintings in Song Shaozu's funerary house (477)," presented at the Fourth Conference of the Early Medieval China Group on March 27, 2021. It is noteworthy that the figures in this depiction are not styled as Xianbei.

kept. Several early members of the Song clan of Dunhuang, to which Song Shaozu may have belonged, had achieved great fame for their erudition in the Confucian Classics. During the last years of the Pingcheng period, Emperor Xiaowen was actively propagating Confucian teachings and morals.[302] Song Shaozu's "Two Peaches" depiction was possibly a herald of this imperial policy, while the same topic in the coffin paintings of Feng Shigong (489) certainly echoed of the reform efforts of the emperor.[303]

Late paintings in Pingcheng tombs

The tomb murals of Periods IV and V became less elaborate.[304] The scenes in the earlier tomb murals were painted within an architectural framework comprised of pillars and beams, creating the impression of being viewed from an interior space. In contrast, the later paintings, such as those in Xiashengjing M1 (Period IV) and the tomb at Chenzhuang (Period V), consist only of the architectural elements. Some other tombs, possibly imitating the elite tombs in south China, were built with stamped bricks with inscriptions or motifs of floral scrolls or "worshipers" 供養人 in Xianbei clothing. One of these was the tomb of the Prince of Danyang 丹揚王, the largest of all Pingcheng tombs, but which also had two painted Maheśvara-like guardians on the walls of the corridor (Fig. 31 *right*).[305]

It is worth noting that early Pingcheng tomb murals, i.e., of Periods II and III, are only painted to the height of the four walls where the ceiling vault begins. Celestial symbols such as the sun, moon, and lotus flowers still adorned the ceilings. They, however, were only painted on small rendering patches on the otherwise unplastered ceiling (Fig. 37).[306] The tomb murals in Pingcheng were much later than those in Koguryo and southern Manchuria in taking up the motifs of the constellations and the Milky Way.[307] The ceiling of the rear chamber of the Chenzhang tomb, for example, was completely painted with stars or

---

302 Jenner 1981, 32; Holcombe 2013, 26.

303 Luo Feng 2020: 49.

304 See Table 2.1. For excavation reports: Appendix I, Nos.2, 7, 11, 22, 25 (Period IV), and 1 (Period V).

305 The discovery of the tomb in 1874 was recorded in the revised chronicle of the Huanren County 懷仁 縣新志, cited in Ni Run'an 2012: 62. The two guardians, each about 150 cm high, were photographed during a reexamination in 1993. The massive construction (four chambers with a floor area of over 140 m²; cf. Note 48) indicates the very high status of the deceased. Danyang 丹揚 is probably a variant of 丹陽. Wang Yintian 2010 and Ni Run'an 2012 argue that Liu Chang 劉昶 (436–497), a prince of the Liu Song dynasty who defected to the Tuoba court, was buried there. If that is the case, it would mean that the Xianbei clothing continued to exist in Pingcheng after the clothing reform in 494.

306 The tomb ceilings generally were destroyed by looters, only two remained intact. The mentioned images are observed in Liang Bahu's tomb (with the sun and moon) and in the newly excavated Qilicun M29 (with a lotus flower).

307 Images of the Milky Way and constellations in Han tombs were found both on the Central Plains and the northern borders (Shaanxi and Jingbian 2017: 12–13). They reappeared in early fifth-century tombs in southern Manchuria and Koguryo, such as Chin's tomb (408) in Taesong-ri, and that of Feng Sufu (415) (Tseng 2003, 378–82) and in the late fifth century in northern China, such as the tombs at Chenzhuang, Xiashenjing (both near Pingcheng), Lincheng (Hebei), and of Feng Shigong (489; Guyuan). The mural in the Wenyinglu Tomb (Period III) contains single small circles and those connected by lines, alluding to constellations. They, however, were only painted on a narrow strip on the upper edge of the mural and do not form a starry vault. Therefore, this depiction hat at best a prototypical character. For the Chenzhaung, Wenyinglu and Xiashenjing tombs, see Table 1, Nos. 1, 19, 20.

Figure 37 Lotus flower painted on plaster on a "bare ceiling," Qilicun M29, Datong, excavated in 2020. Note the upper border of the mural (arrow). The right half of the mural is broken off.

After https://wx3.sinaimg.cn/large/7e7726d7ly1gxzoobsso8j20u00h3773.jpg, retrieved January 22, 2022. With permission of the Datong Archaeological Institute

constellations and the Milky Way (though this latter was largely flaked off), with a lotus flower at its apex. This is surprising, since migrants from these regions made up a sizable share of the inhabitants of Pingcheng. The bare ceilings of the early painted Pingcheng tombs were possibly a result of bans on celestial images imposed by some Tuoba rulers. Although they had a strong interest in the astrological forces that regulated human life and, particularly, politics, they also feared unfavorable prophecies and prognostications through fabricated celestial images or charts.[308] A reemergence of images of heaven in tombs was possibly encouraged by the construction of the Mingtang 明堂 ritual hall between 486 and 490, which is said to have had a light blue-turquoise hemispherical vault (*gaitian* 蓋天) with a mechanical pointer that moved month by month to the corresponding painted lunar lodge.[309] Lin Sheng-chih elucidates that a combination of a star vault and the Milky Way in tombs from this period merely resembled astrological charts, yet did not function as such. This was a compromise to avoid the fear of the rulers and to fulfill the wish to create a private micro-universe for the deceased.[310]

---

308 Tseng 2003, 384–404 and Lin Sheng-chih 2011: 154–55 both point out the strong influence of celestial prognostic charts on the population. At least two bans of the fifth century on astrological charts and prognostications are recorded in the Book of Wei, by Taiwudi in 444 and Xiaowendi in 485. Tseng (2003, 384–87, 398–400) believes that the strong interests in Chinese astrology were the major driving force for early Tuoba rulers to engage Chinese astrologers, with Cui Hao 崔浩 (died 450) as the most prominent of them.

309 *Shuijing zhu* 13.1150–51. See also Tseng 2003, 404–7; 2013, 25–29.

310 Lin Sheng-chih 2011: 154–55.

The tomb ceilings covered with stars and the walls devoid of pictorial depictions also suggest that the configuration of the eternal home underwent an intellectual shift: Emptiness replaced worldly joy, fame, and power, represented by hunting, feasts, and processions. Since the lotus flower motif from the early days remained at the apex of the ceiling, the deceased symbolically lingered in his own cosmos while he enjoyed the blessing of the Buddha.

Notably, no images of filial sons are found in any of the Pingcheng burials. The depiction of the paragons of filial sons on Feng Shigong's (489) coffin in Guyuan is singular for the entire fifth century, which may have been a response to Emperor Xiaowen's reform policies, which will be discussed below.

Tomb figurines in Pingcheng tombs

Figurines were the prominent components in tombs both in the Western Jin Luoyang and the fourth-century Guan-Long regions. From the mid-fifth century onwards, more clay figurines than murals were found in Pingcheng tombs. Ni Run'an sees this phenomenon as a clear sign of the efforts of the Tuoba rulers to enforce the ritual regulations of the Western Jin (*Jin zhi* 晉制) in the realm under their control. The aim was to present the Tuoba as the legitimate heirs of the Western Jin. The impact of the Jin regulations on the burials of the Pingcheng elites was additionally manifested by the square floor plans of the tomb chambers and the use of epitaphs. The results were the vanishing of the tomb paintings and a growing influence of the Guan-Long group in Pingcheng's political and cultural life.[311]

In terms of official prescriptions for burial rituals, it is only known that Emperor Xiaowen reinstated a three-year mourning period for offspring of the deceased, a measure that even had not been followed by all Chinese monarchs.[312] Such an important decision regarding a reorganization of burial rituals (for elites), as proposed by Ni, is not mentioned in written sources.[313] Although paintings in tombs were indeed less prominent and their subjects changed during Period IV, as discussed above, they did not disappear. Further, the so-called Jin funerary regulations *Jin zhi* has been differently interpreted by scholars.[314]

Only 17 of the 252 Pingcheng tombs yield figurines (Table 2.2). Figurines can also be found in fifth-century tombs in other regions: in Hohhot, Inner Mongolia, and Lincheng, Hebei. Given the considerable number of clay figurines without provenance in museums and antique markets around the world, there are undoubtedly more tombs from Pingcheng (or the Pingcheng-period) that contained figurines. The manufacture of clay figurines was probably a branch of the funerary industry in Pingcheng of a size and scale which was not to be scoffed at. Nevertheless, we have only these excavated tombs at our disposal. They do not show a uniform way of arraying figurines in tombs.

---

311 Ni Run'an 2013 and 2016: 221–22.

312 *Wei shu* 13.330 and 108C.2779. Only seven emperors practiced this long mourning period; *Ershiershi zhaji*, 291, only three were Chinese. These were Wudi 晉武帝 (236–290) and Kangdi 晉康帝 (322–344) of the Jin, Xiaowudi of the Liu Song 劉宋孝武帝 (430–464), Yao Xing of the Later Qin 後秦姚興 (366–416), Xiaowendi of the Northern Wei 北魏孝文帝 (467–499), Wudi of the Northern Zhou 北周武帝 (543–578), and Liu Chengjun of the Northern Han 北漢劉承鈞 (926–968).

313 Zhongguo shehui 2018, 101–4, 141.

314 The idea was first proposed by Yu Weichao 1980 and followed up by several eminent Chinese scholars, e.g., Yang Hong 1999; Han Guohe 1999; Huo Wei 2015; Qi Dongfang 2015.

Appendix II lists the assemblages of clay figurines. Since finds are mostly poorly documented, the list conveys only a rough idea. It nevertheless indicates that the use of figurines in the city was a gradual and learning process: Once figurines were introduced, they quickly appeared in burials with funerary houses or beds. Later, figurines appeared mainly in chamber tombs, but never in catacomb tombs, as mentioned above, even though some of them were spacious enough to accommodate some figurines.

Appendix II also shows that the major type for Period III were female attendants, followed by acrobats with music troupes of Central Asians and/or female music ensembles. Large processions with figurines appear at the turn from Period III to Period IV and replace the painted version. However, figurines never depict hunters, described above. Therefore, the decline of hunting scenes can at least partially be attributed to the acceptance of figurines.

Transition from Guanzhong to Pingcheng

In Period III, female figurines were usually put near a stone bed or a coffin,[315] implying that they were supposed to serve the deceased in his/her afterlife. Only the Wenyinglu tomb and the Hudong 2004M11 contained one single male figurine each (Appendix II, Nos. 5, 8). Both were found among female servant figurines, suggesting they had a similar function. Most female figurines (servants, maids, musicians, and dancers) were dressed in Xianbei clothing (Fig. 22). Of the Period III, only the tomb of Zhang Zhilang and the Yunbolu M10 (Appendix II, Nos. 3, 4) are dated to the 460s. The tomb of Lü Xu (dated 456) yields only guardian warriors and beasts, which will not be discussed in this paper.[316]

An earlier tomb with figurines recently excavated from the Dongxing Square cemetery (Appendix II, No. 1) sheds light on the transition from Chang'an-type to Pingcheng-type figurines. This tomb, which the excavators dated to the early Pingcheng period, i.e., before the 440s, contains female figurines dressed in both Xianbei attire and that typical of Chang-an prior to the Tuoba's conquest.[317] One of the female figurines has a high, uncovered forehead and a hairdo commonly found in depictions in the earlier Chang'an region, with a chignon styled from two twisted hair strands (Figs. 38.1, 38.3). The incised lines on the chignon of the female figurine from the Dongxin Square resemble the swirls found on, for example, the aureole of the Buddha Maitreya statue dated to 451 (Liu Song), which is currently in the collection of the Smithsonian's National Museum of Asian Art.[318] The figurine's archaic smile (Fig. 38.2), reminiscent of a bodhisattva, further suggests that the figurine was stylistically more closely associated with the 450s than with the 420s and 430s. The use of figurines in Pingcheng tombs, therefore, seems to have begun around the 450s.

---

315 Next to a stone bed: Tiancun M1, Zhang Zhilang's and Song Shaozu's tomb; next to a coffin: Yunbolu M10.

316 Mentioned in Zhang Zhizhong et al. 2021. No details and photos were provided. Appendix II, No. 2.

317 There is no report available. For a very brief description of some artifacts from the tomb, see Datong bowu 2018, 51, 97 and http://www.360doc.com/content/19/0216/09/33885274_815277513.shtml; accessed April 26, 2020. For female Chang'an-type figurines, see, for example, those from Pingling M1 in Xianyang shi 2006, 92–94.

318 See https://asia.si.edu/object/F1911.121a-b/; accessed July 27, 2020.

Figure 38 (1–2) Figurine of a female servant from the Dongxin Square, Datong, and detail; (3) Head of a female figurine from Pingling M1, Xi'an (late fourth century).

(1–2) After Datong bowu 2018, Cat.-No. 93, with permission of the Datong Museum; (3) Line-drawing by the author based on Xianyang shi 2006, Color pl. 121.

The date and style of the female figurines match well with the historical events of 445–446, when Emperor Taiwu personally led his troops to suppress the large-scale rebellion of Ge Wu 蓋吳, who belonged to the Lushui 盧水 branch of the Xiongnu.[319] The aftermath of the conflict saw the persecution of Buddhists and the relocation of some 2000 craftsmen and their families from Chang'an to Pingcheng. The emigrants most likely brought with them some of their own traditional burial customs. The female figurine from the Dongxin Square was possibly one of the last of the Chang'an style, which quickly vanished from Pingcheng. A weak support for the emigrant hypothesis is the sudden co-occurrence of the above-mentioned oil lamps with multiple arms from Chang'an in Pingcheng during Period III, which were found only in tombs containing figurines (e.g., Appendix II, Nos. 4, 7). However, there is a lack of data for many tombs, making a more detailed study currently impossible. Notably, all the other figurines from this Dongxin Square tomb, including one

---

319 *Wei shu* 4B.100, 111.3033–34. This was one of the largest rebellions in the early Northern Wei dynasty. The region affected included the present-day provinces of Shaanxi, eastern Gansu, and southeastern Shanxi. Rumors had it that Buddhists participated in the rebellion and stored weapons in monasteries. In response to this, Emperor Taiwu initiated the first of the three Buddhist persecutions in Chinese history. Liu Shufen 2002 sees in the rebellion one of the first large-scale ethnic conflicts in the early medieval period; idem 2008, 19–25, 32–45; Pearce 2019, 165–66, 169.

with Central Asian facial characters, are dressed in Xianbei clothing.[320] It appears that the tomb occupant, or his family, adapted to the new living environment and accepted the Xianbei identity, at least in part.

Female musicians and dancers in figurine assemblages and tomb paintings

Music ensembles with mixed musicians of both sexes as well as from Xianbei and Central Asians existed already in the murals in the Shaling M7 (435 or earlier) and the Qilicun 2020M29 (Period III), as well as in the paintings on the funerary houses for Xie Xing's wife (458) and Zhang Zhilang (460). Such an ensemble was also unearthed from the tomb at Dongxin Square, but in a figurine formation (see above). Whether painted or modeled, the ensembles were always part of a banquet, and both types of ensembles existed in parallel for a time. As the theme of tomb paintings changed in the last quarter of the fifth century, mixed ensembles were replaced by all-female ones consisting solely of figurines wearing Xianbei clothing. All-female musician groups were unearthed from five tombs thus far.

The all-female ensembles from the tombs of Chang'an in the Sixteen Kingdoms period are considered to be the most likely prototypes for those of Pingcheng,[321] as the comparable figurines have not been discovered anywhere else in northern China. The remaining pottery music instruments or the gestures of the figurines suggest that the music played originated from the so-called Western Liang music 西涼樂, which swept northern China in the fourth and fifth centuries.[322] Zhou Yang argues that the Chang'an ensembles represented a revival and renewal of the Han tradition.[323] The renewal apparently also affected the musicians. As women began to play an increasingly important role in ritual and banquet music at the Cao Wei court, the rich and powerful followed this new trend and also privately kept large numbers of female musicians as a status symbol.[324] This could explain the early depiction of a music band in the mural from Shaling M7.[325] The figurines of all-female orchestras brought from Chang'an to Pingcheng were almost immediately converted to the Xianbei appearance. Interestingly, despite the alleged bond with the Han tradition, the Chinese in the south regarded the music played by women as belonging to the Qiang and Hu (Central Asian), i.e., people from Guanzhong or further west, even in the late sixth century.[326]

---

320 Personal communication with Wang Yanqing of the Yungang Academy on June 26, 2020. For photos, http://www.360doc.com/content/19/0216/09/33885274_815277513.shtml; retrieved April 26, 2020. In the pre-Northern Wei period, "Central Asian" figurines were found only in the Xinji tomb, Ningxia Guyuan 1988b. Unlike the Central Asian figurines in Pingcheng, the Xinji ones depict warriors.

321 For recent Xi'an finds, see Xi'an shi 2014; Lin Zeyang 2021; Xin Xuefeng and Geng Qinggang 2023.

322 According to *Sui shu* 15.378, Western Liang music was a mixture of the Kuchean and the Liangzhou music. When the new music arrived at Chang'an with the deported people in the fourth century, it had already undergone several transformations. Lawergren 2019, 699.

323 Zhou Yang 2017: 127–31.

324 Xu Jiqi 2018: 69–70, 75.

325 A small band of four musicians, possibly two men and two women, play instruments at the outdoor banquet (south wall). Both men wear Xianbei hats. The images of the women are so damaged that it is difficult to determine their clothing style.

326 An anecdote tells that Zhang Zhaoda 章昭達 (518–571), an official and high military officer of the Chen dynasty, "brought out a large orchestra of women musicians with various instruments to play all the songs of the Qiang and the Hu" to entertain his banquet guests; *Chen shu* 11.184, cited in Pearce 2008: 110.

As in Chang'an, all the female musicians and singers in Pingcheng are depicted in a sitting position. Notably, the Chang'an tombs did not contain any ensembles with musicians of both sexes and from Xianbei and Central Asians. Most instruments of the figurines are not preserved. They may have been flutes, zithers, drums, panpipes, or lutes based on the hand gestures of the figurines. Harps, as they were depicted in the paintings of the funerary house for Xie Xing's wife and the mural in Qilicun M29, were of the angular type and were played by both Xianbei and Central Asian musicians. Although the angular harps originated in the far west, they were regarded as belonging to Kuchean music by the people in northern China.[327]

Other new figurine types

In Period IV, female dancer figurines dressed in Xianbei clothing emerged.[328] There are only a few of them, and they do not seem to have a prototype. They are part of an all-female ensemble, but not all female ensembles include such dancers. Some dancers are adorned with earrings and necklaces that are rarely seen on other types of female figurines. The beaded necklaces in particular convey an impression of wealth and elegance. Some even resemble those worn by bodhisattvas (Fig. 12). The female dancers may have been created to reflect the optimistic economic development in Pingcheng. But it is intriguing why such figurines were not found among the female ensemble in the very rich tomb of Sima Jinlong, whereas two female dancer figurines were integrated into the ensemble discovered in the simple tomb 113 at Yuchang jiayuan.

Yuchang jiayuan M113, excavated in 2013, is one of only two knife-shaped tombs in Pingcheng that was equipped with figurines,[329] and one of the few not looted. The striking stylistic resemblance of its two dancer figurines to those found in Yanbei shiyuan M2, M52, and Erdianchang M36 implies that all these figurines were produced within a short period of time and possibly at the same or related workshops.[330]

Another novel type is the figurine unearthed from the Yuchang jiayuan M113. It depicts a horseman leading an idiosyncratic, perhaps private, funerary procession. This procession comprised a chariot drawn by a fully caparisoned horse and steered by a Xianbei charioteer, as well as an ox cart. To the procession also belong two entertainment troupes, one for banquet music with six female musicians and two female dancers, all in Xianbei clothing, and the other for acrobatics with six male Central Asian musicians and one Central Asian bottom man for pole climbing. Both troupes formed a small arena in which the remaining figurines and clay artifacts were scattered: thirteen male and five female servants, animals, as well as pots and household models. All were arrayed in a shallow depression in front of a side plank of the coffin.[331] There are no other equestrian figurines present, nor are there any

---

327 The mural fragment is preserved in the Museum for Northern Dynasties Arts in Datong. For harps, see Lawergren 2019 and further references there.
328 In addition to those found in Pingcheng, one female dancer figurine was also found in the Daxuelu tomb in Hohhot, Inner Mongolia. See Appendix II, Nos. 5, 10, 16, 19, 20.
329 Datong kaogu 2021b. The other one is Yingbin dadao M76, which was severely robbed. Only a single fragmented figurine is reported, there is no other information available, see Datong kaogu 2006c: 60 and Fig. 33.2.
330 Shanxi and Shanxi 1972, Liu Junxi 2008, 27–39, 40–70, Datong kaogu 2019.
331 The depression is not mentioned in the report, but clearly discernable in Datong kaogu 2021b: Fig. 3.

figurines depicting warriors, weapon bearers, or military standard-bearers. The style of the single rider from this tomb differs from that of all mounted figurines in the procession for Song Shaozu (477). Yet, four comparable riders are present in Sima Jinlong's procession formation (484).[332] The rider figurines from M113 and Sima Jinlong's tomb are similarly modeled: the left hand holds the reins, while the right hand hangs down and is covered by the long sleeve.[333] However, the M113 rider with his marked abdominal girth is in sharp contrast to Sima Jinlong's riders, who have broad shoulders and narrow waists. While the four horsemen from Sima Jinlong's tomb represent merely one of the many cavalry units in the military procession, the horseman from M113, leading a parade without warriors, appears to hold an elevated position and represent the deceased. We do not have any information on the tomb occupant in Yuchang Jiayuan M113, but it appears that he had access to some Pingcheng manufacturers who produced exclusive figurines for prominent people like Song Shaozu and Sima Jinlong. This may explain why such high-quality figurines were found in this late knife-shaped tomb.

Figurines of wood are rarely found due to their difficult preservation. Three wooden tomb guardians—two were warriors and one was a beast—from the tomb of Jia Bao (477) were secured by filling gypsum into the earthen cavities left by the decomposed wood. Fragments of a wooden figure, probably those depicting a Central Asian, and a wooden horse were discovered in Sima Jinlong's tomb as well.[334]

There are more stone figures in tombs than wooden ones. Many skilled stonemasons likely originated from Hexi and Chang'an. After being deported to Pingcheng, they worked primarily on the construction of the royal caves at Yungang. They may have also met certain private demands of rich clients for religious and funerary needs since there are stylistic similarities between tomb finds and the sculptures in Yungang. Since stone embodied religious power and endurance, this material was reserved for sculptures, particularly those of tomb guardians, and for oil lamps. Several stone guardian warriors and beasts, as well as an altar-like stone piece featuring two Xianbei "worshiper" images, were looted from Pingcheng tombs. These are remarkable works of art, but without archaeological contexts, their historical significance is irreversibly lost.[335]

These figures, the altar, and the stone figure found in Yongguling 永固陵, the mausoleum of the Empress Dowager Wenming, are the only known free-standing sculptures of Pingcheng. The stone figure found in Wenming's tomb is dressed in a knee-length jacket with fitted arms and a long six-pieces skirt. The clothing style as well as the remaining flap of the headgear on the shoulders clearly identifies the sculpture as a female attendant in Xianbei garb.[336] She holds a long towel and a long sword with a ring pommel; a similar but

---

332 The excavation report did not document these figurines of Sima Jinlong. But they were on exhibition in the Datong Museum.

333 The right arm of M113's rider is described by the excavators as "broken"; Datong kaogu 2021b: 42.

334 Datong kaogu 2021a: 32; Shanxi and Shanxi 1972: 22–23.

335 Datong bowu 2018, pl. 68; Wang Limin 2016, pls. 75, 78. Wang Yintian and Cao Chenmin 2004: 92.

336 The excavation report (Datong and Shanxi 1978: 32) misinterprets the 57-cm-high statue as a "warrior." Since the tomb has been plundered several times in the past, the initial position of the sculpture cannot be reconstructed. Scholars presume that the figure once stood along the "Spirit Road" or near one of the auxiliary buildings of the mausoleum, see, for example, Du Yixue 2018, 17. I believe the

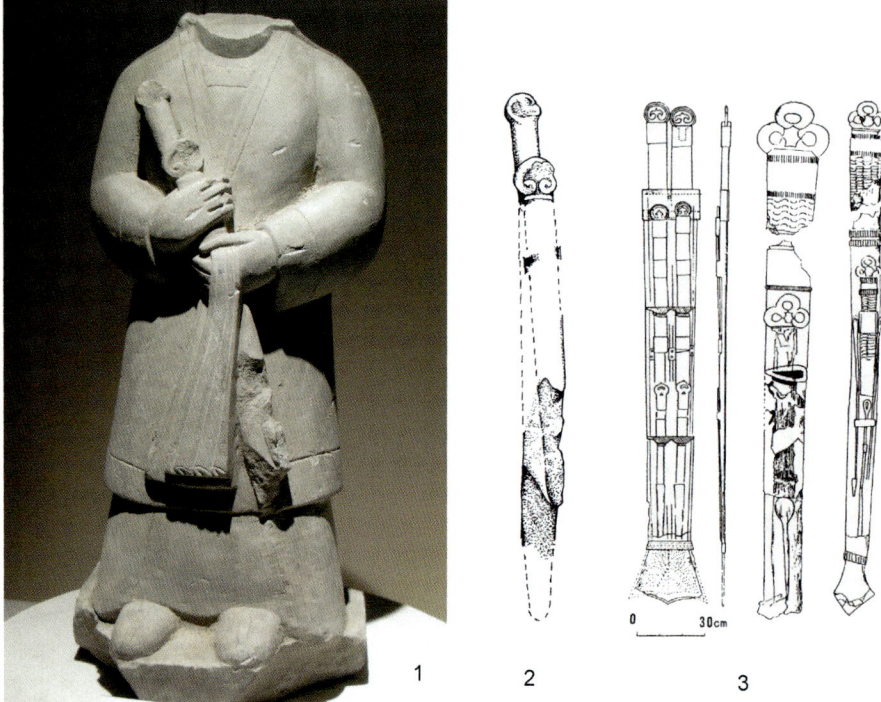

Figure 39 "Parent-and-child" sword. (1) Stone statue of a female attendant dressed in typical Xianbei clothing. Her Xianbei hat can be recognized by the flap on her shoulders; from Yongguling, Datong; (2) Line-drawing of her sword; (3) Swords found in Daegu (far left) and Kyŏngju (middle and far right), Korea.

Photo (in the Datong Museum) and drawing (1, 2) by the author; (3) after Monta Seiichi 2000: 25 Fig. 2.8–10; with permission of Professor Monta Seiichi.

smaller sword is affixed to its scabbard (Figs. 39.1–2). This is clearly the depiction of a "parent-child" sword 親子大刀.[337] The actual swords were found alongside golden crowns from several early fifth-century mounted Silla tombs of noblemen of the maripkan 麻立干 period (Fig. 39.3). Notably, high-ranking women in this polity were not buried with such

---

figure was too small for a guardian on an imperial spirit road. This statue of a weapon-bearing female cannot have been placed in front of one of the auxiliary buildings of Yongguling, either, which, according to the *Shuijing zhu* (13.1138–40), comprised a memorial hall and a Buddhist temple. In my opinion, the only plausible explanation appears to be the "tomb figurine."

337 I am grateful that Professor Wang Yingtian 王銀田, the then vice director of the Datong Museum, brought this stone carved sword to my attention during my first visit to Datong in 1995. For the "parent-child" swords, Monta Seiichi 2000: 253–54. According to Saotome Masahiro (2012: Tables 1 and 2), only a few "parent-child" swords have been unearthed so far. For the maripkans (elevated ruler) and the mounted tombs of Silla, see McBride 2011; Müller 2019.

swords.[338] Interestingly, several stone sarcophagi of the Kofun period in Kenhirora (in modern Kumamoto 熊本県), Japan, were decorated with carved images of such swords. Monta Seiichi argues that an image alone was enough to identify the superiority of the interred nobleman over his peers, as it conveyed his inter-regional connection to Silla.[339]

We may assume that the sword image from Wenming's tomb equally represented an insignia of power, not only because it was a single find from Pingcheng, but also because Wenming was as the de facto ruler of a powerful state in fifth-century East Asia and obviously enjoyed high esteem far beyond its borders. The Book of Wei recorded a large banquet hosted by her and Xiaowendi at the Lingquan Lake 靈泉池 (Numinous Spring) near the Fangshan 方山 Plateau. Court officials, foreign state delegates, and tribal leaders from all regions ("羣臣及藩國使人、諸方渠帥") attended and drank together with Xiaowendi to her health.[340] Notably, the stone statue is unique in shape and style in the early medieval northern China. Figurines with a similar gesture, i.e., holding a long sword with a ring-pommel in both hands in front of the chest, are only attested to in the Hunan and Sichuan regions of the Three Kingdoms and Western Jin period.[341] The stone statue, however, combines the features of a weapon-bearer and female attendant, as she holds a long towel in her left hand.[342] The statue thus probably portrays a high member of the empress dowager's domestic staff. The "parent-child" sword image implies that this empress dowager had contacts with some of the maripkans shortly before Silla emerged as a state, which is not documented in written sources.[343] If this is true, the sword image is further evidence of Wenming's dominance over the Tuoba court until her death.

The sword image is not the only clue for a Korean connection. Ceramic vessels with openwork pedestals, typical of Silla, were found in tombs such as Yingbin dadao M56 in Pingcheng (Fig. 20.1) and Ih-Nur M2 in Inner Mongolia.[344] Since there are only a few of them, the vessels were most likely customized products.

---

338 Saotome Masahiro 2012: 66.

339 Monta Seiichi 2000: 254.

340 *Wei shu* 13.329. The date of the event was not given. Of the many trips to Fangshan, only the one in August 490 coincided with a diplomatic visit from Gaoli 高麗 (Koguryo?). Wenming and Xiaowendi spent ten days there, the longest stay on the site; *Wei shu* 7B.166. This date seems suitable for a largescale tribal convention and celebration. Wenming died in October of the same year.

341 See, for example, Hunan bowu 1959, Pl. 6. 1–2. They were possibly part of a military procession and thus belonged to the category weapon bearers. Notably, some are depicted as Hu males.

342 The Xianbei term for this post, *huluozhen* 胡洛真, only recorded in the *Nan Qi shu* (57.985), referred not only to "weapon bearers" (Ch. *dai zhang ren* 帶仗人), but also the bodyguards of the Tuoba emperors. *Huluo* was reconstructed by Bao Yuzhu 2014 as *yu lak* (defend, seal, circle) or by Shimunek 2017, 151–52 as **qurag* (cognate with Early Middle Mongol *kituquai* "knife"). Figurines of female attendants holding a long towel are evidenced, e.g., in Sima Jinlong's tomb.

343 There are only a few records of diplomatic contacts between Silla and the Southern Liang dynasty, see McBride 2020. The Book of Wei does not contain information about Tuoba's contacts with Silla. Wenming, however, was known for her close relationship with Koguryŏ, Holcombe 2013, 24–25.

344 Yingbin dadao M56's vessel is interpreted as a lamp by the excavators, Datong kaogu 2006c: 58, Fig. 17. For the find of Ih-Nur M2, Chen Yongzhi et al. 2016b: 47. Pottery and lacquer vessels with openwork pedestals are unknown in northern China but are typical for fifth- and sixth-century Silla ceramics, Lee 2013, 71–77. An early example of lacquer, interpreted as "stemmed cup 高杯," was unearthed from Wang Guang's 王光 tomb (first half of the first century BCE) in Pyongyang (Chōsen Koseki 1935, 37). The pedestal form was presumably influenced by bronze cauldrons from the steppe.

Identifying the individuals and tracing their cultural identities

Mono- and multisyllabic names in land purchase contracts and on the roof tiles of the Mingtang ritual hall clearly indicate that people of different ethnicities in Pingcheng were in contact and interacted with each other.[345] While they gradually accepted a Xianbei identity, they surely still preserved their own identities.

How else do people express their Xianbei identity besides wearing Xianbei clothing in public? In mortuary archaeology, the trapezoidal shape of coffins is the primary feature used to identify a tomb as belonging to the Xianbei. It existed prior to their arrival in northern China,[346] and is not observed in other major groups of the eastern steppe, such as the Xiongnu. Since the Xianbei confederation was a loose alliance of diverse steppe groups led by the core clans, the use of trapezoidal coffins was possibly an expression of acceptance or "solidarity" of the associated or submissive tribes with the ruling clans.

This may have maintained the distinctions in material legacy and ritual practices between the Xianbei and the Xiongnu. For example, cauldrons in the Xianbei region are simpler and plainer than those in the Xiongnu domain.[347] The ritual destruction of burial objects among the Xianbei, as mentioned above, was essentially limited to ceramics, whereas the Xiongnu also ritually damaged bronze mirrors and metal fittings for clothing during funerary ceremonies.[348] Below the Xiongnu-Xianbei order, differences in material culture can also be observed between the Xianbei subgroups such as the Murong and the Tuoba. They differed in their preferences for jewelry and sacrificial animals. In the third- to fourth-century Murong burials in southern Manchuria and in burials of the Tuyuhun or other Murong offshoot groups in western Gansu (Hexi), earrings and rings, sometimes also necklaces of gold and silver are frequently discovered. These groups are particularly known for their headdresses, which were made of dangling leaf-shaped sheets of gold or silver. In contrast, colorful stone and glass beads for earrings and necklaces were found primarily in burials from the same era in central and southern Inner Mongolia, the core region of the pre-dynastic Tuoba and its collaborating tribes from western regions.[349] In southern Manchuria, cattle limbs were commonly served as funerary meals, while in Inner Mongolia, sheep and goats were used as food offerings for the deceased.[350] In southern Manchuria,

---

345 A transaction between a group of four landlords Wenniuyu Wuti 文忸于吳提 (a Chi'le?), Helai Tufuyan 賀賴吐伏延, Helai Tugen 賀賴吐根 (both of Helan Xiongnu) and Gaoli Gaoyutu 高梨高郁 吐 (a Korean?) and the burial plot buyer Shen Hongzhi 申洪之 (died 472), was documented in Shen's stone epitaph found in the southern border of Datong in the 1940s. Altogether the landlords sold a lot of 20 *qing* (c. 134 ha) for 100 bolts of officially certified silks 官絹. See Yin Xian 1999: 189–91; Hou Xudong 2008; Luo Xin 2010, Davis 2015, 292. For the inscriptions on roof tiles, Yin Xian 2009.
346 Dien 1991, 41–42.
347 Batsaikhan 2006: 45; Pan Ling 2015, 92–109.
348 Müller Sh. 2000, 89, Note 1; Sun Wei 2009.
349 For southern Manchuria finds, Tian Likun 2001 and Liaoning bowu 2015, 135–48; Laursen 2011, 13–47; Byington 2016, 131–32; Wang Yu and Wan Xin 2017; Satoru Hirose 2017; Dien (forthcoming). For central and southern Inner Mongolian finds, see Wei Jian 2004; Wu Songyan 2015. For the poorly examined steppe-style burials in Hexi and Qinghai; Wu Hong et al. 2012; Li Guohua 2018.
350 For Liaoxi: Liaoning bowu 2015, 109–10; Wang Yu and Wan Xin 2017, 19. For Inner Mongolia: Liu Shuang 2017. Liu, however, did not differentiate between the animals for funerary meals and sacrifices for escorting the souls.

animals were often placed on a built-in platform in the chamber or in a wall niche facing the head panel of the coffin.[351] The data from central and southern Inner Mongolia are meager, but, as was the case during the Xiongnu period, a few animal offerings were found in coffins. Lacquer plates or jars used as serving trays or food containers were discovered in rich tombs in Manchuria and Inner Mongolia, which was, however, a steppe legacy.

It is far more difficult to determine the "ethnic" characteristics of a burial in Pingcheng since people with funerary traditions from many regions were forced to live together in this place. We find, for example, age-old animal sacrifices in tombs with skulls and extremities of horses, sheep, cattle, or dogs, as seen in central Inner Mongolia and Ningxia during the late Bronze Age.[352] However, most of these Pingcheng tombs were no longer pits but catacomb burials with long dromoi, and the sacrificial animals were buried in the dromoi instead of above the coffins. Many catacomb tombs in Pingcheng contained only offerings of sheep or goats, often placed in front of the coffins, while only a few combined animal sacrifices with cattle limbs as food offerings.[353] All these burials with different practices were found next to each other. Quite a few tombs included practices from different sources: Erdianchang M37 (Period II), for example, is a brick-chamber tomb containing two nested coffins, the inner of which bore lacquer paintings with architectural and figural motifs as well as pearl roundels. Animal ribs, most likely from sheep, were placed on a lacquer plate, indicating that this food offering differed from that of the Murong. But the bronze cauldron (Fig. 19.3) has a typical southern Manchurian shape. Among the grave goods were the stone models of a millstone (ø 13.3 cm) and a stove (H. 7.9 cm), which belong to Chinese funerary customs but were rarely made of stone for Chinese burials.[354]

It seems that many Pingcheng residents quickly adapted to the new living environment and organized their burials accordingly. Many people did not seem afraid to approach groups of other cultures. The result was that burial rituals developed early on that were different from those in the ancestral areas. In the process, diverse cultural elements either intermingled, or novel components emerged. The predominance of trapezoidal coffins is one reason, and the emergence of the Xianbei attire is another, why we consider the Pingcheng burials to be Xianbei today. An array of variations lies in between. How did people manage to preserve their recollections of home while adopting a new identity?

Tomb of Poduoluo

Shaling M7 is the earliest Pingcheng tomb with paintings found to date. It was discovered with eleven additional tombs of similar size. Five of them, including Shaling M7, were west-oriented. This tomb is exceptional in that its chamber walls were painted with large-scale murals, and it housed a lacquer-painted coffin with an inscription on the head panel, which gives the date of the interment of the woman in the coffin (435 CE). This is currently the only tomb that contains both tomb murals and coffin paintings.

The inscription also mentions a person who held several high positions, including *shizhong* 侍中 (Inner-court Attendant, personal advisor of a ruler during the Nanbeichao

---

351 See, for example, Babaocun 八寶村 M1 in Chaoyang; Xu Ji 1985: 916–17.
352 Luo Feng 2018: 198.
353 According to my data collection, see, e.g., Dianhanchang M57, Period II; Shanxi daxue et al. 2006, 57.
354 Datong kaogu 2019: 21–24.

period), Director of Receptions 主客尚書, Junior Guardian of the Heir Apparent 太子少保, and General-in-Chief who Pacifies the West 平西大將軍.[355] There is no doubt that the children of the deceased woman ordered the coffin, engaged lacquer painters and a calligrapher, and arranged her funeral. Since, however, the inscription is unfortunately only fragmentarily preserved, the relationship of the high-ranking person to the interred woman is obscured. All that is known is that one of them belonged to a Poduoluo 破多羅 tribe that was conquered by the Tuoba and subsequently resettled in Pingcheng in two waves: one in the 410s and the other in 427.[356] The prevailing opinion is that the high-ranking person was the son, and his mother (*tai furen*) was a member of the Poduoluo tribe. Accordingly, some western scholars refer to her as "Lady Poduoluo."[357] Zhang Qingjie, on the other hand, argues that the woman was the consort (*furen* 夫人) of a high-ranking person named Poduoluo Tai 破多羅太, especially because the burial of the woman was, according to the inscription, a *fuzang* 祔葬, which means that she was interred in an existing tomb of a family member.[358] This viewpoint is, in my opinion, convincing, and would mean that the tomb was not built for the woman, but for the man of the Poduoluo tribe who died earlier. After the death of the mother, the children buried her in the tomb of their father. Interestingly, the portrait of the mother on the coffin provides a clue to her ethnicity, which will be examined in more detail below. For the sake of simplicity, I will refer to the occupant of the tomb as "General Poduoluo" and the woman in the coffin as "Poduoluo's wife" in the following.

One of the major discussions on General Poduoluo's murals is the origins of the motifs and themes, which, according to most contemporary studies, can all be traced back to the

---

355 Zhao Ruimin and Liu Junxi 2006; Ying Xian 2006; Zhang Qingjie 2007.

356 *Bei shi* 98.3277; Yao Weiyuan 1962, 200–4. The tribal name or title Poduoluo first appeared in the *Wei shu* (95.2056; 113.3012), where it was also written Poduolan 破多蘭 (*Wei shu* 2.39; 103.2313). The Book of Jin only records the military affairs of the most famous leader, Moyiyu 沒奕于 or Moyigan 沒奕干, without mentioning the tribe Poduoluo. In the same work, Moyiyu was attributed to the Xianbei (Xianbei Moyiyu/gan). The same person occurs in the *Wei shu* as Muyiyu/gan 木易于/干). But Wei Shou associated Muyiyu/gan either with the Xianbei (*Wei shu* 103.2313) or referred to him as the commander 帥 of a "separate division" 別部 of the Helan 賀蘭 confederation (*Wei shu* 28.681). In any case, the Poduoluo tribe once resided in the mountainous regions between Jincheng 金城 (modern Lanzhou 蘭州) and Anding (modern Jingchuan 涇川). Moyiyu, active for at least 48 years, waged continuous wars, first against the Former and Later Qin states and later against the Tuoba. Gaoping in the Anding Commandery was probably his encampment. When the troops of Tuoba Zun 遵 drove him out of that area in 402, they allegedly captured "40,000 horses, 3,000 camels and yaks, and 90,000 cattle and sheep." Moyiyu fled with the Liu 劉 Xiongnu leaders Weichen 衛辰 and Qugai 屈丐 (*Jin shu* 116.2967) and was granted asylum by the Xiongnu Helian Bobo 赫連勃勃, Moyiyu's son-in-law. Bobo killed Moyiyu in 407.

357 Zhao Ruimin and Liu Junxi 2006 were the first to propose the reading of "*Tai furen* [of the] Poduoluo [tribe]." For the "Lady" translation, see, e.g., Tseng 2013 and Zhang 2018, who possibly assume that the term *tai furen* refers to a noble rank for eminent women. But such a rank is not mentioned in the Book of Wei. During the period of the Western Jin and Sixteen Kingdoms, the title *tai furen* was bestowed by emperors or foreign kings on the elderly mothers of officials of great merit. Otherwise, *tai furen* simply means mothers of high age.

358 Zhang Qingjie 2007. The term *fuzang* originally meant "entombed together," but since Later Han times, it was increasingly used to indicate an interment in the tomb of one's parents, other family members, or ancestors. See the examples listed in https://ctext.org/dictionary.pl?if=gb&char=%E7%A5%94, accessed January 27, 2024.

Han or Jin period.[359] The discussions also revolve around the development of portrait paintings in tombs, such as those found in Shaling M7.[360] While Chinese scholars are generally neutral on the gender issue, some western researchers, who consider the interred woman to be the sole or equal owner of Shaling M7, highlight the feminine aspects of the tomb painting. They demonstrate, for example, how the Lady manifested her status by adopting the symbols of prestige that were traditionally reserved for men.[361]

New details about the headdresses in the portraits of the Poduoluo couple now allow us to take a more differentiated look at how the cultural identities of the deceased were represented in this specific tomb.

Cao Lijuan was the first to notice discrepancies between the wall and coffin paintings of this tomb when she reconstructed the latter from the remaining lacquer fragments. These include: 1) The robes of the deceased couple have different colors (mural: red for ♂ and white for ♀; coffin: brown for ♂ and red for ♀); 2) The couple hold deer tail whisks (mural) and painted round fans (coffin); 3) The screens around the seating daises are decorated with lattice patterns (mural) and fish-scale patterns (coffin); 4) The kitchen scenes located on an outdoor area (mural) and in a wooden architecture (coffin); 5) Agricultural scenes are absent in the mural but present on the coffin.[362]

In 2018, Wang Yanqing examined the portraits of the deceased on the lacquer fragments and supervised a Yungang Academy project to replicate the mural in Shaling M7.[363] Her study brings to light remarkable details that have been previously overlooked. It shows, among other things, that the couple's black Xianbei hats in the lacquer painting are adorned with gold strips hung with small dangling discs (Figs. 40–41), which resemble the cross-shaped gold ornaments for headdresses found both in the tomb of Feng Sufu (d. 415) in Beipiao as well as in Wangzifenshanshan 王子墳山 M1 in Chaoyang (Figs. 42.1–2).[364]

---

359 Cao Lijuan 2009: 23–34; Seo Yun-kyung 2011, 169–72; Lin Sheng-chih 2012: 16–17; Tseng 2013, 78–89; Wei Zheng 2018. They all agree that the portraits and scenes from the kitchen and large-scale processions were influenced by the paintings of Liaodong and Koguryo. Further, Lin Sheng-chih argues that Shaling M7's kitchen and banquet scenes were related to those of Dingjiazha M5 in Gansu. Zhang 2019 believes that the motif of the *cintāmaṇi*, the Buddhist wish-fulfilling jewel, being painted between the world-creating deities Fuxi and Nüwa on the barrel vault of Shaling M7's corridor was brought from Hexi. Lin Sheng-chih (2011, 139) and Seo Yun-kyung (2011, 173–74) have noticed that the murals in Shaling M7 otherwise contain no Buddhist symbols and argue that the *cintāmaṇi* was adopted to serve as a light symbol illuminating the entry of the deceased to the celestial realm. According to Wei Zheng 2018, the dragons alongside Fuxi and Nüwa were meant to help souls ascend to heaven, and the idea and symbol of dragons originated in pre-Han China. For an overview of the discussions on Chinese influences in the Shaling M7 mural, see Lin Sheng-chih 2008.

360 See the section "Portraits of the deceased" above.

361 Tseng, based on her argument that the tomb was built for the lady alone, explores the conceptualization of the murals from the lady's perspective (Tseng 2013, 72–89; 2019: 224–25). Zhang (2018, 72 note 219) surmises that Lady Poduoluo and her no-name husband were interred in the same coffin and proposes that the mural was gender divided into a masculine and feminine half. She argues that the elevated social status of women in Xianbei society made this equal position attainable (ibid., 66–106).

362 Cao Lijuan 2009, 22–25.

363 http://中国考古网.中国/cn/gonggongkaogu/2018/0126/60886.html; accessed Aug. 30, 2020.

364 Wang Yanqing 2018; 2019. Xu Bingkun 2015, 293 specifically points out that the cross-shaped gold strips from the Wangzifenshan tomb (= Shi'ertai 88M1) were cut out in one piece from a sheet of

Figure 40 Lacquer-painted portraits of the deceased (details) on the head panel of the coffin in Shaling M7. Left: Poduoluo's wife; Right: General Poduoluo. Note the wing-shaped flaps framed by gold strips (green arrows) and the rectangular plaque (blue arrow).

Photos and drawings (with modifications by the author): courtesy of Professor Wang Yanqing.

Like the gold headdress ornament for Feng Sufu, the painted gold strips leading to the foreheads on the couple's hats are shorter than other strips extending to the temples and to the back of the head. The painted gold strips on the general's temples are not decorated with discs, although they are on his wife's. In the lacquer painting, the forehead of the general, presumably also of his wife, is additionally adorned with a horizontal gold strip with discs not found on Feng Sufu's headdress.[365] It has often been suggested that two strips with gold leaves found in Fangshen M2 could have been such forehead decorations (Fig. 42.3).[366] Fangshen M2, however, possibly a double burial, otherwise yielded only two gold adornments of the "flowering tree" type (see below), which were more common in the region and were generally sewn directly onto the forehead of a hat. The cross-shaped frames

---

gold, whereas the frame of Feng Sufu's headdress ornament consists of two gold strips riveted together in the middle. Xu also believes that the cross-shaped strips for Feng Sufu's headdress were originally decorated with gold discs, even though sparsely. For details on the finds of Wangzifenshan, Fangshen M2 and Feng Sufu, see Laursen 2011, 56–58, 67–70.

365 The lacquer painting for the forehead of Poduoluo's wife is missing. It is thus uncertain just how the head band looked. Interestingly, Laursen (ibid., 69) notes that the ends of the cross-shaped strips of Feng Sufu's headdress are not perforated. She therefore suggests that these ends were once tucked into a folded-up cuff of the hat. If so, Feng Sufu's gold strip frame did not include a headband. However, this headdress was sometimes shown in exhibitions with one.

366 The two strips of Fangshen M2 are sometimes displayed as *one* diadem (Laursen 2011, 58). One piece of approximately 28 cm in length is long enough to serve as a forehead band. No information is available on the second piece.

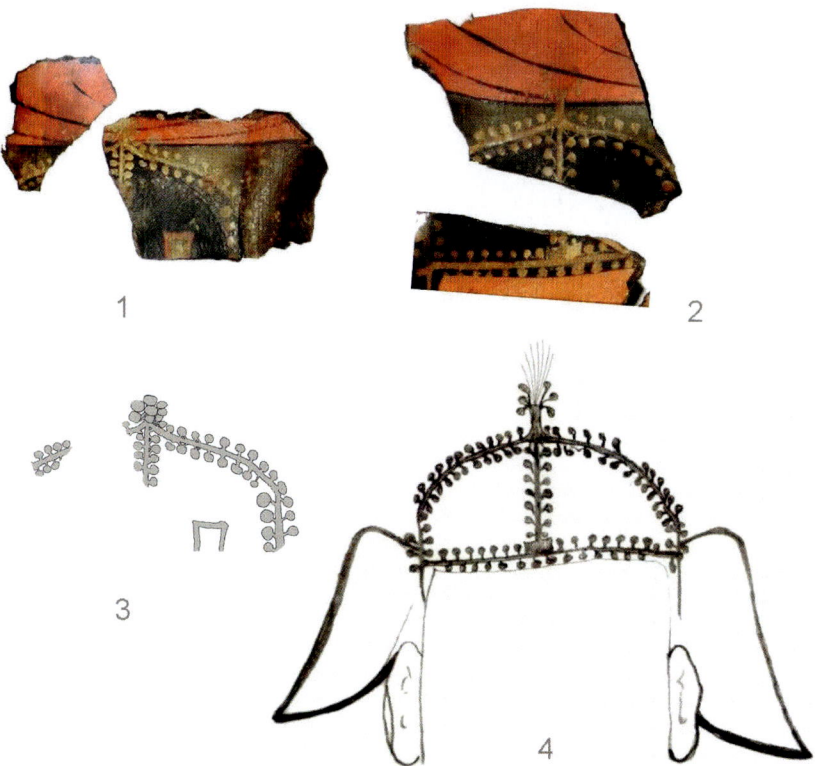

Figure 41 Cross-shaped gold ornaments for the "Xianbei hat" and finials for the wife (1) and Po-duoluo (2) and their reconstructions (3–4).

1–2, 4: Courtesy of Professor Wang Yanqing; 3: Drawing by the author.

were not found in this tomb. The purposes of the two Fangshen M2 strips thus remain obscure. Thus, the horizontal bands on the hats of Poduoluo and his wife in the coffin painting can currently not fully be substantiated by actual artifacts from excavations.

Other details include a small rectangular gold plaque that is attached to the middle of the general's headband and a rectangle plaque with red and gold colors on the left-hand side of the wife's hat (Fig. 41).[367] However, the small middle plaque of the general differs markedly from reconstructed *dang* 鐺 (frontal) plaque for the gold ornament for the hat of

---

367 Wang Yanqing 2019. The rectangular plaque in the middle of the general's headband can be observed clearly on the original lacquer fragment but only vaguely in the photos. I am grateful to the Vice Director of the Datong Museum, Professor Cao Chenming, for his gracious support for my visit on September 16 in 2019 to view the remaining lacquer fragments on the head panel of the coffin.

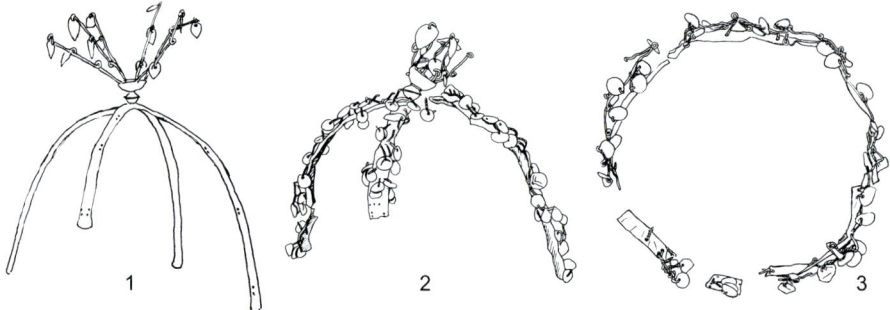

Figure 42 Cross-shaped gold strip ornaments and a headband (?) with dangling leaves from (1) the tomb of Feng Sufu (415) at Beipiao, (2) the tomb at Wangzifenshan (the strip on the back of the head is missing), and (3) Fangshen M2 (originally possibly two strips but broken into four fragments by the time of the excavation).

Line-drawings by the author based on Liaoning bowu 2015, Colorpl. 44.1 (1); Tian Likun 2021, Fig. 8.2 (2); Laursen 2011, Fig.2.10 (3).

Figure 43 Flowery hair ornaments for women. (1) Figurine from the tomb at Caochangpo, Xi'an, late Sixteen Kingdoms period (colors highlighted by the author); (2) Portraits of the wives of Shun (details) on Sima Jinlong's (484) lacquer screen; possibly based on an Eastern Jin painting.

Photo (taken in the China History Museum) and line-drawing by the author.

Figure 44 Portraits of the Poduoluo couple. (*Above*) Mural (replica) on the eastern wall of the tomb chamber; (*below*) Lacquer painting on the head panel of the coffin.

(Above) Courtesy of Professors Wang Yanqing; (below) After Datong kaogu 2006b, Fig. 19 with modifications by the author; with permission of the Datong Museum.

Feng Sufu.[368] Both gold ornaments for the hats in the coffin painting end with a finial. That of the general is made up of six thin wires that imitate twigs, each ending in a small disc. The twigs enclose a tuft of gold filaments (Fig. 41.4). The finial of the wife's gold headdress is in the shape of a flower (Fig. 41.3),[369] reminiscent of some flower-shaped embellishments on women's coiffures from Chang'an (Fig. 43.1) to Turfan during the Sixteen Kingdoms period.[370] Similar flower rosettes for hair can also be observed for noble ladies on Sima Jinlong's (484) lacquer screen (Fig. 43.2). Lastly, the hats in the coffin painting have two decorative wing-shaped flaps framed by gold strips (Fig. 40),[371] which are not seen in other images in Pingcheng. Wang Yanqing proposes referring to these two Poduoluo headdresses as *buyao mao* (步摇帽, "hats with *buyao*," or "hats embellished with gold leaf ornaments that dangle as the wearer walks"). Her conclusion that the Poduoluo couple belonged to the Tuoba leads her to believe that the *buyao* hats were worn by both the Murong in southern Manchuria and the Tuoba in Pingcheng. Most importantly, Wang Yanqing points out that the hats of the couple in the mural are not painted with gold disc ornaments (Fig. 44). Could this discrepancy simply be due to the negligence of the craftsmen, considering that the tomb was built for the general and the coffin for the wife?

Indeed, nearly 20 gold leaf ornaments for headgear dating from the late third to the early fifth century have been unearthed in the Chaoyang and Beipiao regions.[372] The majority are of the so-called "flowering tree"-type (*hua shu shi buyao* 花樹式步搖). Only the ones from the above-mentioned tombs of Feng Sufu and from Wangzifenshan belong to the cross-shaped ornaments. To date, only four gold headdresses, all of the "flowering tree" type, have been unearthed in central Inner Mongolia, the core region of the pre-Tuoba Dai kingdom that remained ritually and militarily important for the Northern Wei state.[373] In other

---

368 See, e.g., Watt 2004, 15, Fig. 9 and Laursen 2011, Fig. 2.32. The clay figurines from Zhongzhaocun M100 (fourth century) show that the *dang* plaques were affixed to the foreheads of military officers' helmets. Similar gold plaques were found in female burials of the same period in present-day Gansu, suggesting that women used the plaques as well. How they used it, is unclear, however. The painting in Lou Rui's (d. 570) tomb indicates that these plaques still adorned official hats in the sixth century. The archaeological finds do not support the pairing of the *dang* plaques and the cross-shaped hat ornaments. The reconstruction of Feng Sufu's headdress with a *dang* is therefore questionable. For *dang*, Laursen 2011, 111–20. For Zhongzhaocun M100, Xin Long et al. 2020, for plaques for women, Wei Zheng 2013, for Lou Rui's painting, Müller Sh. 2019c, Fig. 18.7h.

369 Wang Yanqing's close-up photos (Figs. 40–41) show a flower rosette. However, the piece in question was not in the Museum's storage during my last visit. A personal inspection was thus not possible.

370 See the figurine (Ast.vi.4.04) from an Astana tomb found by Sir Aurel Stein: http://idp.bl.uk/database/oo_scroll_h.a4d?uid=1885730465;recnum=76880;index=1; accessed January 29, 2022.

371 Wang Yanqing 2019.

372 Jiang Nan 2012, Table 1.

373 A "flowering tree"-type of ornament usually has a rectangular plaque as a base, on which tree-like wires with movable droplet-shaped leaves of gold, silver or gilded bronze are attached. They are not only found in the very rich tombs (Jiang Nan 2012: 78). The four Inner Mongolia pieces (from the Darhan Mumingan [Damao] Banner 達茂旗) have inlaid stones and granulation on the animal-shaped bases. They were "wrapped" by a gold chain and obviously cached. As no further objects were found, their dating and attribution to the "Xianbei nobility of the late Northern Wei dynasty" (Lu Sixian and Chen Tangdong 1984) based solely on the historical records is thus problematic. Laursen (2011, 74–77) recognizes the considerable differences in technique and style between the pieces from the Damao Banner and from the Liaoxi region and believes that the former were works of more sophisticated Xiongnu craftsmanship. Wu Songyan and Zhao Fei (2021) date the pieces anew to the fourth century.

words, the cross-shaped gold headdress was clearly limited to the Yan territory. This, in turn, suggests that Poduoluo's wife hailed from this region and held a noble rank comparable to that of Feng Sufu (prince) or the persons buried in the Wangzifenshan tomb.

Poduoluo's wife was therefore conceivably interred and represented according to her past and present status: a noblewoman of a Yan kingdom[374] and the wife of a high-ranking official in the Tuoba state. The cross-shaped gold headdress, which is otherwise found in Pingcheng, showcased her noble origins. The lacquer-painted coffin also corresponded to the mortuary practices of the Yan elites evidenced in the Chaoyang region. On the other hand, some small lacquer fragments suggest that the coffin was also decorated with a scene of a military procession, which was a mark of respect for her husband. Interestingly, the lacquer fragments also contain a scene of two soldiers fighting with swords, which is not depicted in the murals in this and other tombs.[375]

Considering that the Poduoluo were a pastoral tribe from the Guyuan region, where headgear with gold-leaf adornments were not attested, it is questionable why General Poduoluo was also portrayed with Yan-styled decoration on the coffin painting and why his wife is depicted with a Xianbei hat without gold ornaments in the tomb mural.

It must be emphasized that clothing and body ornaments were important components of an individual's social practices and conveyed his or her ethnic identities.[376] If Shaling M7 was built for General Poduoluo, it is safe to assume that the murals were painted from his cultural and social perspective, just as the coffin painting of his wife expressed her perspective. It is therefore understandable that the portraits of the deceased on the mural wore headgear without gold cross-shaped ornaments.

The problem with the coffin portraits is more complicated. The exquisite armor and weapons discovered in both Yan tombs make it clear that this cross-shaped gold ornament, along with the high hat suggested by Laursen, was part of military parade accoutrements for noblemen, not for noblewomen. I assume that the children of the deceased woman considered it necessary to "elevate" their father to the nobility of a Yan state in order to be able to present their mother according to her former status with the cross-shaped gold ornaments, but that for women due to the flower finial. In this context, it is worth noting that although there is no archaeological evidence of a high hat for the nobility in the Yan kingdoms, its existence is nonetheless a reasonable assumption. If this is true, the high hat was a contribution of the Murong or the Yan states to the dress convention of the Tuoba state, since it indeed became the usual headgear from the Northern Wei period onwards.

Other distinctions between the murals and the coffin painting, which Cao Lijuan points out, also strongly support the hypothesis that General Poduoluo and his wife were of different ethnic origins.

The banquet scene on the eastern half of the southern wall of Poduoluo's tomb portrays the host and guests with Xianbei hats but wearing long "Chinese-style" robes.[377] The host,

---

374 The Northern Wei had (military) contacts only with the Later and the Northern Yan kingdoms.
375 Datong kaogu 2006b: 15, Fig. 26.
376 Assmann 1995, 126–27 describes this as a "communicative memory" that an individual repeatedly recalls in order to demonstrate his affinity to a group.
377 Datong kaogu 2006b: 19, Fig. 41.

Figure 45 The host in the banquet scene on the southern wall in Poduoluo's tomb.
Line-drawing by the author based on Datong kaogu 2006: 20 and Xu Guangji 2010, II, 26

presumably representing the deceased general, sits with his legs hanging on a chair in a wooden building (Fig. 45).[378] This pose, normally reserved for Buddha Maitreya, is almost unique in the early fifth-century sepulchral art in East Asia and alludes to the exalted, god-like status of the person depicted. The other half of the same wall bears scenes of the "Arrival of a Lady" and an open-air kitchen scene (Fig. 24). In the foreground, the kitchen staff is bustling around and preparing food and drinks for the banquet, including grilling skewers of meat on the sides of a heated steppe cauldron, drawing water from a well using a windlass on an arched frame,[379] pounding grain in a mortar by stepping on a pestle, and fetching beer from a large brewing vessel set up in a round tent.[380] In addition, two people are busy

---

378 A similar pose is otherwise only observed in the murals of two late fourth- to early fifth-century Koguryo tombs of the Gakjeoch'ong 角抵塚 (Tomb of Wrestlers) and Muyongch'ong 舞踊塚 (Tomb of Dancers) in Ji'an 集安, Jilin (Ikeuchi and Umehara 1940, Pls. 3, 23, 26b, 39). Chairs were introduced into China along with Buddhism and did not come into use in non-religious and domestic environments until Tang times. Kieschnick 2003, 233–49. For another depiction with the same sitting pose, see an early sculpture of Buddha Maitreya in Dunhuang Cave 272; Whitfield 1996, Vol. 1, 10–11. A recent ^{14}C dating placed this cave, along with two other early Dunhuang Caves (268 and 275), between 410 and 440 CE; cf. Guo et al. 2018.

379 The frames of most well models from the Western Jin period in the north (Shandong, Hebei, Shanxi, and Shaanxi) are trapezoidal. The arched shape is therefore unusual.

380 A person waiting in line for the beer probably carries a wineskin on his back. If true, this would be the earliest depiction of a wineskin bearer found in China. In the Tang dynasty, images of a *hu* person, or Persian, carrying a wineskin are most common.

butchering a sheep lying on the ground. All these people wear headgear that is distinct from that of the Xianbei, indicating that they come from various cultures and regions. The clothing of the men and women in the murals of the upper registers of the north, east, and south chamber walls, on the other hand, shows gender differences: men wear hats and tunics and trousers typical of the Xianbei, women wear short jackets, long bell-shaped skirts in two alternating colors and a hairstyle with buns similar to those in the Guanzhong area (Fig. 24). Unlike these "minor characters," the guests in the banquet scene on the south wall are all dressed in Xianbei clothing.

In the fragments of the coffin painting, however, all the persons are shown in Xianbei dress with hats with flaps flying upwards, as was the case in earlier paintings of common people from the Yan kingdoms mentioned above. One fragment (H. 10.3 cm, W. 18 cm) probably depicts an "Arrival" scene as well, as the shape of the small window is reminiscent of the exterior shutters of a square tent.[381] The posture of the person (a woman?) with the eared cup in the "building" shows that she has a high status. The person standing outside holding a staff is most likely her attendant.[382] Another fragment (H. 35.5 cm, W. 52 cm) depicts a roofed kitchen with people carrying out activities such as cooking with a large pot or refilling firewood into the stove. A large brewing vessel is placed in a house next to the kitchen.[383] The well in front of the kitchen has the same square frame as the one found in a Northern Yan mural fragment.[384] Additionally, there are scenes of agricultural activities.

Even though the pictorial programs of the tomb murals and the coffin paintings are broadly similar, the details clearly point to two ecological environments: The scenes of kitchen work in the wooden buildings and agricultural activities in the coffin painting contrast sharply with the scenes of food and drink preparation in an open area or in front of tents in the mural. The former reflect a more agrarian lifestyle, while the latter indicate a pastoral way of life in open landscapes.

If Poduoluo's wife was indeed a noblewoman of a Yan kingdom, it is notable that the "Arrival of a Lady" also adorned her coffin, as there is no trace of such a scene in the fourth-century paintings in southern Manchuria. It is possible that the children transferred to their mother's funeral not only the homage to their father (military parade), but also part of their father's cultural memories.

As mentioned above, the "Arrival" scene was also depicted in the tomb of Liang Bahu (died 461), though inaccurately. Liang's tomb inscription indicates that he was from Gaoping 高平 of the Anding Commandery 安定郡 (present-day Guyuan),[385] the same western region as General Poduoluo. This may explain why the "Arrival" scene appeared in Liang's

---

381 Müller Sh. 2017, 186, Fig. 3.1–2.
382 See Datong kaogu 2006b: 14, Fig. 25.
383 See Datong kaogu 2006b: 13, Fig. 20, Wang Yanqing 2019.
384 The mural painting was found in Beimiaocun 北廟村 M1 in Liaoyang, presently the only Northern Yan depiction of a well in the Daling River Valley; Xu Ji 1985: Pl. 8.5.
385 Ni Run'an 2016: 23. People with the surname Liang in the Anding region were originally members of the Balielan 拔列蘭 clan of the Xiutu 休屠 Xiongnu. Some Balielan people assumed the surname Liang as early as the third century, while others did so during Emperor Xiaowen's reform of surnames in 496. The Balielan acknowledged Tuoba sovereignty in the initial years of the Northern Wei, see Yao Weiyuan 1962, 60–62.

tomb. However, the memory was beginning to fade at this time. One can speculate that Poduoluo and Liang were once much closer to the Xiongnu than to the Xianbei due to their original habitations. The "Arrival" scene in their tombs, as well as in several others, demonstrates their recognition and solidarity with the core group of Xianbei by reciting the myth of the latter. It seems, then, that the Poduoluo were referred to as a "separate stock" 別種 of the Xianbei in the historical records with good reason.[386] It is unclear where the individuals buried in Yunbolu M10 and Yanbei shiyuan M2 came from. On the other hand, based on the arrangement of the clay figurines and the tent models in both burials, the deceased also clearly demonstrated their affiliation with the core Xianbei group.[387]

Mid-Pingcheng (440–476) tombs with inscriptions

Most, though still few, of the excavated Pingcheng epitaphs date from this period. A total of seven were found, four of which were discovered from burials with funerary houses. The remaining three were from a painted brick tomb (of Liang Bahu, 461), an earthen chamber tomb (Chi'gan kehou 叱干渴侯, 466), and from a knife-shaped tomb. According to the inscriptions, the four individuals interred in funerary houses hailed from different regions. The reason for their choice of this type of interment is unknown, except that they could obviously all afford such opulent funerary furniture.[388]

Lü Xu (456)

The funerary house of Lü Xu (456), placed in a south-facing earthen chamber tomb excavated near Zhijiabao, is the earliest datable one from Pingcheng. On one of the front pillars of the house, which formed a veranda, an inscription was carved stating that Lü once held the offices of *lingjiang jiangjun* 凌江將軍 (River-crossing General) and Governor of Fufeng 扶風太守. And he was registered 縣民 in the Huaili District 槐里縣 of the Fufeng Commandery 扶風郡. The "River-crossing General" was a lower-ranking military post (Grade 5) in the Former Qin (350–394) and Liu Song (420–479) dynasties. Just when the Tuoba court integrated this office into the organization of its own army is unclear, since it was first mentioned in the final year of the Pingcheng period (493).[389] Interestingly, the painted reliefs on Lü's funerary house bear a striking resemblance to those in the Xiangyang 襄陽 region, where numerous northerners fled from Guanzhong in the early years of the Liu Song dynasty.[390] Both his military post and the reliefs on the funerary house suggest that Lü spent his earlier life in the Liu Song dynasty. Huaili was incorporated into the Fufeng Commandery in 446 after Emperor Taiwu suppressed the rebellions of Ge Wu and the Buddhists in Chang'an.[391] Lü Xu was possibly first captured by the Tuoba army and, after this event, settled and registered in Huaili before being subsequently deported to Pingcheng. The custom of being buried in a stone house is not attested to in the Guanzhong region of the fourth and fifth centuries, let alone in southern China. Lü's decision to adopt a

---

386 *Wei shu* 103.2313.
387 Qiao Liping and Zhang Zhizhong 2017: 184. Cf. p. 94–95 and Fig. 26.
388 Cf. Müller Sh. 2019a, 412.
389 Lü Zongli 2015, 757.
390 Chittick 2010, 22–23. For the Xiangyang brick reliefs, Xiangyang shi 2019.
391 Liu Shufen 2002: 13–19.

stylish casket known only in Pingcheng was thus influenced by a contemporary trend rather than by tradition. Note that Lü's tomb contained ceramic vessels, bronze belt fittings, lacquer plates, mica flakes, a stone lamp and the figures of a warrior and a beast as tomb guardians. At the same time, other clay figurines and a multi-armed clay lamp, both of which were characteristic of many Guanzhong tombs from the Sixteen Kingdoms period, are lacking, suggesting that he was not a native from that region.

In summary, Lü Xu took pride in his previous official titles, which he had acquired in another state. His affluent life in Pingcheng is indicated by his interment in the stone house, which in turn was protected by the images of the deities he was familiar with from his youth in a southern state. Two painted Xianbei servants on both ends of his body (most likely laid on a funerary bed) and an engraved small Buddha on the western upper corner of the façade were motifs from current Pingcheng art and were possibly intended to further guarantee a pleasant and a blissful afterlife.

Yuchi Dingzhou's wife (457)

This burial at the Shangquan Villag in Yanggao, 30 km northeast of Datong city, well illustrates the interplay of cultures. The skeleton of a woman was found on the stone bed inside a plain stone house with a veranda, which was located in a west-facing brick chamber. A lengthy Chinese inscription was engraved on the door of the house. Skulls and extremities of horses, cattle, sheep, and dogs were buried in the fillings of the long dromos.

The chamber was roofed with a "fan-like" vault, which, as mentioned above, was primarily known in southern China from the period between the Eastern Han and Eastern Jin dynasties. Since the construction of such ceilings required professional knowledge and experience, it is likely that the work was executed by Chinese masons. The stone house was also probably built by Chinese or those who had rudimentary knowledge of the Chinese characters.[392]

The inscription was in fact a brick purchase contract, which did not mention the interred woman. Thus, nothing is known about her, and her relationship to Yuchi Dingzhou, the builder of the tomb, is not clear. For simplicity, she is referred to here as "Yuchi Dingzhou's wife." However, her bronze chinstrap suggests that she came from a western region. Notably, the practice of burying animal skulls and extremities in the dromos is not evidenced in other tombs of chinstrap users or in tombs with stone funerary houses. Therefore, this practice may be attributed to the burial customs of Yuchi himself, since he belonged to a tribe with the same appellation that was ruled by the Tuyuhun in the fourth century. In the early Tuoba Wei period, the Yuchi migrated to the Shuofang commandery 朔方郡 in modern northern Shaanxi, where they most likely came into close contact with the Xiongnu members,[393] who had long practiced animal sacrifices using skulls and extremities as part of burial rites.[394] Further, the inscription mentions Yuchi Dingzhou's position as *moti* 莫堤 (a

---

392 The components of the stone house were labeled with the characters, according to Hao Junjun 2022, from the Han text *Jijiupian* 急就篇 (Quick Access [to Characters]) to facilitate the assembly.

393 Yao Weiyuan 1962, 193–95; I wrongly equated Yuchi with Viśa in Müller Sh. 2019a: Note 129. The royal Khotan members were mentioned in Gandhari as Vij'ida Siṃha but referred to in Khotanese as Viśa, a title. Yuchi appeared in the early seventh century as the surname of Khotan kings, Wen 2016.

394 See p. 66.

Tuoba term for "regional inspector" *cishi* 刺史, rank 3 or 4),[395] similar to that of Song Shaozu. Hence, he could apparently afford to build a brick chamber tomb with a custom-made funerary house. Dingzhou purchased 8,000 bricks from two tribesmen, Chang Maide 常買得 and Houmochen Rangan 侯莫陳染干, for six bolts of officially certified silk tabby (*guanjuan* 官絹), to build the tomb chamber.[396] The absence of any mention of the acquisition of the burial plot suggests that Dingzhou was the landowner. Regardless, this type of interethnic transaction has been practiced in the multiethnic regions of the Northwest since the fourth century.[397] The migrants brought their experiences of dealing with different kinds of people to Pingcheng, which undoubtedly facilitated interethnic intercourse there.

Xie Xing's wife (458)

The funerary house of Xie Xing's wife was discovered, but not officially excavated, in an area east of the Yu River 御河東岸. It is one of the only two painted funerary houses with portraits of the deceased couple. The other one was found in Zhijiabao in 1997 (Fig. 35). Xie Xing and his wife are both portraited on the rear wall, wearing Xianbei hats and long robes fastened with a long sash,[398] although according to the inscription, this house was dedicated to the wife. The surrounding male servants are all clad in Xianbei clothing, while the female servants wear hip-length Chang'an-style jackets and long skirts, suggesting that Xianbei clothing for women has not yet been completely established. The inscription on the lintel of the house states that Xie Xing was from Yanmen 雁門 (modern northern Shanxi) but contains no information about his deceased wife.[399] Only the soft pink shade of the painting, which is not observed in all earlier murals in northern China but has in common with that of the wall painting on the Zhijiabao house and some Koguryo tomb murals in southern Manchuria, may indicate that Xie Xing's wife originally hailed from that region.[400] Although Xie Xing may have been a member of the Chinese Yanmen Xie family, he is portrayed wearing a Xianbei hat and a *kandys* cloak, suggesting that he was a military officier. In any case, he was wealthy. This latter may be supported by the embroidered pearls or beads on the robes of Xie Xing's wife and her female servants.

Xing Hejiang (469)

The funerary house of Xing Hejiang is remarkable in that, as mentioned above, its inner walls are entirely painted with Buddhas, Bodhisattvas, and other Buddhist figures. It was

---

395 Yin Xian and Liu Junxi 2011: 49. The phonetic reconstruction by Shimunek is **modɪ*. According to him, this term is cognate to Middle Mongol *muji* for province and position (idem. 2017, 156, 354).

396 For Houmochen, see Yao Weiyuan 1962, 180–82 and Long Chengsong 2016: 304–10. The surname Chang is not clearly associated with any ethnic group. During the Northern Wei period, however, Maide was frequently used as a name by non-Chinese members (Yin Xian and Liu Junxi 2011: 50). Chang Maide, in this case, was most likely a tribesman as well.

397 Evidenced by land purchase contracts; Lu Xiqi 2010. See Davis 2015, 127–32 for such contracts in general.

398 The clothing style of Xie Xing's wife differs from those in other contemporary paintings in northern China. This needs to be studied more in detail but cannot be carried out within the scope of this paper.

399 Müller Sh. 2019a, 386 Note 12, 420–21.

400 Müller Sh. 2019a, 411. Considering the dominant pink color tone and the Type II bronze cauldron (Fig. 19.5) found in the same tomb together, it can be assumed that the occupant(s?) of the Zhijiabao tomb were indeed related to the Liao River Valley region, see p. 79.

discovered in 2015 in a largely destroyed tomb in the Tongjiawan Village south of Datong City. The stone stele coming with the funerary house is probably the first in Pingcheng to contain some information about the buried women. According to it, Xing Hejiang of Jianhe 澗河 in Dingzhou was the wife of Han Shouluoba 韓受洛拔 of the Yan commandery 燕郡 (present-day Beijing) in Youzhou. The stele also states that Xing was deported to Chang'an and lived there for a time before being resettled by the Tuoba to Pingcheng. Li Yuqun points out that the motif of Buddhas Shakyamuni and Prabhutaratna on the rear wall of Xing's house was not found in Liangzhou but was popular in Chang'an during the Sixteen Kingdoms period. However, the worship of the Seven Buddhas painted on the southern inner wall was widespread in the Hexi region. The Buddhist paintings in this funerary house thus show an early hybridization of religious teachings and art.[401] The fact that all the worshipers were depicted in Xianbei clothing suggests that she identified herself as a member of the Buddhist community in Pingcheng. Her husband's multisyllabic name Shouluoba indicates that Han was not Chinese.[402]

Jianhe could be a scribal error of Hejian, as there was no Jianhe commandery in Dingzhou, only a Hejian commandery. It is possible that Xing Hejiang was Chinese, although she did not necessarily belong to the most famous Hejian Xing family.[403] The epitaph documents a life of hardship, while the house of Buddhas, although it reveals nothing about her origins and family, reflects Xing Hejiang's longing to rest in the blessing and peace.

Song Shaozu (477)

Although both belong to the beginning of Period IV (477–494), Song Shaozu and Jia Bao (both were buried in 477) owned the last two dated funerary houses in Pingcheng known to date. The well-preserved stone house of Song Shaozu is exploited here to illustrate the adaptation to a new cultural and political environment. The brick epitaph found in the dromos gives only information about the date of his death or burial, his origins and last post. Accordingly, Song Shaozu, who died in his 50s, was probably relocated from Dunhuang to Pingcheng as an adolescent after the fall of the Northern Liang in 439. He probably had made a successful military and administrative career as the inspector of the superior region Youzhou under the Tuoba rule. This is indicated by the second-largest military procession in Pingcheng, represented by an assemblage of high-quality figurines. The figurine formation arrayed around his stone house symbolically made the stone house the center of the procession and at the same time displayed his identification with the Tuoba state. His long-term and rigorous horseback riding activity is suggested by his rather pronounced "bowed legs," or *genu varum*.[404] He however retained memory of his homeland, which is perceivable in the wall paintings inside his funerary house. The poorly preserved paintings show

---

401 Li Yuqun 2022.
402 For the southern Xiongnu connection of the surname Han, Yao Weiyuan 1962, 126–27; More to the Xiongnu and the name Shouluoba, Müller Sh. 2019a, 421 Note 136.
403 Only a few tombs of the Hejian Xing family members have been found to date. Nevertheless, the two reported tombs are the earliest Chinese ones of the Luoyang period (494–534), which were located in their home cemeteries, cf. Müller Sh. 2000, Map 5.2, 234. It was clearly in violation of the imperial edict that all people who relocated from Pingcheng to Luoyang should be buried in Luoyang (*Wei shu* 7B.178), and it demonstrates the strong self-assurance of this family.
404 Liu Junxi 2008, 210; Tseng 2013, 91 Note 72.

human figures in non-Xianbei clothing, including a pictorial representation probably of the vernacular literature "Killing Three Warriors with Two Peaches," circulating among Chinese or in Chinese-dominated regions since the Han period. Since Song Shaozu and his wife were interred together in the stone house, without coffins, they adopted the fashionable burial form in Pingcheng and thus deviated from Chinese funerary rituals.

Han Farong (Period III)

The intact knife-shaped tomb (DHAM13) of Han Farong 韓法蓉 was excavated in 2011 at Heng'anjie 恆安街. The brick epitaph identifies Han Farong as the wife of Cui Lingzhen 崔令珍, but otherwise mentions nothing further about her. Cui was undoubtedly Chinese, as evidenced by the aesthetic calligraphy on the brick epitaph, which is the only one found so far in a knife-shaped tomb. The epitaph was carefully buried in the dromos filling, as was common in the Guan-Long region, suggesting that Cui was not necessarily a member of the famous Qinghe 清河 or Boling 博陵 Cui families in present-day Shandong. Han's luxurious necklace with strings of numerous tiny glass beads, pearls, and gold beads resembles that of a Bodhisattva.[405] The jewelry, as well as a stone lamp with handsome relief carvings of lotus petals, provide clues to Han's inclination towards Buddhism and to the enormous wealth of Cui (and Han?). The contrast between the sumptuous jewelry and the simple construction of the tomb is striking. Given the fortune Cui spent on Han's sartorial elegance for the afterlife, they likely could have afforded a brick tomb for her funeral. Since knife-shaped tombs were not part of Chinese mortuary tradition, Cui probably built the tomb to fulfill his wife's wishes rather than his own. As mentioned above, knife-shaped tombs may have been brought to Pingcheng by migrants from western Gansu or further west. Han's origin could therefore be traced to the west or to ancestors who immigrated from that direction. While Han Farong's cultural identity was maintained through the construction of a knife-shaped tomb, her husband, like Yuchi Dingzhou, also left traces in the funerary rites, in this case, in the form fine calligraphy on the brick epitaph.

Merging together and creating new traditions

The above examples elucidated that cultural boundaries in Pingcheng were permeable from the beginning. The practice of adopting and reinterpreting cultural elements from others continued until the end of Pingcheng's time as a capital.

Yang Zhongdu (484)

The burial of Yang Zhongdu 楊眾度[406] from Chouchi 仇池 (roughly present-day Longnan 隴南 in southeastern Gansu) demonstrates once again the great efforts made by immigrants to adapt to a new living condition, and how they embraced new trends in Pingcheng. The brick-chambered M35 is the only one among the 34 excavated tombs in 2001 at the Qilicun site that contains a tomb inscription. The inscription was engraved on at least two bricks, but only one bears the complete text. The inscribed bricks were deposited in the dromos.

---

405 See p. 59 and Fig. 12.
406 His name was first read as Yang Zhongqing 楊眾慶. Yin Xian 2007 rectifies it to Yang Zhongdu.

Yin Xian argues that Yang Zhongdu was of the Di 氐 ethnic group and a member of the ruling clan of the Chouchi polity. According to the tomb inscription, Yang died in 484 at the age of 67. Thus, he was born in 417 during the reign of Yao Hong 姚泓 of the Later Qin State. Yin Xian also reckons that Yang defected from Chouchi and came to Pingcheng well before the Tuoba troops finally crushed the Chouchi Yang rebellions in 442.[407] He possibly also brought with him members of his own tribe to Pingcheng, which apparently pleased the Tuoba court, for not without reason the Tuoba bestowed on him the title "Submitted and Proselytized Visitor" (*touhua ke* 投化客),[408] making him a member of a highly privileged group in the Tuoba state. The title was mentioned with pride in Yang's epitaph. His loyalty was rewarded with offices and ranks as well. At his death, the title of Jianwei 建威 General ("General Establishing Sovereignty," rank 4B), and the noble rank of Viscount (*zi* 子) were bestowed upon him.

His wealth was reflected in the construction and furnishings of his tomb, which included a square brick chamber and a long dromos (bearing in mind that all Guanzhong tombs from the Sixteen States period to the early years of the Tuoba occupation were earthen chamber tombs). With a floor area of 4.28 m × 4.62 m,[409] the chamber is larger than the average (3 m × 3 m) and even slightly larger than that of Song Shaozu (4.13 m × 4.24 m). The chamber was constructed entirely of bricks with impressed floral motifs, a trend from the south that grew in popularity for later brick tombs in Pingcheng and Inner Mongolia. His coffin was embellished with intricately crafted animal masks, although these were made of lead. Six hooked finials, also made of lead, were given to the deceased as *mingqi* 明器 (spirit objects).[410] The tomb of Feng Sufu, brother of the king of the Northern Yan State, is the only one to date that yielded six hooks, however of bronze.[411] In Pingcheng, only two high-ranking tombs contain such hooks, all bronze cast.[412] The lead-made animal masks and hooks may have been employed to create the impression of a noble burial. On the other hand, a general development can be observed in Period IV: articles for sepulchral use, such as animal masks for coffins or chinstraps, were made of lead or tin-lead alloy instead of bronze. The reason for this is not yet known, as small pieces of jewelry and belt

---

407 Yin Xian 2007: 81–82. For the Yang clans, see *Song shu* 98.2043–11, *Wei shu* 101.2227–33. The original text of the latter was already lost in Tang times and reconstructed with the text of *Song shu*.

408 For *touhua*, see Zhang Zhizhong 2006: 83.

409 Zhang Zhizhong 2006: 82. The tomb is facing south.

410 Depending on their intended function, such metal artifacts are given different names, such as *zhanggou* 帳鉤 ("canopy hook") or *gantou* 桿頭 ("finial of a staff"). The former interpretation implies that they held tassels on the four corners of an (imagined) canopy, which could be the reason why they were occasionally found in a square arrangement in tombs. But some tombs yield more than four, as in the case of Qilicun M35, or in some tombs the hooks were placed together. Therefore, the hook was also explained as the finial attached to the top of a wooden pole to hold a pennant. Such poles, in turn, adorned a high-ranking chariot or were carried in a funeral procession; cf. Liaoning bowu 2015, 121–23, 186–94.

411 Liaoning bowu 2015, 52–53.

412 The tomb of General Poduoluo, with one bronze hook, and the Erdianchang M36 (Period IV, chamber size: 5.8 m × 5.9 m), with two bronze hooks. However, both tombs were plundered. Additionally, the Ih-Nur M3 found in Xilin-Gol, Inner Mongolia (Phase III), not discussed in this article, also yield two bronze hooks. More bronze hooks were found in Pingcheng, however, without corresponding information about the tombs.

fittings remained made of bronze. In Yang Zhongdu's case, both factors may have played a role. Yang, whose noble rank was relatively low, presumably appropriated a symbol of prestige that was superior to his own. The clay figurines of servants, animals, and models of household goods deposited in the tomb were crudely crafted compared to those of Song Shaozu (477) and Sima Jinlong (484), suggesting that Yang did not have access to the tomb figurine workshops that supplied the high nobility in Pingcheng. Alongside this appropriation was his (of his family's) endeavor to preserve part of the identity of his homeland in the Guan-Long region by placing a multiarmed lamp in his chamber and burying his brick epitaph in the dromos filling.

Qutu Longye (490)

An example from the last years of Pingcheng as capital is Erdianchang (Second Power Station) M16 in the southern suburb of modern Datong. This is, again, the only one of the 27 excavated tombs that yielded an epitaph. The inscription mentions only the name of the occupant (Qutu Longye 屈突隆業) and his death or burial date (490). However, since the tomb was neither plundered nor disturbed, it was suitable for an examination of the burial rites.

This was a simple, south facing, and rectangular brick chamber tomb. The coffin stood in the middle of the rear half of the chamber, with the foot end directly on the back wall (Fig. 46). Two large, round lacquer trays for serving the funerary meal were placed directly in front of the coffin. On one tray there was lacquer tableware, including an eared cup and six round bowls of different sizes, on the other there was the ribcage and forearms of a sheep or goat, as well as a jar for an (alcoholic) beverage. The brick epitaph leaned against the head panel of the coffin. No further grave goods are found in the spacious chamber.[413]

The sex of the deceased has not been determined, but based on the first name, the person was most likely a man. Qutu, the "surname", also indicates that he may have been a member of a tribe of the same name that once joined the Kumoxi 庫莫奚, or Qay, confederation in Northeast Asia.[414] Following their integration into the Yuwen branch of the Xianbei, the Qutu were forced to relocate first to Changli 昌黎 (present-day Jingzhou 錦州 in Liaoning) in the Former Yan State in 343 and then to Chang'an in the Former Qin State after Fu Jian defeated the Murong in 370. In 384, part of the Xianbei in Chang'an founded the Western Yan State, but they lost the battle against the Later Yan State in 394. After the Tuoba conquered the Later Yan in 395, the Qutu were again compelled to relocate east to Boling 博陵 in present-day Shandong and then to Pingcheng.[415] After their brief stay in

---

413 The excavation report contains little information about this tomb; see Datong kaogu 2019: 19, 36. The description here is mainly based on a photo of the chamber published in Wang Yanqing and Gao Feng 2013: 26 Fig. 9.2 and their report on the lacquerware found in this tomb. I am grateful to Professor Wang Yanqing for providing me with a higher-resolution image.

414 For Qutu, see Yao Weiyuan 1962, 137–42. In *Wei shu* 113.3010, only a Shitu 尸突 clan is recorded. Shitu is obviously a copyist error of Qutu 屈突 due to the graphic similarity of shi and qu (*Wei shu* 113.3021; Shimunek 2017, 145). Shimunek also reconstructed Qutu as *kʰurtʰ or *kʰurdor (op. cit.). For Kumoxi, Kumo-xi, or Xi, a Khitan related group ("Kitanic" according to Shimunek), see *Wei shu* 100.2222–23; Golden 1986 [1988]: 16–17; Golden 2022; Shimunek 2017, 61–64.

415 Yao Weiyuan 1962, op. cit.; *Zizhi tongjian* 118.3717–18.

Figure 46 Qutu Longye's tomb (Erdianchang M16). *Left*: the floorplan; *Middle*: the tomb interior. *Right*: The Brick epitaph (date of death: November 30, 490). (1) Brick epitaph; (2) Jar; (3) Large lacquer tray with seven lacquer vessels; (4) Animal offering on a large lacquer tray.

Drawings and photo by the author based on Datong kaogu 2019: 16 Fig. 2 (far left), Wang Yanqing and Gao Feng 2013: 26 Fig. 9.2 (middle), and in the Datong Museum (far right).

Changli, the Qutu claimed to be the Tuhe of Changli 昌黎徒河人,[416] thereby acknowledging the supremacy of the Murong.

Given this historical context, one would expect the Qutu to make every effort to conform some part of their material culture as closely as possible to that of the Murong. Unfortunately, we do not have any identifiable first-generation Qutu burials in Pingcheng, such as that of Qu Zun or those of his tribesmen, to conduct such a study.[417] The late date of Erdianchang M16 (490) indicates that Qutu Longye belonged to the second or a later generation of immigrants. Since the epitaph only mentions his death (or burial) date and name, he probably did not hold an office. But he (or his family) was evidently rich enough to build a brick tomb, which corresponds to the medium-sized burials we find in Pingcheng. As with many other later Pingcheng tombs with brick chambers, the animal offerings in front of Longye's coffin represent a steppe burial custom that was present in catacomb tombs throughout the Pingcheng era. In Longye's case, however, the choice of sacrificed

---

416　See, for example, the biography of the first prominent member, Qu(tu) Zun 屈遵 (329–398) in *Wei shu* 33.777. The constructed identity persisted into Tang times; see the rubbing of the epitaph of the famous Tang general Qutu Tong 屈突通 in the Beijing Library 北京圖書館藏中國歷代石刻拓本匯編 (http://csid.zju.edu.cn/tomb/stone/detail?id=8a8fbda74ca22703014ca22820d50010&rubbingId=8a8fb da74d093780014d26fd6c190023; retrieved February 3, 2021). Tuhe was a toponym for the region close to the modern Jinxi 錦西, Liaoning, see Wang Miaohou 1990. It was written 屠和 during the Warring States period, 徒河 in Han times. The Murong Xianbei in the area were accordingly named Tuhe, written in 徒何, see Ai Yingfan 2010.

417　See Note 416. Qu Zun died in Pingcheng and was possibly buried there.

animals seems to correspond more to the early Tuoba Xianbei rites of southern Inner Mongolia than to those of southern Manchuria, since he was offered parts of a sheep or goat instead of cattle limbs, as was more common among the Murong. Chicken bones, however, without zoological identification, in the eared cup indicate that the ritualized stereotypical sacrifice was supplemented by some possibly personal favorite foods. In addition, Longye's tomb was furnished with an epitaph that, although gradually becoming common in the later Pingcheng period, was not anchored in the sepulchral tradition of Inner Mongolia and Manchuria. The placement of the epitaph on the head panel of the coffin as well as the position of the body were unique in Pingcheng. The deceased was lying on his left side; his left arm and legs were flexed, and his left hand was under his head. This recalls the posture of the dying Buddha, only on the wrong side. Besides, a brick was placed at his feet, similar to a late burial with a funerary bed in Pingcheng.[418]

In summary, it seems that Longye's burial conformed to the usual funerary rites of the middle-class in the late Pingcheng period: a brick chamber, a funeral meal with sheep or goats, lacquerware, and an epitaph. However, some details, such as the placement of the epitaph, did not follow any known rules. Without the epitaph, it would be impossible to determine the origin of the deceased. Only the body arrangement could possibly reveal something about the self-identity of the deceased. However, comparable cases are lacking for further investigation.

Feng Shigong (490)

The last example is Feng Shigong's tomb (489). Although not discovered in Pingcheng, it also well illustrates the high degree of cultural hybridity that characterized the final years of the Pingcheng era. Juliano and Dien (2002) have expertly explicated this topic using the coffin paintings, but the tomb furnishings and some less noticed painting topics can provide further insights. The tomb was not robbed, but it was badly damaged by a drilling machine for a railway track construction and the ensuing water ingress. Nevertheless, the poorly documented and rarely noticed grave goods do provide some information about the burial. The tomb was re-excavated in the 2010s. The discovery of an epitaph masoned in the wall made it possible to determine the date and the tomb occupant.[419]

The tomb was oriented towards the west. Although the chamber was medium-sized (L. 3.8 m, W. 3.8 m, H. 3.9 m), it was partly built with bricks with incised motifs. The deceased were provided with rich grave goods and their coffins lavishly decorated. Feng Shigong's lacquer-painted coffin stood in the middle of the chamber, while his wife's coffin, unpainted but embellished with bronze studs and gilded bronze rings,[420] lay close to the rear wall. The grave goods were found scattered throughout the chamber due to mechanical and water damage, and we do not know whether they were originally deposited in the chamber or in the coffins or both. The small bronze angular *fang* 鈁 and round *hu* 壺

---

418 Datong kaogu 2014: 12; Müller Sh. 2019a, 394.

419 The following description is based on the floor plan given in Ningxia Guyuan 1988a, 3. For the destruction and the recent excavation, see Luo Feng 2019.

420 The gilded rings were mounted on decorative eight-petaled bases. They scattered on the site where the wife's coffin lay; at least five of these rings have been documented (Ningxia Guyuan 1988a, 6). But Luo Feng (Ningxia and Zhong Ri 1999, 15) speaks of only two such rings affixed to the wife's coffin.

bottles as well as the turtle-shaped stove excavated from this tomb are all reminiscent of certain prestige grave goods found in some tombs (of the Southern Xiongnu?) in southern Inner Mongolia and northern Shanxi from the last years of the Han dynasty.[421] Since similar bronze bottles and stoves disappeared from the fourth- and fifth-century burials in northern China, the ones from this tomb were probably heirlooms. Since they were found in front of the head of the wife's coffin, it is probable that they belonged to her. Mackenzie (2002) observed traces of soot on the firebox of the stove. Additionally, a tiny piece of bread dough (dia. 4.5 cm; height 0.5 cm) was discovered in the steamer on the stove.[422] The findings seem to suggest that these artifacts were part of the presentation of the funerary banquet. Due to the damage to the tomb, we do not know whether animal offerings were made during the burial ceremony. There were no figurines in this tomb.

Two leather belts with buckles and fittings were discovered,[423] at least (fragmented) one of which was securely located in the middle section of the destroyed coffin of the wife. It is plausible that she wore a belted garment. A short knife was also found on her side, another one lay more to the husband. And the wife probably wore jewelry made of amber, pearls, and crystal. This reminds of a clothing style found in some catacomb tombs for females in Pingcheng. Next to the head of each deceased lay an iron mirror wrapped in textile. Two crescent-shaped earrings of gold were located on the side of the husband. These traces suggest that both were buried in accordance with a certain steppe clothing style, even though the husband may be of Chinese descent based on his surname Feng. The tomb construction conformed to the Pingcheng format. Additionally, the double-edged long sword of iron and the unusual find of a pair of iron stirrups (probably for actual use) were signs of the high military posts Shigong once held and may also indicate his close relationship with Empress Dowager Wenming (died 490), as mentioned above.[424]

Due to the extensive damage, we do not know whether the coffin was painted with a procession scene, which Shigong was surely entitled to. Two lacquer fragments show hunting scenes, reminiscent of the painting themes on coffins from the early Pingcheng period. They were probably painted on both side planks. The much-discussed portrait of Feng Shigong on the head panel of the coffin shows that the depiction followed a general trend among the upper-class residents of Pingcheng, who presented their noble status using means familiar from the Persian world, such as the princely sitting posture with hanging legs and the elegant manner of holding a goblet with the outstretched little finger.[425] Otherwise, Buddhist and Daoist motifs are also prominently represented, as are narrative depictions of filial sons and a small fragment of the "Killing Three Warriors with Two Peaches"

---

421 For the Guyuan finds, see Ningxia Guyuan 1988a, 3rd b/w plate page; see also Mackenzie 2002, 85; Dien 2007a, 308–9. Similar stoves were found, for example, in tombs from Nalintaohai 納林套海 and Shajintaohai 沙金套海, Inner Mongolia, or Shuozhou 朔州, Shanxi. All these Han tombs appear to be very richly furnished, cf. Wei Jian 1998, 38–41, 98; Pingshuo 1987, Pl. 6.2.

422 Guyuan xian 1984: 48. The dough was however not examined.

423 Ningxia Guyuan 1988a, 5. The excavators assume that some of the fittings are ornaments for horse harnesses. As no other horse-related objects were found, this assumption seems rather unlikely.

424 Luo Feng 2019, 142–45. The titles mentioned in the inscription are "Commissioned with Extraordinary Power, the West Conquering General" 使持節鎮西將軍 and "Commander-in-Chief of the Gaoping Garrison" 高平鎮督[都]大將, the most important garrison on the northwest border of the Tuoba.

425 According to *Nan Qi shu* (57.986), the Tuoba rulers sat with hanging legs on the throne in Pingcheng.

story, which also appeared in Song Shaozu's stone house. All human images in the stories about filial sons and the hunting scenes are dressed in Xianbei garb. Even the King Father of the East and the Queen Mother of the West were painted on the coffin lid with headgear reminiscent of Xianbei hats, as Sun Ji points out.[426] Only the two surviving figures from the "Two Peaches" tale are dressed in different attire and headgear, which could have been influenced by Han reliefs. This suggests that the depiction adhered to an old-fashioned template. The choice of the topic of filial piety may have been a remote display of loyalty and support for Xiaowen's reforms in the capital (Wenming died slightly later) and the effort to translate the Classic of Filial Piety *Xiaojing* into the "national language," which was later committed to paper in Luoyang.[427] Regardless, the theme of the "Two Peaches" narrative may indicate Shigong's cultural ties to certain northwestern regions such as Dunhuang, possibly through a Ru education.

Women in Pingcheng

The sources for studies on the life and role of women in the Xianbei society are mainly written sources, such as literary works, dynastic records, and Buddhist or funerary inscriptions.[428] Recent bioarchaeological studies have also shed light on some physical aspects of women, i.e., aspects of their ways of living. The previously mentioned isotopic analyses of bone collagen extracted from several large graveyards in Pingcheng show that there were no significant differences in the food intake between men and women, i.e., there does not seem to be any gender discrimination in food distribution, at least among the skeletons examined. In fact, women consumed slightly more meat than men.[429] Furthermore, my data from the few burials with gender-identified individuals (including those in catacomb, earthen, and brick chambered tombs) suggest that women's tombs were as well furnished as men's tombs, if not better. One could conclude that women were equally treated as men in many aspects in life and death, which seems to have been a widespread phenomenon in the steppe.[430] A similar result is shown by the burial practices of women who came from the steppe. In the tombs of these women, one finds hunting utensils and tools such as arrowheads, bow strengtheners for reflex bows, and iron knives. These artifacts indicate their actual, anticipated, or desired active role in hunting or even in combat.

---

426 Sun Ji 1989. See also Juliano and Dien 2002; Dien 2007a, 296–99, and the detailed study by Kuroda Akura 2022; 2023 on the textual sources for the stories of filial sons in the Guyuan coffin painting. For the depiction of the "Two Peaches" story, identified by an inscription, see Luo Feng 2020.

427 Knapp 2010, 171–73, 180, 192. Müller Sh. 2019a, 405 note 76. Ōnishi Yumiko 2020: 207 suggests on the other hand that the depictions could have been based, at least partially, on the Buddhist "Transformation Tableau of the young Shun" 舜子變. In this case, Xiaowendi's reform did not play a major role in the adoption of the filialty topics on this coffin. For the translation of the *Xiaojing* into the Xianbei language, *Sui shu* 32.935.

428 See, for example, Hinsch 2018; Holmgren 1979, 1991; Luo Xin 2022.

429 Hou Liangliang et al. 2019: 289; Zhang Guowen et al. 2020.

430 Shelach 2008, 101. The samples of the skeletal remains for the analyses are taken from the recently excavated graveyards at Shuibosi and Jinmaoyuan. Hou Liangliang et al. 2019: 280–81, Zhang Guowen et al. 2020: 8.

Inscriptions and burial evidence point to intertribal or interethnic marriages. Some husbands or children appear to have made efforts to retain the ethnic or religious identities of their deceased wives or mothers, or to display their high ranks. This is shown by the burials of Han Farong and Xing Hejiang, as well as the coffin of General Poduoluo's wife. However, tomb inscriptions generally contained more information about the husband than about the wife, who in most cases was mentioned only briefly or not at all. This phenomenon probably had its roots in the Chinese tradition of epitaph production. Already during the Jin period, it was common to mention women only in the context of their husband's career, with the result that "the identity of the dedicatee is almost lost among the extensive résumé of her husband."[431]

The relatively large number of "paired burials" in Pingcheng shows a different fate for women. Such burials suggest that women—provided that the gender of the tomb occupants was correctly identified—were killed, or committed suicide, either voluntarily or under pressure from their family, community, or certain tribal codes of honor, in order to follow their husbands into death. Therefore, the position of women in Pingcheng society was not clear and was probably determined by ritual rules of the families or communities in which they lived.

Conclusion

The burial culture of Pingcheng was subject to rapid changes. The period between the 450s and 460s saw the greatest variety of tomb types, mortuary furniture, interior furnishing, and burial practices. This was clearly the result of several mass relocations of peoples from all northern regions to Pingcheng. The most striking features of this short period included funerary houses and beds, metal chinstraps, knife-shaped tombs, paired burials in a single coffin, large-scale wall paintings, and clay figurines. Moreover, those tombs, built prior to the construction of the Yungang caves, already demonstrate strong Buddhist influences. Pingcheng prospered despite several natural catastrophes in the Taihe era (477–499). It is possible that more brick chamber tombs were built. Some of them were embellished with wall paintings, though the themes differed from those of the earlier murals. Some were built with bricks that bore impressed ornaments or inscriptions. But more brick tombs were furnished with clay figurines. Only a few had both figurines and murals.

Not all types of tombs existing in northern China during the Three Kingdoms, the Western Jin and the Sixteen Kingdoms periods are found in this city. The stone slab tombs typical of southern Manchuria and the narrow brick chamber tombs with barrel vaults that were common in northern Hebei in the third and fourth centuries, for example, have not yet been observed in Pingcheng. On the other hand, neither the knife-shaped tomb construction nor the burial of a man and a woman in a single coffin, which occurred in several tomb types, had ever been documented in northern China. Now they suddenly appeared in the city.

Based on the tomb finds typical of the steppe, such as cauldrons, belt fittings, and animal offerings, as well as painting themes in tombs or on coffins, some of the brick tombs appear to have been built for high-ranking or wealthy people with pastoral roots. Good

---

431 Davis 2015, 278.

examples are the painted tomb of General Poduoluo and the Yunbolilu M1. The painting contents in these tombs, at least until the mid-Pingcheng period, were similar, though with individual variations. These include scenes of funerary feasts or festive drinking with portraits of the deceased, a procession or a hunting scene—depending on the rank and status of the deceased—, and an outdoor banquet scene in connection with female guests who came with square tents. After the introduction of figurines in Pingcheng, most likely by peoples from the Guanzhong area, some of these themes were gradually depicted by figurines rather than paintings. Figurines were capable of rendering any subject matter, but there was no depiction of hunting through figurines. Thus, hunting as a theme demonstrating the North and West Asian way of life retreated from tomb art after the mid-Pingcheng period and did not return until the mid-sixth century. Sogdian *sabaos* also adopted this topic to decorate their house-shaped sarcophagi. The ethnicities of the occupants using funerary houses in Pingcheng are less obvious. Inscriptions on such mortuary furniture suggest that many of them were possibly sedentary people. Most of them did not adhere to the above-mentioned compositions when decorating their funerary houses. The subjects they chose tended to express personal wishes, such as the blessing of the Directional Animals or Buddhas, or were simply memories of their own past.

Some catacomb tombs contained only undecorated coffins. But these coffins were filled with a wealth of imported or locally manufactured luxury goods, such as jewelry or vessels made of precious metals, glass, or lacquer. Some of the treasures were not simply silent companions of the deceased in the afterlife, stored in coffins. Given their in-situ positions, it is likely that the famous Greco-Bactrian silver bowls from Dianhanchang M107 and Ih-Nur M1 in Inner Mongolia served a ritual function during the burial ceremonies, such as for libation. These cases show that, despite their less complex tomb structures, the tomb occupants had access to the resources of a much larger world, from which they were able to extract luxuries and, ultimately, could afford to take the treasures into the afterlife. "Simple" tombs in Pingcheng were therefore not necessarily synonymous with tombs of the "poor people" or "commoners." They represented another great sepulchral tradition, that of the steppe, which was not in line with that of the sedentary population. Brick tombs in Pingcheng constitute a small fraction. Additionally, the sheer number of the pit and catacomb tombs indicates that Pingcheng was indeed primarily inhabited by steppe peoples.

Written sources are silent on how the different population groups coexisted in Pingcheng. Recent studies of skeletal injuries suggest that only a small percentage of the deceased died violent deaths.[432] Cemeteries generally contained the burials of people from different cultural backgrounds. Since burials seldom overlapped, peoples apparently peacefully shared burial grounds. A number of Pingcheng tombs exhibit burial features or rituals from other cultures. Regardless of whether the hybridization occurred at the request of the deceased or his or her family, the peoples of Pingcheng did not seem to be anxious about contact or interaction across tribal or ethnic boundaries. This can also be confirmed by some purchase contracts between buyers and vendors from different tribes or ethnic groups. Adopting elements from other cultures was, in fact, an ongoing process that did not take a particular course or adhere to predetermined "recipes."

---

432 Cui Hexun 2021, 51; Li Pengzhen 2021, 139; Ruansun Zifeng 2022, 49.

In Pingcheng's funerary art, the "Central Asians" are the only group that is visually distinct from the Xianbei. Written sources indicate that wealthy Sogdians resided in Pingcheng, but we do not have precise information about their burials. Likewise, a "Chinese" burial in the typical Western Jin style is not discernible in Pingcheng, although high-ranking Chinese officials served at court because of their expertise in domestic administration. Tomb inscriptions, techniques for brick chamber construction and brick firing, and lacquer painting are regarded as the legacy of the Han, Wei, or Jin traditions. But these traditions could also have come from the descendants of those Chinese who fled to border areas and lived there for generations. Among them, the heritages from Hexi and the Guanzhong region, which have already adapted to local cultures, appear to be the most influential. The Chinese influence on the inhabitants of Pingcheng was undeniable, but it was only one of many.

The Book of Wei does not mention any court-organized military processions for the funerals of dignitaries during the Pingcheng period; the only exception was a burial of a Tuoba prince in 487.[433] However, the symbolic presence of soldiers and military bands at funerals, expressed through tomb paintings or the arrangement of figurines, was documented in Pingcheng tombs early on. It was undoubtedly a continuation of the funerary practice that was developed during the third and fourth centuries for the high-ranking military elites and was clearly intended to demonstrate one's status and to impress others. There is also no written evidence that the imperial court regulated such depictions at funerals. The depiction of a military procession was only present in the tombs of very high-ranking officers and their spouses, such as those of General Poduoluo and his wife, General Mao Dezu's wife Zhang Zhilang, Song Shaozu, and Sima Jinlong (possibly also his wife). Hence, this symbolic presence was obviously not within the means or power of access of every affluent inhabitant who wished to be buried in a blaze of glory.

According to the available data for Pingcheng, it is generally difficult to clearly identify a "typical" Tuoba or Xianbei burial. This is partly because the steppe peoples had more or less common mortuary customs due to the similar ecological environment in which they lived. For the pre-dynastic period, the trapezoid-shaped coffins and a few small bronze plaques with horse or deer motifs are the archaeological indications of a Tuoba or Xianbei burial. The occurrence of both in the first century CE was confined to the area of the Far Eastern steppe and forest-steppe, which corresponds to the geographical distribution of the Xianbei in historical works. The rise and expansion of the Murong and Tuoba resulted in the spread of trapezoidal coffins to other regions. In Pingcheng, this coffin shape was clearly accepted by all inhabitants despite their different origins. Another novel development from the early fifth century was even more remarkable. At least in the sepulchral and religious art, such as murals and votive stelae, elites and commoners in Pingcheng began to present themselves as Xianbei dignitaries and donors by wearing Xianbei clothing instead of Chinese official robes or various regional costumes. And the paintings of historical (Chinese) or religious (Buddhist) stories were narrated with Xianbei images. As Albert Dien notes, the new look was not dictated by the authorities, as there is "no indication ...

---

433 *Wei shu* 16.396. Xiaowendi ordered a *guchui* troop to attend the funeral of Pingyuan 拓跋平原, a prince of Tuoba Gui's lineage and important commander against the Ruru invasions. All other military bands at funerals are documented for the Luoyang period.

that there was any imposition of signs of fealty and submission such as the forced wearing of the queue during Manchu rule" from the side of the Tuoba rulers.[434] The uniform appearance of Xianbei attire in Pingcheng and elsewhere in fifth century northern China indicates that a collective identity or "group solidarity" with the Tuoba leadership emerged within the populace and strengthened over time. This development corresponds to the observation by Matsushita Ken'ichi that in most inscriptions on epitaphs and funerary or Buddhist stelae, the state in Pingcheng was not named after the officially proclaimed "Wei" but after "Da Dai" 大代 (Great Dai), the name of the dominion of the pre-dynastic Tuoba lords in central and southern Inner Mongolia. He perceives this as a sign of the populace's endorsement of a steppe state, rather than that of the Chinese.[435] The trend most likely threatened Emperor Xiaowen's ambitions to attain absolute power as befitted a Chinese emperor and may have been one of the reasons why he moved the capital to Luoyang at all costs, where he could make a fresh start.

Pingcheng's burial and material cultures pioneered those of the later Northern Dynasties and the Tang Dynasty. Although not all inventions originated in Pingcheng, its inhabitants modified and popularized them. The practice of laying the body on a funerary bed (made of earth, brick, or stone) without using a coffin spread from Pingcheng to other parts of northern China, and was most popular in present-day Liaoning, Hebei, Henan, and Ningxia during the sixth and seventh centuries. After the Pingcheng era, knife-shaped tombs and tombs with paired burials in one single coffin were also discovered in several northern provinces, particularly in garrison towns in the border areas. And they were clearly associated with (Xianbei?) soldiers or non-Chinese people. Techniques, such as pottery with glazed appliqués imitating enamel works, pottery with polychrome glazes, or glazed roof-tiles, which are not covered in this paper, led to a new era of ceramic production in northern China. Many creative works that were the results of inspiration from cultural contacts did not survive in the new capital Luoyang, such as the grayware jar with a Garuda-similar bird appliqué which emulated the "chicken-head" ewers from the south, or a blown-glass vessel in the shape of a Xianbei-style grayware jug. It is also interesting to note that many steppe-related burial cultures, such as animal offerings, jewelry with colorful stones, and coffin paintings did not re-appear in Luoyang. One can argue that Luoyang was a completely Sinicized city. But if the techniques and traditions of the steppe people and Central Asians declined so drastically or came to a standstill, one must ask who moved to Luoyang with Emperor Xiaowen.[436]

---

434 Dien 2007a, 319.
435 Matsushita Ken'ichi 2007, 111–58; Müller Sh. 2013.
436 This was the topic of my zoom-presentation at the worldwide conference of the Society of East Asian Archaeology 2022 in Daegu, Korea.

Bibliography

Ai Yinfan 艾蔭范. 2010. "Xianbei xingshi Han yi he Liaoxi guguo Tuhe" 鮮卑姓氏漢譯和遼西古國屠何. *Bohai daxue xuebao* (*zhexue shehui kexueban*) 5: 156–159.

Akiyama Terukazu, Andō Kōsei, Matsubara Saburo, Okazaki Takashi, Sekino Takeshi, Coordinated by Mary Tregear. 1968. *Arts of China*. Volume 1 *Neolithic Cultures to the T'ang Dynasty: Recent Discoveries*. Tokyo: Kodansha International.

Allsen, Thomas T. 2006. *The Royal Hunt in Eurasian History*. Philadelphia: University of Pennsylvania Press.

An Jiayao. 2004. "The Art of Glass Along the Silk Road," in Watt 2004, 57–65.

Assmann, Jan. 1995. "Collective Memory and Cultural Identity," transl. John Czaplicka, *New German Critique*, no. 65, Cultural History/Cultural Studies (Spring – Summer): 125–133 (from the original "Kollektives Gedächtnis und kulturelle Identität," in *Kultur und Gedächtnis*, edited by Jan Assmann und Tonio Hölscher, 9–19. Frankfurt/Main: Suhrkamp, 1988).

Bai Shuli 白述禮. 2007. "Shi lun Ningxia Yanchi xin faxian de huangjin fangqi" 試論寧夏鹽池新發現的黃金方奇, *Ningxia daxue xuebao* (*Renwen shehui kexueban*) 4: 82–87.

Bao Yuzhu 寶玉柱. 2014. "Mongguyu xɔrtʃh in in ciyuan tanxi" 蒙古語 xɔrtʃh in 詞源探析, *Manyu yanjiu* 1: 71–74.

Batsaikhan, Zagd. 2006. "Foreign Tribes in the Xiongnu Confederation," *The Silk Road* 4.1: 45–47.

Beckwith, Christopher I. 2005. "The Chinese Names of Tibetans, Tabghatch, and Turks," *Archivum Eurasiae Medii Aevi* 14: 5–19.

Bei shi 北史. Compiled by Li Yanshou 李延壽 (Tang) et al. Beijing: Zhonghua shuju, 1974.

Beijing shi wenwu yanjiusuo 北京市文物研究所. 2017. "Beijing Fangshan Shuiniantun Xi Jin mu fajue jianbao" 北京房山水碾屯西晉墓發掘簡報, *Wenwu* 1: 4–14.

—— and Yanqing xian wenwu guanlisuo 延慶縣文物管理所. 2012. "Beijing shi Yanqing xian Xitun mudi xiqu (I qu) kaogu fajue jianbao" 北京市延慶縣西屯墓地西區 (I 區) 考古發掘簡報, *Beijing wenbo* 4: 19–30.

Bemmann, Jan, and Michael Schmauder. ed. 2015. *Complexity of Interaction along the Eurasian Steppe Zone in the First Millennium CE*. Bonn Contributions to Asian Archaeology Vol. 6. Bonn: Vor- und Frühgeschichtliche Archäologie, Rheinische Friedrich-Wilhelms-Universität Bonn.

Bray, Francesca. 2018. "Where Did the Animals Go? Presence and Absence of Livestock in Chinese Agricultural Treatises," in *Animals through Chinese History: Earliest Times to 1911*, edited by Roel Sterckx, Martina Siebert and Dagmar Schäfer, 118–138. Cambridge: Cambridge University Press.

——. 2019. "Agriculture," in Dien and Knapp 2019, 355–373.

Bromberg, Carol A. 1983. "Sasanian Stucco Influence: Sorrento and East-West," *Orientalia Novaniensia Periodica* 14: 247–267.

Brosseder, Ursula B. 2015. "A Study on the Complexity and Dynamics of Interaction and Exchange in Late Iron Age Eurasia," in Bemmann and Schmauder 2015, 199–332.

—— and Bryan K. Miller. eds. 2011. *Xiongnu Archaeology: Multidisciplinary Perspectives of the First Steppe Empire in Inner Asia*. Bonn Contributions to Asian Archaeology, Vol. 5. Freiburg: Vor- and Frühgeschichtliche Archäologie, Rheinische Friedrich-Wilhelms-Universität Bonn.

Brück, Joanna, and David Fontijn. 2013. "The Myth of the Chief: Prestige Goods, Power, and Personhood in the European Bronze Age," in *The Oxford Handbook of the European Bronze Age*, edited by Harry Fokkens and Anthony Harding, 197–215. Oxford: Oxford University Press. https:// doi.org/10.1093/oxfordhb/9780199572861.001.0001

Byington, Mark E. 2016. *The Ancient State of Puyŏ in Northeast Asia: Archaeology and Historical Memory*. Cambridge, MA and London: Harvard University Asia Center.

Cao Chenming 曹臣明. 2010. "Qiantan Datong Caochangcheng Bei Wei yihao yizhi de xingzhi" 淺談大同操埸城北魏一號遺址的性質. *Beichao yanjiu* 7: 122–126.

——. 2016. "Pingcheng fujin Xianbei ji Bei Wei muzang fenbu guilü kao" 平城附近鮮卑及北魏墓葬分佈規律考. *Wenwu* 5: 61–69.

Cao Lijuan 曹麗娟. 2009. "Datong Shaling Bei Wei bihuamu yanjiu" 大同沙嶺北魏壁畫墓研究, MA thesis, Zhongyang meishu xueyuan.

Chavannes, Eduard. 1909. *Mission archéologique dans Chine septentrionale*. Paris: Imprimerie nationale.

Chen shu 陳書. Compiled by Yao Silian 姚思廉 (557–637). Beijing: Zhonghua shuju, 1972.

Chen Xiaolu 陳曉露. 2012. "Loulan bihuamu suojian Guishuang wenhua yinsu" 樓蘭壁畫墓所見貴霜文化因素, *Kaogu yu wenwu* 2: 79–84.

Chen Yongzhi 陳永志, Song Guodong 宋國棟, Li Chunlei 李春雷 and Cao Peng 曹鵬. 2016a. "Neimenggu Zhengxiangbaiqi Yihe Nao'er muqun" 內蒙古正鑲白旗伊和淖爾墓羣, in *2015 Zhongguo zhongyao kaogu faxian* 2015 中國重要考古發現, edited by Guojia wenwuju 國家文物局, 92–95. Beijing: Wenwu chubanshe.

Chen Yongzhi, Song Guodong and Ma Yan. 2016b. "The Results of the Excavation of the Yihe-Nur Cemetery in Zhengxiangbai Banner (2012–2014)," *The Silk Road* 14: 42–57.

Ch'en, Kenneth. 1964. *Buddhism in China: A Historical Survey*. Princeton: Princeton University Press.

Cheng, Bonnie. 2014. "Exchange across Media in Northern Wei China," in *Face to Face: The Transcendence of the Arts in China and Beyond*, edited by Rui Oliveria Lopez, 126–158. Lisbon: Centro de Investigação e Estudos em Belas-Artes.

Chin, Connie. 2008. "Climate Change and Migrations of People during the Jin Dynasty," *Early Medieval China* 2: 49–78.

Chittick, Andrew. 2010. *Patronage and Community in Medieval China: The Xiangyang Garrison, 400–600 CE*. Albany: State University of New York Press.

——. 2020. *The Jiankang Empire in Chinese and World History*. Oxford: Oxford University Press.

Chizhi 持志 and Liu Junxi 劉俊喜. 2014. "Bei Wei Mao Dezu qi Zhang Zhilang shiguo mingke" 北魏毛德祖妻張智朗石槨銘刻, *Zhongguo shufa* 4: 120–122.

Chōsen Koseki Kenkyūkai 朝鮮古蹟研究會. 1935. *Rakurō Ō Kō bo* 樂浪王光墓. Sŏul: Kyŏngin Munhwasa.

Compareti, Matteo. 2009. "Sasanian Textile: An Iconographical Approach," in *Encyclopaedia Iranica*, edited by E. Yarshater. Online version: http://www.iranicaonline.org/articles/sasanian-textiles, last updated December 15, 2009.

——. 2014. "Some Examples of Central Asian Decorative Elements in Ajanta and Bagh India," *The Silk Road* 12: 39–48.

——. 2016. "Observations on the Rock Reliefs at Taq-i Bustan: A Late Sasanian Mounument Along the 'Silk Road'," *The Silk Road* 14: 71–83.

——. 2020. "'Iranian' Decorative Patterns on Enigmatic Central Asian Ceramics," *Journal of Asian Civilization* 43.1: 2–40.

de Crespigny, Rafe. 1977. "The Ch'iang Barbarians and the Empire of Han: A Study in Frontier Policy I," *Papers on Far Eastern History* 16: 1–25.

——. 1978. "The Ch'iang Barbarians and the Empire of Han: A Study in Frontier Policy II," *Papers on Far Eastern History* 18: 193–243.

Cui Hexun 崔賀勛. 2021. "Shanxi Datong Huayu mudi Bei Wei shiqi rengu yanjiu" 山西大同華宇墓地北魏時期人骨研究. MA thesis; Jilin University.

Dai Chunyang 戴春陽 and Zhang Long 張瓏. 1994. *Dunhuang Qijiawan: Xi Jin Shiliuguo muzang fajue baogao* 敦煌祁家灣：西晉十六國墓葬發掘報告. Beijing: Wenwu chubanshe.

Datong shi bowuguan 大同市博物館. 1989. "Datong dongjiao Bei Wei Yuan Shu mu" 大同東郊北魏元淑墓, *Wenwu* 8: 57–65.

——. 2018. *Ronghe zhi lu–Tuoba Xianbei qianxi yu fazhen lichen* 融合之路—拓跋鮮卑遷徙與發展歷程. Hefei: Anhui meishu chubanshe.

——. 2019a. *Yi cai qiannian: Datong diqu muzang bihua* 熠彩千年：大同地區墓葬壁畫. Beijing: Kexue chubanshe.

——. 2019b. "Shanxi Datong Shitoucun Bei Wei mu chutu de qiwu" 山西大同石頭村北魏墓出土的器物, *Zhongguo guojia bowuguan guankan* 11: 6–22.

Datong shi bowuguan 大同市博物館 and Shanxi sheng wenwu gongzuo weiyuanhui 山西省文物工作委員會. 1978. "Datong Fangshan Bei Wei Yongguling" 大同方山北魏永固陵, *Wenwu* 7: 29–35.

Datong shi kaogu yanjiusuo 大同市考古研究所. 2004a. "Shanxi Datong Xiashenjing Bei Wei mu fajue jianbao" 山西大同下深井北魏墓發掘簡報, *Wenwu* 6: 29–34.

——. 2004b. "Datong Hudong Bei Wei yihao mu" 大同湖東北魏一號墓, *Wenwu* 12: 26–34.

——. 2006a. "Shanxi Datong Qilicun Bei Wei muqun fajue jianbao" 山西大同七里村北魏墓群發掘簡報, *Wenwu* 10: 25–49.

——. 2006b. "Shanxi Datong Shaling Bei Wei bihuamu fajue jianbao" 山西大同沙嶺北魏壁畫墓發掘簡報, *Wenwu* 10: 4–24.

——. 2006c. "Shanxi Datong Yingbin dadao Bei Wei muqun" 山西大同迎賓大道北魏墓群, *Wenwu* 10: 50–71.

——. 2010. "Shanxi Datong nanjiaoqu Tiancun Bei Wei mu fajue jianbao" 山西大同南郊區田村北魏墓發掘簡報, *Wenwu* 5: 4–18.

——. 2011a. "Shanxi Datong Yunbolilu Bei Wei bihuamu fajue jianbao" 山西大同雲波里路北魏壁畫墓發掘簡報, *Wenwu* 12: 13–25.

——. 2011b. "Shanxi Datong Wenyinglu Bei Wei bihuamu fajue jianbo" 山西大同文瀛路北魏壁畫墓發掘簡報, *Wenwu* 12: 26–60.

——. 2011c. "Shanxi Datong Yanggao Bei Wei Yuchi Dingzhou mu fajue jianbao" 山西大同陽高北魏尉遲定州墓發掘簡報, *Wenwu* 12: 4–12, 51.

——. 2014. "Shanxi Datong Shaling xincun Bei Wei mudi fajue jianbao" 山西大同沙嶺新村北魏墓地發掘簡報, *Wenwu* 4: 4–15.

——. 2015. "Shanxi Datong Heng'anjie Bei Wei mu (11DHAM13) fajue jiabao" 山西大同恆安街北魏墓 (11DHAM13) 發掘簡報, *Wenwu* 1: 13–21.

——. 2017. "Shanxi Datong Yunbolu Bei Wei mu (M10) fajue jianbao" 山西大同雲波路北魏墓 (M10) 發掘簡報, *Wenwu* 11: 4–20.

——. 2019. "Shanxi Datong Erdianchang Bei Wei muqun fajue jianbo" 山西大同二電廠北魏墓群發掘簡報, Wenwu 8: 15–37.

——. 2021a. "Shanxi Datong Bei Wei Jia Bao mu fajue jianbao" 山西大同北魏賈寶墓發掘簡報, *Wenwu* 6: 23–37.

——. 2021b. "Shanxi Datong Yudong xinqu Yuchang jiayuan Bei Wei mu M113 fajue jianbao" 山西大同御東新區御昌佳園北魏墓 M113 發掘簡報, *Kaogu yu wenwu* 4: 39–51.

——. 2022. "Shanxi Datong Tongjiawan Bei Wei Xing Hejiang shiguo diaocha jianbao" 山西大同全家灣北魏邢合姜墓石槨調查簡報, *Wenwu* 1: 18–34.

——. 2023. "Shanxi Datong Qilicun Bei Wei muqun M29 fajue jianbao" 山西大同七里村北魏墓群 M29 發掘簡報. *Wenwu* 1: 30–60.

Davis, Timothy M. 2015. *Entombed Epigraphy and Commemorative Culture in Early Medieval China: A History of Early Muzhiming*. Leiden: Brill.

Delacour, Catherine. 2002. "A propos de trois récentes acquisitions de la section Chine du musée Guimet : une épée Donghu, une paire de boucles d'oreilles Xianbei et une aiguière Liao," *Arts asiatiques* 57.1: 179–193.

Deng Tianzhen 鄧天珍, Shi Shaohua 史少華, Bai Yunxing 白雲星 and Fang Beisong 方北松. 2019. "Yumen Huahai Bijiatan guanban 'Jin lü zhu' de baohu xiufu yanjiu" 玉門花海畢家灘 '晉律注' 的保護修復研究, *Wenwu baohu yu kaogu kexue* 3: 44–51.

Dien, Albert E. 1991. "A New Look at the Xianbei and their Impact on Chinese Culture," in *Ancient Mortuary Traditions of China: Papers on Chinese Ceramic Funerary Sculptures*, edited by George Kuwayama, 40–59. Los Angeles: Los Angeles County Museum of Art.

——. 2001. "Developments in Funerary Practices in the Six Dynasties Period: The Duisuguan 堆塑罐 or 'Figured Jar' as a Case in Point," in Wu Hung 2001, 509–546.

——. 2004. "Xianbei Drummer / Xianbei Horn Player" in Juliano and Lerner 2004, 92–93.

——. 2007a. *Six Dynasties Civilization*. New Haven and London: Yale University Press.

——. 2007b. "Lighting in the Six Dynasties Period," *Early Medieval China* 1: 1–32. DOI: 10.1179/152991007791330337

——. 2014. "Light after Dark: Artificial Illumination in the Six Dynasties Period—Lamps," in *Willow Catkins: Festschrift for Dr Lily Xiao Hong Lee on the Occasion of Her 75th Birthday*, edited by Shirley Chan, Barbara Hendrischke and Sue Wiles, 285–322. Sydney, Australia: The Oriental Society of Australia.

——. forthcoming. "Liaoning in the Six Dynasties period: Aspects of its cultural heritage," Submitted for inclusion in Proceedings of the UNESCO International Workshop on the Cultural Heritage of the Northern Kingdoms in northeast China.

—— and Keith N. Knapp. eds. 2019. *The Cambridge History of China*, Volume 2: *The Six Dynasties, 220–589*. Cambridge: Cambridge University Press.

Dong Ruishan 董睿山. ed. 2008. *Bei Wei Pingcheng yanjiu wenji* 北魏平城研究文集. Taiyuan: Shanxi renmin chubanshe.

Du Linyuan 杜林淵. 2007. "Nan Xiongnu muzang chubu yanjiu" 南匈奴墓葬初步研究, *Kaogu* 4: 74–86.

Du Yixue 杜一雪. 2018. "Bei Wei Fangshan Yongguling yanjiu" 北魏方山永固陵研究. MA thesis, Zhongyang meishu xueyuan.

Duthie, Nina. 2015. "Origins, Ancestors, and Imperial Authority in Early Northern Wei Historiography." Ph.D. diss., Columbia University.

Eisenberg, Andrew. 2008. *Kingship in Early Medieval China*. Leiden, Bosten: Brill.

Erdenebaatar, Diimaazhav, Tömör-Ochir Iderkhangai, Baatar Galbadrakh, Enkhbaiar Minzhiddorzh, Samdanzhamts Orgilbaiar. 2011. "Excavations of Satellite Burial 30, Tomb 1 Complex, Gold Mod 2 Necropolis," in Brosseder and Miller 2011, 303–314.

Ershiershi zhaji 二十二史札記. *Ershiershi zhaji jiaozheng* 二十二史札記校證. By Zhao Yi 趙翼 (1727–1814). Annotated by Wang Shumin 王樹民. Beijing: Zhonghua shuju, 1984.

Fan Xin 樊欣. 2020. "Shanxi Datong Jingangyuan mudi rengu yanjiu" 山西大同金港園墓地人骨研究. MA thesis; Zhengzhou University.

Fisch, Jörg. 1998. *Tödliche Rituale. Die indische Witwenverbrennung und andere Formen der Totenfolge*. Frankfurt am Main: Campus Verlag.

Fisher, Genevieve, and Diana DiPaolo Loren. 2003. "Introduction (SPECIAL SECTION: Embodying Identity in Archaeology)," *Cambridge Archaeological Journal* 13.2: 225–230. doi:10.1017/S0959774303210143

Fleming, Robin. 2021. *The Material Fall of Roman Britain, 300–525 CE*. Philadelphia: University of Pennsylvania Press.

Gansu sheng wenwu kaogu yanjiusuo 甘肅省文物考古研究所. 2005. "Gansu Yumen Guanzhuang Wei Jin muzang fajue jianbao" 甘肅玉門官莊魏晉墓葬發掘簡報, *Kaogu yu wenwu* 6: 8–13.

Gao Feng 高峰. 2008. "Bei Wei Pingcheng muzang huihua jianshu" 北魏平城墓葬繪畫簡述, in Dong Ruihshan 2008, 313–327.

Geng Shuo 耿朔. 2015. "Beifang diqu chutu Xi Jin ciqi chutan" 北方地區出土西晉瓷器初探. *Gugong bowuyuan yuankan* 3: 34–50.

Gervers-Molnár, Veronika. 1973. *The Hungarian Szür: An Archaic Mantle of Eurasian Origin*. ROM HTA Monograph 1. Toronto: The Royal Ontario Museum.

Golden, Peter B. 1986 [1988] "The Ölberli (Ölperli): The Fortunes and Misfortunes of an Inner Asian Nomadic Clan," *Archivum Eurasiae Medii Aevi* 6: 5–29.

——. 2018. "The Stateless Nomads of Central Eurasia," in *Empires and Exchanges in Eurasian Late Antiquity: Rome, China, Iran, and the Steppe, ca. 250–750*, edited by Nicola Di Cosmo and Michael Maas, 317–332. Cambridge: Cambridge University Press.

——. 2022. "The Kaepiči [Каепичи]," in *Historical Linguistics and Philology of Central Asia: Essays in Turkic and Mongolic Studies*, edited by Bayarma Khabtagaeva, 39–89. Leiden, Boston: Brill.

Gu Shunfang 古順芳 and Lü Xiaojing 呂曉晶. 2022. "Bei Wei Pingcheng muzang chutu shiguo qiantan" 北魏平城墓葬出土石槨淺探, *Yungang yanjiu* 2: 57–74.

Guo, Qinglin, Richard A. Staff, Chun Lu, Cheng Liu, Michael Dee, Ying Chen, A Mark Pollard, Jessica Rawson, Bomin Su, and Ruiliang Liu. 2018. "A New Approach to the Chronology of Caves 268/272/275 in the Dunhuang Mogao Grottoes: Combining Radiocarbon Dates and Archaeological Information within a Bayesian Statistical Framework," *Radiocarbon* 60.2: 667–679. DOI:10.1017/RDC.2018.4

Guo Wu 郭物. 2007. "Di'erqun qingtong (tie) fu yanjiu" 第二群青銅（鐵）鍑研究, *Kaogu xuebao* 1: 61–96.

Guo, Zhiyong, Shiqi Cai, Zhanyun Zhu, Yaling Qin, Xiuya Yao, Jia Wang, Wenxiao Jin, Meifeng Shi, Lanfang Li, Junchang Yang, and Liu Liu. 2023. "Multi-Analytical Investigation into the Material Techniques of Paintings on Northern Wei Dynasty (398–494 CE) Coffin Planks Excavated from Shanxi, China," *Humanities & Social Sciences Communications* 10:682. Open access: https://doi.org/10.1057/ s41599-023-02166-z, accessed June 13, 2024.

Guyuan xian wenwu gongzuo zhan 固原縣文物工作站. 1984. "Ningxia Guyuan Bei Wei mu qingli jianbao" 寧夏固原北魏墓清理簡報, *Wenwu* 6: 46–56.

Han Guohe 韓國河. 1999. "Wei Jin shiqi sangzang lizhi de chengchuan yu chuangxin" 魏晉時期喪葬禮制的承傳與創新, *Wen shi zhe* 1: 31–36.

Han Huarui 韓化蕊, Han Shuya 韓書亞, Jing Yongjie 靜永杰, Wang Xiaokun 王曉琨 and Li Yanxiang 李延祥. 2019. "THM-Py-GC/MS fenxi Neimenggu Yihe naoer chutu zhaoming ranliao" THM-Py-GC/MS 分析内蒙古伊和淖爾出土照明燃料, *Guangpuxue yu guangpu fenxi* 12: 3868–3872.

Han Lisen 韓立森, Zhu Yanshi 朱岩石, Hu Chunhua 胡春華, Okamura Hidenori 岡村秀典, Mamoru Hirokawa 広川 守 and Mukai Yusuke 向井佑介. 2013. "Hebei sheng Dingzhou Bei Wei shihan chutu yiwu zai yanjiu" 河北省定州北魏石函出土遺物再研究. *Kaoguxue jikan* 19: 277–299.

Han Shengcun 韓生存, Cao Chenmin 曹臣民 and Hu Ping 胡平. 1996. "Datong chengnan Jinshu meichang Bei Wei muqun" 大同城南金屬鎂廠北魏墓群, *Beichao yanjiu* 1: 60–70.

Hao Junjun 郝軍軍. 2022. "Bei Wei 'Yuchi Dingzhou mu' suojian Jijiupian kezi kao" 北魏"尉遲定州墓"所見《急就篇》刻字考. *Beifang wenwu* 2022.4: 90–92.

Harada Yoshito 原田淑人. 1967. *Kan rikuchō fukusoku* 漢六朝の服飾. Tokyo: Tōyō Bunko.

Hebei sheng wenhuaju wenwu gongzuodui 河北省文化局文物工作隊. 1966. "Hebei Dingxian chutu Bei Wei shihan" 河北定縣出土北魏石函, *Kaogu* 5: 252–259.

Hebei sheng wenwu yanjiusuo 河北省文物研究所, Lincheng xian wenwu baoguansuo 臨城縣文物保管所. 2001. "Lincheng xian Nanmeng cun Tang mu fajue baogao" 臨城縣南孟村唐墓發掘報告, in *Hebei sheng kaogu wenji* 河北省考古文集, vol. 2, edited by Hebei sheng wenwu yanjiusuo 河北省文物研究所, 244–255. Beijing: Yanshan chubanshe.

Heller, Amy. 2016. "Obervations on Painted Coffin Panels of the Tibetan Empire," *Zentral-Asiatische Studien* 45: 147–202.

Henansheng wenwu zanjiusuo 河南省文物研究所. 1993. *Mixian Dahuting Han mu* 密縣打虎亭漢墓. Beijing: Wenwu chubanshe, 1993.

Hinsch, Bret. 2018. *Women in Early Medieval China*. Lanham: Rowman & Littlefield.

Höllmann, Thomas O., Shing Müller and Sonja Filip. 2016. "Steppenkrieger am Gelben Fluss. Nordchina unter fremder Herrschaft (4. bis 6. Jh.)," *Antike Welt* 3: 70–75.

Holcombe, Charles. 2013. "The Xianbei in Chinese History," *Early Medieval China* 19: 1–38.

——. 2019. "The Sixteen Kingdoms," in Dien and Knapp 2019, 119–144.

Holmgren, Jennifer. 1979. "Women's Biographies in the Wei-shu," PhD diss., Canberra: Australian National University.

——. 1982. *Annals of Tai: Early T'o-pa History according to the First Chapter of the Wei-shu.* Canberra: Australian National University Press.

——. 1991. "Imperial Marriage in the Native Chinese and Non-Han State, Han to Ming," in *Marriage and Inequality in Chinese Society*, edited by Rubie S. Watson and Patricia Buckley Ebrey, 58–96. Berkeley: University of California Press.

Hou Liangliang 侯亮亮 and Gu Shunfang 古順芳. 2018a. "Datong diqu Bei Wei jumin shengye jingji de kaoguxue guancha" 大同地區北魏居民生業經濟的考古學觀察, *Zhengzhou daxue xuebao (zhexue shehui kexueban)* 6: 115–118.

—— and ——. 2018b. "Datong diqu Bei Wei shiqi jumin shiwu jiegou de zhuanbian" 大同地區北魏時期居民食物結構的轉變, *Bianjiang kaogu yanjiu* 23: 297–313.

——, ——, Su Junji 蘇俊吉, Xiao Xiaoming 蕭曉鳴, Lü Xiaojing 呂曉晶, Zheng Hui 鄭惠 and Guo Yi 郭怡. 2019. "Datong Shuibosi Bei Wei muqun ren he dongwu guge de wending tongweisu: Shi xi Bei Wei nüxing de diwei" 大同水泊寺北魏墓群人和動物骨骼的穩定同位素：試析北魏女性的地位. *Bianjiang kaogu yanjiu* 2: 279–295.

Hou Xiaogang 侯曉剛. 2020. "Datong shi Yunboli Huayu erqi bihuamu de niandai" 大同市雲波里華宇二期壁畫墓的年代, *Wenwu shijie* 2020.1: 12–15.

Hou Xiaogang 侯曉剛 and Chen Xiaochun 陳小春. 2023. "Shanxi Datong Qilicun Bei Wei mu M29 bihua" 山西大同七里村北魏墓 M29 壁畫, *Yungang yanjiu* 2: 79–85.

Hou Xudong 侯旭東. 1998. *Wu, liu shiji beifang minzhong fojiao Xinyang: yi zaoxiangji wei Zhongxin de kaocha* 五、六世紀北方民眾佛教信仰：以造像記為中心的考察. Beijing: Zhongguo shehui kexue chubanshe.

——. 2008. "Bei Wei Shen Hongzhi muzhi kaoshi" 北魏申洪之墓誌考釋, in *1–6 shiji Zhongguo beifang bianjiang, minzu, shehui guojixueshu yantaohui lunwenji* 1–6 世紀中國北方邊疆、民族、社會國際學術研討會論文集, edited by Jilin daxue guji yanjiusuo 吉林大學古籍研究所, 207–223. Beijing: Kexue shubanshe.

Hsing I-t'ien 邢義田. 2000. "Gudai Zhongguo ji Ouya wenxian, tuxiang yu kaogu ziliao Zhong de 'Huren' waimao" 古代中國及歐亞文獻、圖象與考古資料中的'胡人'外貌. *Guoli Taiwan daxue meishu shi yanjiu jikan* 9: 15–100.

Hsu Sheng-I 徐勝一. 2003. "Xiaowendi qiandu Luoyang yu qihou bianhua zhi yanjiu" 孝文帝遷都洛陽與氣候變化之研究, *Shida dili yanjiu baogao* (Geographical Reserach) 38: 1–12. https://www.geo.ntnu.edu.tw/wp-content/uploads/2022/01/381.pdf; accessed August 17, 2017.

Huairen xian wenwu guanlisuo 懷仁縣文物管理所. 2010. "Shanxi Huairen Bei Wei Danyangwang mu ji huawen zhuan" 山西懷仁北魏丹陽王墓及花紋磚, *Wenwu* 5: 19–26.

Huangfu Jiang 皇甫江. 2007. *Zhongguo dao jian* 中國刀劍. Jinan: Mingtian chubanshe.

Hunan sheng bowuguan 湖南省博物館. 1959. "Changsha Liang Jin Nanchao Sui mu fajue baogao" 長沙兩晉南朝隋墓發掘報告, *Kaogu* 3: 75–105.

Huo Wei 霍巍. 2007. "Qinghai chutu Tubo mu guanban hua renwu fushi de chubu yanjiu" 青海出土吐蕃木棺板畫人物服飾的初步研究, *Yishushi yanjiu* 9: 257–276.

——. 2015. "Liuchao lingmu zhuangshi zhong ruishou de shanbian yu 'Jin zhi' de xingcheng" 六朝陵墓裝飾中瑞獸的嬗變與'晉制'的形成, *Kaogu* 2: 103–113.

Ikeuchi Hiroshi 池内宏 and Umehara Sueji 梅原末治. 1940. *Tsūkō* 通溝. Vol. 2 *Manshūkoku Tonhoa-shō Chian-ken Kōkuri hekigafun* 滿洲國通化省輯安縣高句麗壁畫墳 (T'ung-kou, Vol. 2 Kao-kou-lian Tombs with Wall Paintings in Chi-an District, T'ung-hua Province, Manchoukuo). Tōkyō and Hsin-ching: Nichiman Bunka Kyōkai.

Jenner. W. J. F. 1981. *Memories of Loyang: Yang Hsüan-chih and the Lost Capital (493–534)*. Oxford: Clarendon Press.

Jiang Nan 江楠. 2012. "Jin buyao shipin de faxian yu yanjiu" 金步摇飾品的發現與研究, *Caoyuan wenwu* 2: 74–83.

Jilin sheng wenwu kaogu yanjiusuo 吉林省文物考古研究所 and Ji'an shi bowuguan 集安市博物館. 2004. *Ji'an Gaogouli wangling: 1990–2003 nian Ji'an Gaogouli wangling diaocha baogao* 集安高句麗王陵：1990–2003 年集安高句麗王陵調查報告. Beijing: Wenwu chubanshe.

Jin shu 晉書. Compiled by Fang Xuanling 房玄齡 (579–648) et al. Beijing: Zhonghua shuju, 1974.

Jing Minghan 經明漢 and Liu Wenjin 劉文金. 2010. "Chuantong jiaju wenhua wenxian zhong 'humen' yu 'kunmen' zhi zheng wu bianxi" 傳統家具文化文獻中‘壼門’與‘壼門’正誤之辨析, *Jiaju yu shinei zhuangshi* 7: 54–55.

Jinno Megumi 神野恵. 2021. "Kodai Higashi Ajia no tōkaki" 古代東アジアの灯火器, in *Kodai no tomoshibi—senshi jidai kara kinsei ni itaru tōmyōgu ni kansuru kenkyū* 古代の灯火——先史時代から近世にいたる灯明具に関する研究, edited by Fukasawa Yoshiki 深澤芳樹, 41–64. Nara: Nara bunkazai kenkyūsho. http://doi.org/10.24484/sitereports.97121

Juliano, Annette L. 1980. *Teng-Hsien: An Important Six Dynasties Tomb*. Ascona: Artibus Asiae.

—— and Albert E. Dien 2002, "16a–d. Lacquered Coffin" in Juliano and Lerner 2002, 77–81.

—— and Judith A. Lerner, eds. 2002. *Monks and Merchants: Silk Road Treasures from Northwest China*. New York: The Asia Society.

Kang Le 康樂. 1995. *Cong xijiao dao nanjiao: Guojia jidian yu Bei Wei zhengzhi* 從西郊到南郊：國家祭典與北魏政治. Taibei: Daohe chubanshe.

Kaufmann, Walter. 1981. *Musikgeschichte in Bildern*, vol. II: *Musik des Altertums*, Lieferung 8: *Altindien*. Leipzig: VEB Deutscher Verlag für Musik.

Kenoyer, Jonathan Mark, Asa Cameron, Dashzeveg Bukhchuluun, Chunag Amartuvshin, Batdalai Byambatseren, William Honeychurch, Laure Dussubieux, and Randall Law. 2022. "Carnelian Beads in Mongolia: New Perspectives on Technology and Trade," *Archaeological and Anthropological Sciences* 14:6. https://doi.org/10.1007/s12520-021-01456-4

Kieschnick, John. 2003. *The Impact of Buddhism on Chinese Material Culture*. Princeton and Oxford: Princeton University Press.

Kieser, Annette. 2002. *Landadel – Emigranten – Emporkömmlinge. Familienfriedhöfe des 3.–6. Jahrhunderts n. Chr. in Südchina*. Wiesbaden: Harrassowitz.

——. 2018. "Six Dynasties (220–589) Lacquer Ware—a Survey," in *Production, Distribution, and Appreciation: New Aspects of East Asian Lacquer Ware*, edited by Patricia Frick and Annette Kieser, 64–84. Leiden: Brill.

——. 2019. "Southern Material Culture," in Dien and Knapp 2019, 418–442.

Kim Wŏn-yong 金元龍. 1983. *Han'guk pyŏkhwa kobun* 韓國壁畫古墳. Sŏul: Ilchisa.

Kleemann, Jörg. 2010. "Frühmittelalterliche Bestattungen als Projektionen kontextueller Identitäten," in Pohl and Mehofer 2010, 79–92.

Knapp, Keith Nathaniel. 2010. "Borrowing Legitimacy from the Dead: The Confucianization of Ancestral Worship." In *Early Chinese Religion*. Part Two: *The Period of Division (220–589)*, Vol. 1, edited by John Lagerwey and Lü Pengzhi, 143–192. Leiden: Brill.

——. 2019. "The Use and Understanding of Domestic Animals in Early Medieval Northern China," *Early Medieval China*, 25: 85–99. DOI: 10.1080/15299104.2019.1660090

Knechtges, David R. 1997. "Gradually Entering the Realm of Delight: Food and Drink in Early Medieval China," *Journal of the American Oriental Society* 117.2: 229–239.

Kobayashi Hitoshi 小林仁. 2012. "Bei Qi qianyouqi de dingwei he yiyi" 北齊鉛釉器的定位和意義. *Gugong bowuyuan yuankan* 5: 104–111.

Kong Sŏk-ku 孔錫龜 (Kong Xigui). 1998. "Guanyu Anyue 3 hao mu muzhu guanmao" 關於安岳 3 號墓墓主冠帽, transl. Zheng Jingri 鄭京日 and Zheng Chunying 鄭春穎, *Dongbeiya yanjiu lun-*

cong 東北亞研究論叢, edited by Changchun shida 1: 195–221 (originally published in *Koguro̜ Parhae yo̜n'gu* 고구려발해연구 [高句麗渤海研究] 5 (1998): 157–193).

Kradin, Nikolai N. 2010. "Structure of Society and Power in the Ancient Inner Asian Nomadic Empires: Xiongnu and Xianbei," in *Representing Power in Ancient Inner Asia: Legitimacy, Transmission and the Sacred*, edited by Isabelle Charleux, Grégory Delaplace, Roberte Hamayon, and Scott Pearce, 307–341. Bellingham, WA: Center for East Asian Studies, Western Washington University.

Kubozoe Yoshifumi 窪添慶文. 2015. *Wei Jin Nanbeichao guanliaozhi yanjiu* 魏晉南北朝官僚制研究. Translated into Chinese by Zhao Lixin 趙立新, Tu Zongcheng 涂宗呈, Hu Yunwei 胡雲薇, Wei Yuxin 魏郁欣, Lu Yating 呂雅婷, He Yuanhu 何源湖 and Huang Huqun 黃胡群. Taibei: Guoli Taiwan daxue chuban zhongxin. (From the original Kubozoe Yoshifumi, Gi Shin Nanbokuchō kanryōsei kenkyū. Tōkyō: Kyūko Shoin, 2003).

Kuroda Akira 黒田彰. 2022. "Kogen shitsukan no kōshidenzu nit suite (ue)" 固原漆棺の孝子傳について(上), *Joshi dai kokubun* 171: 31–59.

——. 2023. "Kogen shitsukan no kōshidenzu nit suite (naka)" 固原漆棺の孝子傳について(中), *Joshi dai kokubun* 172: 20–43. http://hdl.handle.net/11173/3541; accessed December 11, 2023

de la Vaissière, Étienne. 2005. *Sogdian Traders: A History*. Translated into English by James Ward. Leiden: Brill.

——. 2011. "Two Sogdian(?) Tombs from Gansu: A Preliminary Note," *Journal of Inner Asian Art and Archaeology* 6: 137–148.

—— and Éric Trombert. 2004. "Des Chinois et des Hu: Migrations et intégration des Iraniens orientaux en milieu chinois durant le haut Moyen Âge," *Annales. Histoire, Sciences Sociales* 5/6: 931–969.

Laufer, Bertold. 1919. *Sino-Iranica: Chinese contributions to the history of civilization in ancient Iran, with special reference to the history of cultivated plants and products*. Fild Museum of Natural History Publication 201. Chicago: Field Museum of Natural History.

Laursen, Sarah. 2011. "Leaves that Sway: Gold Xianbei Cap Ornaments from Northeast China." Ph.D. diss., University of Pennsylvania.

Lawergren, Bo. 2019. "Music," in Dien and Knapp 2019, 698–720.

Lee, James. 1978. "Migration and Expansion in Chinese History," in *Human Migration. Patterns and Policies*, edited by William H. McNeill and Ruth S. Adams, 20–47. Bloomington: Indiana University Press.

Lee, Soyoung. 2013. "Vessels for the Afterlife: Silla Pottery, ca. 400–800," in *Silla: Korea's Golden Kingdom*, edited by Soyoung Lee and Denise Patry Leidy, 69–85. New York: Metropolitan Museum of Art.

Leidy, Denise Patry. 2004a. "Acrobats," in Watt 2004, 144–145, Cat. No. 53.

——. 2004b. "Stand," in Watt 2004, 163–164, Cat. No. 72.

Lewis, Mark Edward. 2009. *China between Empires: The Northern and Southern Dynasties*. Cambridge, MA: Harvard University Press.

Li Guohua 李國華. 2018. "Qinghai chutu Xianbei dongwu paishi yanjiu" 青海出土鮮卑牌飾研究. *Beifang wenwu* 4: 57–61.

Li Jiaxin 李佳欣. 2021. "Shanxi Datong Yufu mudi Bei Wei shiqi rengu yanjiu" 山西大同御府墓地北魏時期人骨研究. MA thesis; Jilin University.

Li Meitian 李梅田. 2016. "Xiquge yu wenkangwu: Dengxian Nanchao huaxiang zhuanmu yuewutu xinshi" 西曲歌與文康舞: 鄧縣南朝畫像磚墓樂舞圖新釋. *Gugong bowuyuan yuankan* 4: 82–94.

—— and Zhang Zhizhong 張志忠. 2022. "Bei Wei Xing Hejiang shiguo bihua yanjiu" 北魏邢合姜石槨壁畫研究. *Meishu yanjiu* 2: 28–32.

Li Ming 李明. 2019. "Yunnan Zhaotong Houhaizi Dong Jin Huo Chengsi muzang yishu yanjiu" 雲南昭通後海子東晉霍承嗣墓葬藝術研究. *Sichuan wenwu* 4: 61–69.

Li Pengcheng 李鵬程. 2018. "Shanxi sheng Datong shi Suibosi lianzufang mudi rengu yanjiu" 山西省大同市水泊寺廉租房墓地人骨研究. MA thesis; Liaoing University.

Li Pengzhen 李鵬珍. 2021. "Shanxi Datong Dongxin guangchang Bei Wei mudi rengu yanjiu" 山西大同東信廣場北魏墓地人骨研究. PhD diss., Jilin University.

Li Ping 李憑. 2011. *Bei Wei Pingcheng shiqi (xiudingben)* 北魏平城時期 (修訂本). Shanghai: Shanghai guji chubanshe.

Li Qiliang 李啓良 and Xu Xinyin 徐信印. 1986. "Shaanxi Ankang Changling Nanchao mu qingli jianbao" 陝西安康長嶺南朝墓清理簡報. *Kaogu yu wenwu* 3: 16–21.

Li Shuyun 李樹雲. 2008. "Datong Bei Wei mu chutu de ciqi" 大同北魏墓出土的瓷器, in Dong Ruishan 2008, 328–334.

Li Weimin 李偉敏. 2012. *Beijing kaogu zhi: Fangshan juan* 北京考古志: 房山卷. Shanghai: Shanghai guji chubanshe.

Li Ye 李曄. 2018. "Shanxi Beichao pusa touguan de leixing yanjiu" 山西北朝菩薩頭冠的類型研究, *Xibei meishu* 4: 95–100.

Li Yuqun 李裕群. 2022. "Fodian de xiangzheng: Shanxi Datong Tongjiawan Bei Wei fojiao bihua shiguo" 佛殿的象徵: 山西大同全家灣北魏佛教壁畫石槨, *Wenwu* 1: 52–61.

Liang shu 梁書. Compiled by Yao Silian 姚思廉 (557–637). Beijing: Zhonghua shuju, 1973.

Liaoning sheng bowuguan 遼寧省博物館. 1984. "Liaoning Benxi Jin mu" 遼寧本溪晉墓. *Kaogu* 8: 715–720.

——. 2015. *Bei Yan Feng Sufu mu* 北燕馮素弗墓. Beijing: Wenwu chubanshe.

——. Chaoyang diqu bowuguan wenwudui 朝陽地區博物館文物隊 and Chaoyang xian wenhuaguan 朝陽縣文化館. 1984. "Chaoyang Yuantaizi Dong Jin bihuamu" 朝陽袁台子東晉壁畫墓. *Wenwu* 6: 29–45.

Liaoning sheng wenwu kaogu yanjiusuo 遼寧省文物考古研究所. 2002. *San Yan wenwu jingcui* 三燕文物精粹. Shanyang: Liaoning renmin chubanshe.

—— and Chaoyang shi bowuguan 朝陽市博物館. 1997. "Chaoyang Shiertaixiang zhuanchang 88M1 fajuejianbao" 朝陽十二台鄉磚廠 88M1 發掘簡報. *Wenwu* 11: 19–32.

——, Chaoyang shi bowuguan 朝陽市博物館, and Beipiao shi wenwu guanlisuo 北票市文物管理所. 2004. "Liaoning Beipiao Lamadong mudi 1998 nian fajue baogao" 遼寧北票喇嘛洞墓地 1998 年發掘報告. *Kaogu xuebao* 2: 209–242.

Lin Hao 林浩. 2020. "Datong diqu Bei Wei muzang chutu de hupo qiwu yanjiu" 大同地區北魏墓葬出土的琥珀器物研究. *Wenwu tiandi* 11: 89–91.

Lin Sheng-chih 林聖智. 2008. "Muzang, zongjiao yu quyu zuofang" 墓葬、宗教與區域作坊, *Meishushi yanjiu* 24: 1–42.

——. 2011. "Zhongguo zhonggu shiqi muzang Zhong de tianjie biaoxiang: Dongya de bijiao shiye" 中國中古時期墓葬中的天界表象: 東亞的比較視野, in Wu and Zheng 2011, 131–162.

——. 2012. "Bei Wei Shaling bihuamu yanjiu" 北魏沙嶺壁畫墓研究, *Zhongyang yanjiuyuan lishi yuyan yanjiusuo jikan* 83.1: 1–95.

——. 2019. "Fansi Bei Wei de zongjiao yu muzang tuxiang" 反思北魏的宗教與墓葬圖像, in Müller, Höllmann and Filip 2019, 81–111.

Lin Zeyang 林澤洋. 2021. "Guanzhong Shiliuguo taoyong yanjiu" 關中十六國陶俑研究, *Zhongguo guojia bowuguan guankan* 5: 42–55.

Lingley, Kate A. 2014. "Silk Road Dress in a Chinese Tomb: Xu Xianxiu and Sixth-Century Cosmopolitanism," *The Silk Road*, 12: 1–12.

Liu Daiyun 劉呆運, Xu Yongchu 徐雍初 and Su Qingyuan 蘇慶元. 2010. "Shaanxi Xianyang Weicheng Dizhang muzang ji taoyao 2009 nian fajue" 陝西咸陽渭城底張墓葬及陶窯 2009 年發掘, in *2009 Zhongguo zhongda kaogu faxian* 2009 中國重大考古發現, edited by Guojia wenwuju 國家文物局, 122–127. Beijing: Wenwu chubanshe.

Liu Junxi 劉俊喜. 2008. *Datong Yanbei shiyuan Bei Wei muqun* 大同雁北師院北魏墓群. Beijing: Wenwu chubanshe.

—— and Gao Feng 高峰. 2004. "Datong Zhijiabao Bei Wei mu guanbanhua" 大同智家堡北魏墓棺板畫, *Wenwu* 12: 35–47.

Liu Meiyun 劉美雲 and Wei Haiqing 魏海清. 2014. "Shoulie xisu dui Bei Wei qianqi zhengquan de yingxiang" 狩獵習俗對北魏前期政權的影響, in *Beichao shi: Zhongguo Wei Jin Nanbeichao shi guoji xueshu yantaohui lunwenji* 北朝史：中國魏晉南北朝史國際學術研討會論文集, edited by Yin Xian 殷憲, 423–427. Beijing: Shangwu yinshuguan.

Liu Rui'e 劉瑞娥 and Zhu Jialong 朱家龍. 1999. "Jimingyi Bei Wei bihuamu qingli suixiang" 雞鳴驛北魏壁畫墓清理隨想, *Huhehaote wenwu* 9: 49–51.

Liu Ruimin 劉瑞民 and Liu Junxi 劉俊喜. 2006. "Datong Shaling Bei Wei bihuamu chutu qipi wenzi kao" 大同沙嶺北魏壁畫墓出土漆皮文字考, *Wenwu* 10: 78–81.

Liu Shan 劉珊, Gong Yue 弓月, Zhang Guowen 張國文, Wang Xin 王欣, Chen Tao 陳濤 and Hou Liangliang 侯亮亮. 2022. "Sichou zhi lu dongduan daduhui liangchang Zhong de guwu: Datong Caochangcheng Bei Wei taiguan liangchu yizhi tanhua su de C, N wending tongweisu fenxi" 絲綢之路東端大都會糧倉中的穀物：大同操場城北魏太官糧儲遺址炭化粟的 C, N 穩定同位素分析, *Disiji yanjiu* 1: 144–157. https://kns.cnki.net/kcms/detail/11.2708.p.20211202.1007.046.html.

Liu Shuang 劉驥. 2017. "Liang Han shiqi Neimenggu zhongnanbu xunsheng xianxiang shixi" 兩漢時期內蒙古中南部殉牲現象試析. *Caoyuan wenwu* 1: 76–84.

Liu Shufen. 2022. "Ethnicity and the Suppression of Buddhism in Fifth-Century North China: The Background and Significance of the Gaiwu Rebellion." *Asia Major*, third series, 15.1: 1–21.

Liu, Yan, Jianjun Yu, Junchang Yang, and Wenying Li. 2021. "Long-Distance Relationship with the Mediterranean World? Gold Beech-Nut Pendants Found in the Early Iron Age China and the Eurasian Steppe," *Mediterranean Archaeology and Archaeometry* 21.2: 259–280.

Liu Yuyang 劉羽陽 and Wang Hui 王輝. 2017. "Xianqin shiqi xibei youmu diqu dongwu maizang xisu—cong maizang tou ti de xianxiang tanqi" 先秦時期西北游牧地區動物埋葬習俗—從埋葬頭蹄的現象談起. *Kaogu yu wenwu* 1: 61–69.

Liu Zhaomin 劉昭民. 1994. *Zhongguo lishi shang qihou zhi bianqian* 中國歷史上氣候之變遷. Taipei: Taiwan shangwu yinshuguan.

Long Chengsong 龍成松. 2016. "Zhonggu huxiang jiazu yanjiu—yi zuyuan, diyu, wenhua wei zhongxin" 中古胡姓家族研究—以族源、地域、文化為中心. PhD diss., Wuhan: Wuhan University.

Lorge, Peter A. 2011. *Chinese Martial Arts: From Antiquity to the Twenty-First Century*. Cambridge: Cambridge University Press.

Lu Bin 逯斌 and Wang Aiguo 王愛國. 2016. "Shanxi Bei Wei youtao yanjiu" 山西北魏釉陶研究, *Wenwu shijie* 1: 14–19.

Lu Sixian 陸思賢 and Chen Tangdong 陳棠棟. 1984. "Damao qi chutu de gudai beifang minzu jinshijian" 達茂旗出土的古代北方民族金飾件, *Wenwu* 1: 81–83, 29.

Lu Xiqi 魯西奇. 2010. "Gansu Lingtai Shaanxi Changwu suo chutu Bei Wei diquan kaoshi" 甘肅靈臺、陝西長武所出土北魏地券考釋. *Zhongguo jingjishi yanjiu* 4: 10–17.

Lucy, Sam. 2005. "Ethnic and Cultural Identities," in *The Archaeology of Identity: Approaches to Gender, Age, Status, Ethnicity and Religion*, edited by Margarita Díaz-Andreu, Sam Lucy, Staša Babić and David N. Edwards, 86–109. London: Routledge.

Lü Pengzhen 呂朋珍. 2013. "Bei Wei bihuamu yanjiu" 北魏壁畫墓研究. MA thesis. Hohhot: Neimenggu shifan daxue.

Lü Zongli 呂宗力. 2015. *Zhongguo lidai guanzhi da cidian* 中國歷代官制大辭典 (修訂版) (revised edition). Beijing: Shangwu yinshuguan.

Lugli, Federico, Giulia Di Rocco, Antonino Vazzana, Filippo Genovese, Diego Pinetti, Elisabetta Cilli, Maria Cristina Carile, Sara Silvestrini, Gaia Gabanini, Simona Arrighi, Laura Buti, Eugenio Bortolini, Anna Cipriani, Carla Figus, Giulia Marciani, Gregorio Oxilia, Matteo Romandini, Rita Sorrentino, Marco Sola and Stefano Benazzi. 2019. "Enamel Peptides Reveal the Sex of the Late

Antique 'Lovers of Modena'," *Scientific Reports* 9, 13130. https://doi.org/10.1038/s41598-019-49562-7

Luo Feng 羅豐. 2018. "Beifangxi qingtong wenhua mu de xunsheng xisu" 北方系青銅文化墓的殉牲習俗, *Kaogu xuebao* 2: 183–200.

——. 2019. "Guyuan Bei Wei qiguanhua niandai de zai queding" 固原北魏漆棺畫年代的再確定, in Müller, Höllmann and Filip 2019, 133–149.

——. 2020. "Yige zhihui de yinmou—Bei Wei qiguanhua Zhong de 'ertao sha sanshi' gushi" 一個智慧的陰謀—北魏漆棺畫中的'二桃殺三士'故事. *Gudai meishushi* 5: 31–51.

Luo Xin 羅新. 2010. "Shen Hongzhi muzhi bushi" 申洪之墓誌補釋, in *Chutu wenxian yanjiu* 出土文獻研究, vol. 9, edited by Zhongguo wenhua yichan yanjiuyuan 中國文化遺產研究院, 332–344. Beijing: Zhonghua shuju.

——. 2022. *Manchang de yusheng: yige Bei Wei gongnü he ta de shidai* 漫長的餘生：一個北魏宮女和她的時代. Beijing: Beijing ribao chubanshe.

Luoyang qielan ji 洛陽伽藍記. *Luoyag qielan ji jiaozhu* 洛陽伽藍記校注. By Yang Xuanzhi 楊衒之 (fl. 547). Annotated by Fan Xiangyong 范祥雍. Shanghai: Shanghai guji chubanshe, 1978.

Luoyang shi wenwu gongzuodui 洛陽市文物工作隊. 2005. "Xi Jin Su Huazhi mu" 西晉蘇華芝墓, *Wenwu* 1: 27–28.

Ma Boyao 馬伯垚. 2021. "Muzang zhong de shiku: Xing Hejiang shitang bihua luelun" 墓葬中的石窟：邢合姜石堂壁畫略論, *Gugong bowuyuan yuankan* 11: 81–90.

Ma Changshou 馬長壽. 1985. *Beiming suo jian Qian Qin zhi Sui chu de Guanzhong buzu* 碑銘所見前秦至隋初的關中部族. Beijing: Zhonghua shuju.

Ma Yuji 馬玉基. 1983. "Datong shi Xiaozhancun Huagetai Bei Wei mu qingli jianbao" 大同市小站村花圪台北魏墓清理簡報, *Wenwu* 8: 1–4.

Mackenzie, Colin. 2002. "19a. Stove (zao) with Steamer (zeng)," in Juliano and Lerner 2002, 85.

Martin, Hélène. 2011. "The Animal in the Xiongnu Funeral Universe: Companion of the Living, Escort of the Dead," in Brosseder and Miller 2011, 229–242.

Masana Maeda 前田正名. 1994. *Pingcheng lishidilixue yanjiu* 平城歷史地理學研究. Transl. into Chinese by Li Ping 李憑, Sun Yao 孫耀 and Sun Lei 孫蕾. Beijing: Shumu wenxian chubanshe.

Matsushita Ken'ichi 松下憲一. 2007. *Hokugi kozoku taiseiron* 北魏胡族体制論. Sapporo: Hokkaido daigakuin bungau kenkyuka kenkyu sosyo.

McBride, Richard D., II. 2011. "When did the Rulers of Silla Become Kings," *Han'guk kodaesa tam'gu* 8: 215–255.

——. 2020. "Making and Remaking Silla Origins," *Journal of American Oriental Society* 140.3: 531–548.

Meister, Michael W. 1970. "The Pearl Roundel in Chinese Textile Design," *Ars Orientalis* 8: 255–267.

Miller, Bryan K. 2015. "The Southern Xiongnu in Northern China: Navigating and Negotiating the Middle Ground," in Bemmann and Schmauder 2015, 127–198.

Monta Seiichi 門田誠一. 2000. "Sōshoku kofun no gadai kara mita chiiki kan kōshō no ichisokumen: Kumamoto Kenhirora kofun no sekkan ni arawasareta oyako tachi" 裝飾古墳の画題からみた地域間交渉の一側面—熊本県広浦古墳の石棺に表された親子大刀, *Ōryō shigaku* 26: 245–264.

Müller, Sebastian. 2019. "Monumental Burial Mounds in Kyŏngju: Remarks on their Socio-political Meaning," *International Journal of Korean History* 24.2: 133–169.

Müller, Shing. 2000. "Die Gräber der Nördlichen Wei-Dynastie (386 - 534)." PhD diss., University of Munich.

——. 2003 [2006]. "Chin-straps of the Early Northern Wei: New Perspectives on the Trans-Asiatic Diffusion of Funerary Practices," *Journal of East Asian Archaeology* 5, 1–4: 27–71.

——. 2009. "Horses of the Xianbei, AD 300–600: A brief Survey," in *Pferde in Asien: Geschichte, Handel und Kultur / Horses in Asia: History, Trade and Culture*, edited by Bert G. Fragner,

Ralph Kauz, Roderich Ptak and Angela Schottenhammer, 181–193. Wien: Verlag der Österreichischen Akademie der Wissenschaften.

——. 2013. "From Dai to Northern Wei: The Transformation of the Tuoba Xianbei Society," in
Metamorphoses. Proceedings of the Seventh International Conference on Oriental Studies (*Tor-
chinov Readings*) [Пахомов, Сергей Владимирович (Автор), Метаморфозы: седьмая
Международная востоковедная конференция (Торчиновские чтения), 22–25 июня 2011 г.],
edited by Sergey V. Pakhomov. Part II, 83–92. St. Petersburg: Saint-Petersburg State University.

——. 2017. "Zelte der Tuoba-Xianbei im 5. Jh.: Eine vorläufige Untersuchung," in *Über den Alltag
hinaus. Festschrift für Thomas O. Höllmann zum 65. Geburtstag*, edited by Shing Müller and
Armin Selbitschka, 177–200. Wiesbaden: Harrassowitz.

——. 2019a. "Funerary Beds and Houses of the Northern Dynasties," in Müller, Höllmann and Filip
2019, 383–474.

——. 2019b. "A Preliminary Study of the Lacquerware of the Northern Dynasties, with a Special
Focus on the Pingcheng Period (398–493)," *Early Medieval China* 25: 42–63.

——. 2019c. "Northern Material Culture," in Dien and Knapp 2019, 384–417.

——, Thomas O. Höllmann and Sonja Filip, eds. 2019. *Early Medieval North China: Archaeological
and Textual Evidence*. Asiatische Forschungen 159. Wiesbaden: Harrassowitz.

Mukai Yusuke 向井佑介. 2010. "Hokugi Heijo jidai ni okeru bosei no hen'you" 北魏平城時代にお
ける墓制の變容, *Tōhō gakuhō* 85: 133–177.

Muzio, Ciro Lo. 2019. "Persian 'Snap': Iranian Dancers in Gandhāra," in *The Music Road: Coher-
ence and Diversity in Music from the Mediterranean to India*, edited by Reinhard Strohm, 71–86.
Oxford: Oxford University Press.

Nan Qi shu 南齊書. Compiled by Xiao Zixian 蕭子顯 (498–537). Beijing: Zhonghua shuju, 1972.

Nan shi 南史. Compiled by Li Yanshou 李延壽 (Tang). Beijing: Zhonghua shuju, 1975.

Nanjing bowuyuan 南京博物院. 2018. *Langya wang: Cong Dong Jin dao Bei Wei* 瑯琊王：從東晉
到北魏. Nanjing: Yilin chubanshe.

Nanyang shi wenwu yanjiusuo 南陽市文物研究所 and Xichuan xian bowuguan 淅川縣博物館.
1996. "Henan sheng Xichuan xian Xiling Sui huaxiangzhuan mu" 河南省淅川縣西嶺隋畫像磚
墓, *Zhongyuan kaogu* 3: 26–28, 46.

Neimenggu bowuyuan 內蒙古博物院, Neimenggu zizhiqu wenwu kaogu yanjiusuo 內蒙古自治區文
物考古研究所. ed. 2015. *Zhongguo beifang ji Menggu, Beijiaer, Xiboliya diqu gudai wenhua
(zhong)* 中國北方及蒙古、貝加爾、西伯利亞地區古代文化 (中). Beijing: Kexue chubanshe.

Neimenggu zizhiqu wenwu kaogu yanjiusuo 內蒙古自治區文物考古研究所, Xilin Guole meng
wenwu baohu guanlizhan 錫林郭勒盟文物保護管理站, Zhengxiang baiqi wenwu guanlisuo 正
鑲白旗文物管理所. 2016. "Zhengxiang baiqi Yihe naoer muqun M2 fajue jianbao" 正鑲白旗伊
和淖爾墓群 M2 發掘簡報, *Caoyuan wenwu* 1: 46–51.

Ni Run'an 倪潤安. 2004. "Hebei Lincheng 'Meng Bin mu' wei Bei Wei muzang" 河北臨城'孟賓墓'
為北魏墓葬, *Zhongguo lishi wenwu* 6: 51–58.

——. 2011a. "Bei Wei Pingcheng diqu muzang wenhua laiyuan luelun" 北魏平城地區墓葬文化來
源略論, *Xibu kaogu* 1: 291–309.

——. 2011b. "Bei Wei Pingcheng shidai Pingcheng diqu mzang wenhua de laiyuan" 北魏平城時代
平城地區墓葬文化的來源, *Shoudu shifan daxue xuebao* (*shehui kexue ban*) 6: 26–34.

——. 2012. "Danyang wang bukao" 丹陽王補考, *Kaogu yu wenwu* 1: 62–67.

——. 2013. "Nanbeichao muzang wenhua de zhengtong zhengduo" 南北朝墓葬文化的正統爭奪.
Kaogu 12: 71–83.

——. 2014. "Bei Wei Pingcheng shidai Pingcheng muzang de wenhua zhuanxing" 北魏平城時代平
城墓葬的文化轉型, *Kaogu xuebao* 1: 33–66.

——. 2016. "Guan Long yu Pingcheng zhijian Bei Wei muzang wenhua de hudong" 關隴與平城之
間北魏墓葬文化的互動, *Shixue yuekan* 2: 22–28.

——. 2017. *Guang zhai Zhongyuan: Tuoba zhi Bei Wei de muzang wenhua yu shehui yanjin* 光宅中原：拓跋至北魏的墓葬文化與社會演進. Shanghai: Shanghai guji chubanshe.

——. 2018. "Bei Wei Pingcheng muzang fenqi biaozhun tantao" 北魏平城墓葬分期標準探討, *Beifang minzu kaogu* 5: 86–106.

Ni Yuzhan 倪玉湛, Wang Wenguang 王文廣. 2016. "Baiwu ernian jin fangqi niandai buzheng" 白烏二年金方奇年代補正, *Zhuangshi* 11: 82–84.

Ningxia Guyuan bowuguan 寧夏固原博物館. 1988a. *Guyuan Bei Wei mu qiguanhua* 固原北魏墓漆棺畫. Yinchuan: Ningxia renming chubanshe.

——. 1988b. "Pengyang Xinji Bei Wei mu" 彭陽新集北魏墓, *Wenwu* 9: 26–42.

Nylan, Michael. 2016. "At Table: Reading and Misreading Funerary Images of Banquets in Early China," in *Dining and Death: Interdisciplinary Perspectives on the 'Funerary Banquet' in Ancient Art, Burial and Belief*, edited by Catherine M. Draycott and Maria Stamatopoulou, 627–662. Leuven-Paris-Bristol, CT: Peeters.

Okamura Hidenori 岡村秀典 and Mukai Yusuke 向井佑介. 2007. "Hokugi Hōzan Eikoryō no kenkyū: Tōa kōko gakkai 1939nen shūshūhin wo chūshin to shite" 北魏方山永固陵の研究: 東亞考古學會一九三九年收集品を中心として, *Tōhō gakuhō* 80: 69–150.

Ōnishi Yumiko 大西由美子. 2020. "'Shunko hen' ni tsuite: Shunsetsuwa no hikaku o tōshite" 「舜子変」について: 舜説話の比較を通して, *Ochanomizu joshi daigaku Chūgoku bungaku kaihō* 39: 214–196.

Otani Ikue 大谷育恵. 2012. "Kan–Hokugi-ki ni okeru mimikazari no tenkai to sono kakki – Chūgoku hokuhen o taishō to shita kinzoku-sei sōshingu no kenkyū (1)" 漢－北魏期における耳飾の展開とその画期－中国北辺を対象とした金属製装身具の研究 (1). In *Yamaguchi daigaku kōkogaku ronshū: Nakamura Tomohiro sensei tainin kinen ronbunshū* 山口大学考古学論集: 中村友博先生退任記念論文集, edited by Yamaguchi Daigaku Jinbun Gakubu 山口大学人文学部考古学研究室, 317‒334. Yamaguchi: Nakamura Tomohiro sensei tainin kinen jigyōkai.

——. 2019. "Hokugi–Hokucho heikoki no iseki yori shutsudo shita kinzokusei tōbu kessokugu to keibushoku: Yūrashia tōbu sōgen chitai de no hirogari ni chakumoku shite" 北魏―北朝並行期の遺跡より出土した金属製頭部結束具と頸部飾: ユーラシア東部草原地帯での広がりに着目して, *Kanazawa daigaku kōkogaku kiyō* 40: 123–140.

——. 2021. "Mongoru kuni de aratani kakunin sa reta kinzokusei no tōbu kessokugu to keibushoku o tomonau maisō jirei ni tsuite" モンゴル国で新たに確認された金属製の頭部結束具と頸部飾を伴う埋葬事例について, *Kindaikouko* 79: 1–7. http://doi.org/10.24517/00061892

——. 2022. "Hokugi-ki no shinkei tarekazari-tsuki mimikaza—Muda Tomohiro-shi shozō shiryō to sono ruirei" 北魏期の針形垂飾付き耳飾―六田知弘氏所蔵資料とその類例, *Dazaifu-shi: Kyūshū Kokuritsu Hakubutsukan* (the Bulletin of Kyushu National Museum) 18: 59–66.

Pan Ling 潘玲. 2015. *Zhongguo beifang wanqi fu yanjiu* 中國北方晚期鍑研究. Beijing: Kexue chubanshe.

—— and He Yumeng 何雨萌. 2015. "Zhongguo beifang wanqi fu laiyuan fenxi" 中國北方晚期鍑來源分析, in Neimenggu and Neimenggu 2015, 448–457.

Pearce, Scott. 1991. "Status, Labor, and Law: Special Service Households under the Northern Dynasties," *Harvard Journal of Asiatic Studies* 51.1: 89–138.

——. 2008. "The Way of the Warrior in Early Medieval China, Examined through the 'Northern Yuefu'," *Early Medieval China* 13–14.2: 87–113.

——. 2019. "Northern Wei," in Dien and Knapp 2019, 155–183.

——. 2023. *Northen Wei (386–534): A New Form of Empire in East Asia*. New York, N.Y.: Oxford University Press.

Pearson, Mike Parker. 2001. *The Archaeology of Dearth and Burial*. 2nd Printing. College Station: Texas A&M University Press.

Perrin, Ariane. 2016. "The Image of the Deceased in Koguryŏ Funerary Art (4th–5th Centuries AD): A Comparison between the Ji'an (China) and Pyongyang (Korea) Regions," *Arts Asiatiques* 71: 77–99.

Pingshuo kaogudui 平朔考古隊. 1987. "Shanxi Shuoxian Qin Han mu fajue jianbao" 山西朔縣秦漢墓發掘簡報, *Wenwu* 6:1–52.

Pirazzoli-t'Serstevens, Michèle. 2002. "From the Ear-cup to the Round Cup. Changes in Chinese Drinking Vessels (2nd to 6th century AD)," *Oriental Art* 48.3: 17–27.

——. 2008. "Inner Asia and Han China: Borrowings and Representations," transl. Margaret McIntosh. *In New Frontiers in Global Archaeology: Defining China's Ancient Traditions (Proceedings of the International Symposium Celebrating the Tenth Anniversary of the Arthur M. Sackler Museum of Art and Archaeology at Peking University)*, edited by Thomas Lawton, 1–19. Tokyo: AMS Foundation for the Arts, Sciences and Humanities.

Pohl, Walter. 2010. "Archaeology of Identity: Introduction," in Pohl and Mehofer 2010, 10–23.

—— and Mathias Mehofer. 2010. *Archaeology of Identity – Arhchäologie der Identität*. Forschungen zur Geschichte des Mittelalters, Vol. 17. Wien: Verlag der Österreichischen Akademie der Wissenschaften.

Pulleyblank, Edwin G. 1983. "The Chinese and their Neighbors in Prehistoric and Early Historic Times," in *The Origins of Chinese Civilization*, edited by David N. Keightley, 411–466. Berkeley: University of California Press.

——. 1991. *Lexicon of Reconstructed Pronunciation in Early Middle Chinese, Late Middle Chinese, and Early Mandarin*. Vancouver: University of British Columbia.

Qi Dongfang 齊東方. 2015. "Zhongguo gudai sangzang zhong de Jin zhi" 中國古代喪葬中的晉制. *Kaogu xuebao* 3: 345–366.

Qiao Liping 喬麗萍 and Zhang Zhizhong 張志忠. 2017. "Datong Yunbolu Bei Wei shiguomu xiangguan wenti" 大同雲波路北魏石槨墓相關問題, *Beichao yanjiu* 8: 181–194.

Qimin yaoshu 齊民要術. *Qimin yaoshu jiaoshi* 齊民要術校釋. By Jia Sixie 賈思勰 (fl. 533–544). Comm. by Miao Qiyu 繆啟愉 and Miao Guilong 繆桂龍. Beijing: Nongye chubanshe, 1982.

Qingyang shi bowuguan 慶陽市博物館 and Qingcheng xian bowuguan 慶城縣博物館. 2008. "Gansu Qingcheng Tangdai Youji jiangjun Mu Tai mu" 甘肅慶城唐代游擊將軍穆泰墓, *Wenwu* 3: 32–51.

Rawson, Jessica. 1991. "Central Asian Silver and its Influence on Chinese Ceramics," *Bulletin of the Asia Institute*, new series 5: 139–151.

——. 2010. "Carnelian Beads, Animal Figures and Exotic Vessels: Traces of Contact between the Chinese States and Inner Asia, ca. 1000–650 BC," in Wagner and Wang 2010, 1–42.

Ruansun Zifeng 阮孫子鳳. 2022. "Shanxi Datong Yuchang jiayuan mudi Bei Wei shiqi rengu yanjiu" 山西大同御昌佳園墓地北魏時期人骨研究. MA thesis; Jilin University.

Rudenko, S. I. 1969. *Die Kultur der Hsiung-Nu und die Hügelgräber von Noin Ula*, Transl. by Karl Jettmar. Bonn: Rudolf Habelt Verlag.

Sanguo zhi 三國志. Compiled by Chen Shou 陳壽 (233–297). Beijing: Zhonghua shuju, 1982.

Santai xian wenhua tiyuju 三台縣文化體育局 and Santai xian wenwu guanlisuo 三台縣文物管理所. 2002. "Sichuan Santai Qijiang yamuqun 2000 niandu qingli jianbao" 四川三台郪江崖墓羣 2000 年度清理簡報, *Wenwu* 1: 16–41.

Saotome Masahiro 早乙女雅博. 2012). "Kōkogaku kara mita Shiragi no kokka keisei" 考古学からみた新羅の国家形成, *Metoroporitan shigaku* 8: 59–77.

Satoru Hirose 廣瀨覚. 2017. "Zaoqi Murong Xianbei de muzhi he qinzu guanxi de guancha: yi Beipiao Dabanyingzi mudi weili" 早期慕容鮮卑的墓制和親族關係的觀察——以北票大板營子墓地為例, in *Liaoxi diqu Dong Jin Shiliuguo shiqi ducheng wenhua yanjiu* 遼西地區東晉十六國時期都城文化研究, edited by Liaoning sheng wenwu kaogu yanjiusuo 遼寧省文物考古研究所 and Nara Bunkazai Kenkyūjo 奈良文化財產研究所, 91–106. Shenyang: Liaoning renmin chubanshe.

Schafer, Edward. 1963. *The Golden Peaches of Samarkand: A Study of T'ang Exotics*. Berkeley: University of California Press.

Shaling Home Depot. 2018a. https://read01.com/zh-sg/PM8KGgz.html?__cf_chl_tk= J2S2kPWIv D3imZmBdTCVFPIgZcc_sC3NLkGuy_hVAeY-1639477962-0-aNycGzNCVE#.Ybh1oVkxmcw; accessed December 14, 2021.

——. 2018b. http://sx.people.com.cn/n2/2018/ 0420/c189130-31485018.html; accessed April 23, 2018.

Schreiber, Gerhard. 1947. "Das Volk der Hsien-pi 鮮卑 zur Han-Zeit," *Monumenta Serica* 12: 145–203.

Sengupta, Arputharani. 2019. *Buddhist Jewels in Mortuary Cult: Magic Symbols*. Delhi: Agamkala Prakashan.

Seo, Yun-kyung 徐潤慶. 2011. "Cong Shaling bihuamu kan Bei Wei Pingcheng shiqi de sangzang meishu" 從沙嶺壁畫墓看北魏平城時期的喪葬美術. In Wu and Zheng 2011, 163–190.

Shaanxi sheng kaogu yanjiuyuan 陝西省考古研究院 and Jiangbian xian wenwu guanliban 靖邊縣文物管理辦. 2017. "Shaanxi Jingbian xian Yangqiaopan Qushuhao Dong Han bihuamu fajue jianbao" 陝西靖邊楊橋畔渠樹壕東漢壁畫墓發掘簡報, *Kaogu yu wenwu* 1: 3–26.

Shaanxi sheng wenwu guanli weiyuanhui 陝西省文物管理委員會. 1959. "Xi'an nanjiao Caochangpo cun Beichao mu de fajue" 西安南郊草廠坡村北朝墓的發掘, *Kaogu* 6, 285–287.

Shang Gang 尚剛. 2011. "Xishou yu gaizao—6 zhi 8 shiji de Zhongguo lianzhu quanwen zhiwu" 吸收與改造—6至8世紀的中國聯珠圈紋織物, in Zhao Feng and Qi Dongfang 2011, 18–23.

Shanxi daxue lishi wenhua xueyuan 山西大學歷史文化學院, Shanxi sheng kaogu yanjiusuo 山西省考古研究所 and Datong shi bowuguan 大同市博物館. 2006. *Datong nanjiao Bei Wei muqun* 大同南郊北魏墓群. Beijing: Kexue chubanshe.

Shanxi sheng Datong shi bowuguan 山西省大同市博物館 and Shanxi sheng wenwu gongzuo weiyuanhui 山西省文物工作委員會. 1972. "Shanxi Datong Shijiazhai Bei Wei Sima Jinlong mu" 山西大同石家寨北魏司馬金龍墓, *Wenwu* 3: 20–64.

Shanxi sheng kaogu yanjiusuo 山西省考古研究所. 2006. "Datong xian Guoying liangshi yuanzhongchang Bei Wei mu" 大同縣國營糧食原種場北魏墓, in *San Jin kaogu* 三晉考古, vol. 3, edited by Shanxi sheng kaogu yanjiusuo and Shanxi sheng kaogu xuehui 山西省考古學會, 850–860. Taiyuan: Shanxi renmin chubanshe.

Shanxi sheng kaogu yanjiusuo 山西省考古研究所 and Datong shi kaogu yanjiusuo 大同市考古研究所. 2011. "Shanxi Datong shi Datong xian Chenzhuang Bei Wei mu fajue jianbao" 山西大同市大同縣陳莊北魏墓發掘簡報, *Wenwu* 12: 37–46.

——, ——. 2014. "Shanxi Datong xian Hudong Bei Wei mu (M11) fajue jianbao" 山西大同縣湖東北魏墓 (M11) 發掘簡報, *Wenwu* 1: 28–36.

——, ——. 2015. "Shanxi Datong nanjiao Tongjiawan Beiweimu (M7, M9) fajue jianbao" 山西大同南郊全家灣北魏墓 (M7, M9) 發掘簡報, *Wenwu* 12: 4–22.

——, ——. 2016. "Shanxi Datong Caochangcheng Bei Wei erhao yizhi fajue jianbao" 山西大同操場城北魏二號遺址發掘簡報. *Wenwu* 4: 4–25.

——, ——. 2018. "Shanxi Datong Hudong Bei Wei muqun fajue jianbao" 山西大同湖東北魏墓群發掘簡報, *Zhongguo guojia bowuguan guankan* 2: 47–77.

——, ——, Datong shi bowuguan 大同市博物館, and Shanxi daxue kaoguxi 山西大學考古系. 2005. "Datong Caochangcheng Bei Wei jianzhu yizhi fajue baogao" 大同操場城北魏建築遺址發掘報告, *Kaogu xuebao* 4: 485–513.

Shelach, Gideon. 2008. "He Who Eats the Horse, She Who Rides It?" in *Are All Warriors Male? Gender Roles on the Ancient Eurasian Steppe*, edited by Katheryn M. Linduff and Karen S. Rubinson, 93–109. Lanham: AltaMira Press.

Shimunek, Andrew. 2017. *Languages of Ancient Southern Mongolia and North China: A Historical-Comparative Study of the Serbi or Xianbei Branch of the Serbi-Mongolic Language Family, with an Analysis of Northeastern Frontier Chinese and Old Tibetan Phonology*. Wiesbaden: Harrassowitz.

Shiozawa Hirohito 塩沢裕仁. 2007. "Senpi no tojō 'heijo' sono toshi kūkan no yōsō" 鮮卑の都城・平城: その都市空間の様相, *Hōsei shigaku* 68: 1–27.

Shuijing zhu 水經注. *Shuijing zhu shu* 水經注疏. By Li Daoyuan 酈道元 (fl. 540). Comm. by Yang Shoujing 楊守敬 (1839–1915) and Xiong Huizhen 熊會貞 (?–1936). Nanjing: Jiangsu guji chubanshe, 1988.

Sichuan sheng wenwu kaogu yanjiuyuan 四川省文物考古研院, Mianyang shi bowuguan 綿陽市博物館 and Santai xian wenwu guanlisuo 三台縣文物管理所. eds. 2007. *Santai Qijiang yamu* 三台郪江崖墓. Beijing: Wenwu chubanshe.

Simpson, St John, and E. V. Stepanova. 2017. "Eating, Drinking and Everyday Life," in *Scythians: Warriors of Ancient Siberia*, edited by St John Simpson and Svetlana Pankova, 152–191. London: Thames & Hudson, The British Museum.

Smith, Judith G. ed. 1998. *Arts of Korea*. New York: The Metropolitan Museum of Art.

Smith, Stuart Tyson. 2013. "Identity," in *The Oxford Handbook of Archaeological Theory*, edited by Andrew Gardner, Mark Lake and Ulrike Sommer. Oxford: Oxford University Press. https://doi.org/10.1093/oxfordhb

Song shu 宋書. Compiled by Shen Yue 沈約 (441–513). Beijing: Zhonghuashuju, 1987.

Song Xin 宋馨. 2002. "Beiwei Sima Jinlong muzang de chongxin pinggu" 北魏司馬金龍墓葬的重新評估, *Journal of Chinese Studies* (Chinese University of Hong Kong) n.s. 11: 273–298.

——. 2006. "Bei Wei Pingcheng qi de Xianbei fu" 北魏平城期的鮮卑服, in Zhang Qingjie et al. 2006, 84–107.

——. 2023. "Beichao de xin zangshi: shuangren danguanzang" 北朝的新葬式：雙人單棺葬. *Wei Jin Nanbeichao shi yanjiu*, Vol. 1: 154–185.

Soper, Alexander. 1960. "South Chinese Influence on the Buddhist Art of the Six Dynasties Period," *Bulletin of the Museum of Far Eastern Antiquities* (Stockholm) 32: 47–112.

Spengler III, Robert N. 2019. *Fruit from the Sands: The Silk Road Origins of the Foods We Eat*. Oakland: University of California Press.

Spiro, Audrey. 1990. *Contemplating the Ancients: Aesthetic and Social Issues in Early Chinese Portraiture*. Berkeley: University of California Press.

——. 2001. "Hybrid Vigor: Memory, Mimesis, and the Matching of Meanings in Fifth-Century Buddhist Art," in *Culture and Power in the Reconstitution of the Chinese Realm, 200–600*, edited by Scott Pearce, Audrey Spiro, and Patricia Ebrey, 128–148. Cambridge MA: Harvard University Press.

Stark, Sören. 2021. "A 'Rouran Perspective' on the Northern Chinese Frontier during the Northern Wei Period. Some Thoughts on the Yihe-Nur Tombs (Inner Mongolia)," in *Von den Hunnen zu den Türken – Reiterkrieger in Europa und Zentralasien. From the Huns to the Turks – Mounted Warriors in Europe and Central Asia*, edited by Falko Daim, Harald Meller und Walter Pohl, 59–87. Tagungen des Landesmuseums für Vorgeschichte Halle, Volume 23. Halle a. d. Saale: Landesamt für Denkmalpflege und Archäologie Sachsen-Anhalt.

Stockhammer, Philipp W. 2012. "Performing the Practice Turn in Archaeology," *Transcultural Studies* 1: 7–42. http://archiv.ub.uni-heidelberg.de/ojs/index.php/transcultural/article/view/9263/3238.

Stöllner, Thomas, Rainer Slotta, Abdolrasool Vatandoust. eds. 2004. *Persiens Antike Pracht. Bergbau – Handwerk – Archäologie*. Exhibition catalogue, 2 vols. Bochum: Deutsches Bergbaumuseum.

Su Bai 宿白. 1991. "Pingcheng shili de jiju he 'Yungang moshi' de xingcheng yu fazhan" 平城實力的集聚和‘雲岡模式’的形成與發展 in *Zhongguo shiku. Yungang shiku (yi)* 中國石窟・雲岡石窟（一）, edited by Yungang shiku wenwu baoguansuo 雲岡石窟文物保管所, 176–197. Beijing: Wenwu chubanshe.

Sui shu 隋書. Compiled by Wei Zhong 魏徵 (580–643). Beijing: Zhonghua shuju, 1973.

Sun Ji 孫機. 1989. "Guyuan Bei Wei qiguan yanjiu" 固原北魏漆棺研究. *Wenwu* 9: 38–44.

Sun Jingguo 孫靖國. 2012. "Zhonggu shiqi Sangganhe liuyu nongmu huanjing de bianqian: jianlun Bei Wei weihe ding du Pingcheng" 中古時期桑乾河流域農牧環境的變遷: 兼論北魏為何定都平城. *Nandu xuetan (renwen shehui kexue xuebao)* 3: 22–32.

Sun Wei 孫危. 2009. "Xianbei 'huiqi' zangsu yanjiu" 鮮卑'毀器'葬俗研究. *Bianjiang kaogu yanjiu* 8: 139–147.

Sun Yan 孫彥. 2006. "Han, Wei, Nanbeichao yuren tuxiang kao" 漢魏南北朝羽人圖像考. *Nanfang wenwu* 1: 69–74.

Taiping yulan 太平御覽. Compiled by Li Fang 李昉 (925–996) et al. Shanghai: Shanghai guji chubanshe, 1990.

Taiyuan shi wenwu kaogu yanjiusuo 太原市文物考古研究所. 2003. "Taiyuan Bei Qi Heba Chang mu" 太原北齊賀跋昌墓, *Wenwu* 3: 11–25.

——. ed. 2020. *Taiyuan Bei Qi Han Zujian mu* 太原北齊韓祖念墓. Beijing: Kexue chubanshe.

Tang Changru 唐長孺. 1955. "Wei Jin za hu kao" 魏晉雜胡考, in idem., *Wei Jin Nanbeichao shi luncong* 魏晉南北朝史論叢, 382–450. Beijing: Sanlian shudian.

Tian Likun 田立坤. 2001. "San Yan wenhua muzang de leixing yu fenqi" 三燕文化墓葬的類型與分期, in Wu Hung 2001, 205–230.

Tong Tao and Patrick Wertmann. 2010. "The Coffin Paintings of the Tubo Period from the Northern Tibetan Plateau," in Wagner and Wang 2010, 187–213.

Tseng, Chin-Yin. 2013. *The Making of the Tuoba Northern Wei: Constructing Material Culture Expressions in the Northern Wei Pingcheng Period (398–494 CE)*. BAR International Series 2567. Oxford: Archaeopress.

——. 2019. "The Representation of Military Troops in Pingcheng Tombs and the Private Household Institution of Buqu in Practice," *Asian Studies* 7.2: 221–243. DOI: 10.4312/as.2019.7.2.221-243

Tseng, Lilian Lan-ying. 2013. "Visual Replication and Political Persuaion: The Celestial Image in Yuan Yi's Tomb," in *Han Tang zhi jian de shijue wenhua yu wuzhi wenhua* 漢唐之間的視覺文化與物質文化 *Between Han and Tang: Visual and Material Culture in a Transformative Period*, edited by Wu Hung 巫鴻, 377–424. Beijing: Wenwu chubanshe.

Varenov, Andrey V. and Maria A. Kudinova. 2020. "Siberian and central asian turkic-time personages in three-horned headdresses and petroglyphs of the Wujiachuan rock-art site," *Bulletin of Tomsk State University. History* 68: 35–42 (Варенов, А.В., М.А. Кудинова. 2020. "СИБИРСКИЕ И ЦЕНТРАЛЬНОАЗИАТСКИЕ ПЕРСОНАЖИ ТЮРКСКОГО ВРЕМЕНИ В ТРЕХРОГИХ ГОЛОВНЫХ УБОРАХ И ПЕТРОГЛИФЫ ПАМЯТНИКА УЦЗЯЧУАНЬ," Вестник Томского государственного университета. История. История 68: 35–42).

Vickers, Michael. 1999. *Skeuomorphismus oder die Kunst, aus wenig viel zu machen*. Mainz: Philipp von Zabern.

Wagner, Mayke and Wang Wie. ed. 2010. *Bridging Eurasia* 跨越歐亞. Mainz: Philipp von Zabern.

Walker, Joel. 2018. "Luminous Markers: Pearls and Royal Authority in Late Antique Iran and Eurasia," in *Empire and Exchanges in Eurasian Late Antiquity: Rome, China, Iran, and the Steppe, ca. 250–750*, edited by Nicola di Cosmo and Michael Maas, 253–267. Cambridge: Cambridge University Press.

Wallace, Leslie. 2010. "Chasing the Beyond: Depictions of Hunting in Eastern Han Dynasty Tomb Reliefs (25–220 CE) from Shaanxi and Shanxi," PhD diss., University of Pittsburgh.

——. 2019. "Dual Portraits of the Deceased in Yangqiaopan M1, Jingbian, Shaanxi." *Asian Studies* 7.2: 203–219.

Wang Dafang 王大方 and Chen Heling 陳鶴玲. 2015. "Beifang caiguan xin faxian" 北方彩棺新發現. in Wei Jian and Wu Yan, 302–304.

Wang Feifeng 王飛峰. 2019. "Bei Wei lianhua huasheng wadang tanxi" 北魏蓮花化生瓦當探析, *Sichuan wenwu* 3: 67–73.

Wang Jiang 王江. 2021. "Bei Wei Pingcheng jianzhu yizhi yanjiu" 北魏平城建築遺址研究. *Yungang yanjiu* 3: 57–65.

Wang Limin 王利民. ed. 2016. *Pingcheng wenwu jingcui: Datong shi bowuguan cang jingpin lu* 平城文物精粹：大同市博物館藏精品錄. Shanghai: Jiangsu Fenghuang meishu chubanshe.

Wang Miaohou 王綿厚. 1990. "Guanyu Jinxi Taijitun sanzuo gucheng de lishi kaocha—jianlun Xianqin 'Tuhe' yu 'Han Tuhe'" 關於錦西台集屯三座古城的歷史考察—兼論先秦‘屠何’與‘漢徒河’, *Shehui kexue zhanxian* 3: 213–218.

Wang Yanqing 王雁卿. 2006. "Bei Wei Pingcheng muzang faxian jiqi xingzhi yanjiu" 北魏平城墓葬發現及其形制研究, *Shanxi sheng kaogu xuehui lunwen ji 4* 山西省考古學會論文集四, edited by Shanxi sheng kaogu yanjiusuo 山西省考古研究所 and Shanxi sheng kaogu xuehui 山西省考古學會, 182–190. Taiyuan: Shanxi renmin chubanshe.

——. 2012. "Bei Wei Pingcheng Hu ren de kaogu xue guancha" 北魏平城胡人的考古學觀察, in *Zhongguo Wei Jin Nanbeichaoshi xuehui: di shi jie nianhui ji guoji xueshu yantaohui lunwenji* 中國魏晉南北朝史學會：第十屆年會暨國際學術研討會論文集, edited by Zhongguo Wei Jin Nanbeichaoshi xuehui 中國魏晉南北朝史學會, Shanxi daxue lishi wenhua xueyuan 山西大學歷史文化學院, 567–577. Taiyuan: Beiyue wenyi chubanshe.

——. 2017. "Bei Wei daiju kao" 北魏帶具考. *Beichao yanjiu* 8: 166–180.

——. 2018. "Tou an jin buyao, yaoyi zai Pingcheng" 頭安金步搖，搖曳在平城, http://www.sohu.com/a/299537117_526303, accessed April 18, 2019.

——. 2019. "Shaling Bei Wei bihuamu qihua zhaji" 沙嶺北魏壁畫墓漆畫札記, paper submitted to the International Symposium on Tomb Mural Arts between the Han and Tang Dynasties (*Han Tang muzang bihua yishu guoji xueshu yantaohui* 漢唐墓葬壁畫藝術國際學術研討會, organized by Shanxi bowuyuan 山西博物院, Zhongguo kaogu xuehui Sanguo zhi Sui Tang kaogu zhuanye weiyuanhui 中國考古學會三國至隋唐考古專業委員會 and Shanxi sheng kaogu yanjiusuo 山西省考古研究所, in Taiyuan on December 14, 2019 (unpublished).

—— and Gao Feng 高峰. 2013. "Bei Wei qi yingshiqi leixing tanwei" 北魏漆飲食器類型探微, *Wenwu shijie* 5: 20–28.

—— and Gao Feng 高峰. 2016. "Shanxi Datong chutu de Bei Wei Qiguan" 山西大同出土的北魏漆棺, *Xibu kaogu* 2: 188–203.

Wang Yintian 王銀田. 1989. "Yuan Shu muzhi kaoshi: Fu Bei Wei Gao Kun muzhi xiaokao" 元淑墓志考釋：附北魏高琨墓志小考, *Wenwu* 8: 66–68.

——. 2008. "Shilun Datong Caochengcheng Bei Wei jianzhu yizhi de xingzhi" 試論大同操場城北魏建築遺址的性質. *Kaogu* 2: 67–69.

——. 2010. "Danyangwang muzhu kao" 丹陽王墓主考, *Wenwu* 5, 44–50.

——. 2019. "Beichao shiqi de shoumianwen: yi pushou xianhuan wei li" 北朝時期的獸面紋：以鋪首銜環為例, in Müller, Höllmann and Filip 2019, 183–200.

—— and Cao Chenmin 曹臣民. 2004. "Bei Wei shidiao sanpin" 北魏石雕三品, *Wenwu* 6, 89–93.

—— and Han Shengcun 韓生存. 1995. "Datong shi Qijiapo Bei Wei mu fajue jianbao" 大同市齊家坡北魏墓發掘簡報, *Wenwu jikan* 1, 14–18.

—— and Liu Junxi 劉俊喜. 2001. "Datong Zhijiabao Bei Wei mu shiguo bihua" 大同智家堡北魏墓石槨壁畫, *Wenwu* 7: 40–51.

——, Cao Chenming 曹臣明 and Han Shengchun 韓生存. 2001. "Shanxi Datongshi Bei Wei Pingcheng Mingtang yizhi 1995 nian de fajue" 山西大同市北魏平城明堂遺址 1995 年的發掘. *Kaogu* 3: 26–34.

——, Song Jianzhong 宋建忠, and Yin Xian 殷憲. 2010. "Shanxi Datong Bei Wei Xicetian zhitao yizhi diaocha jianbao" 山西大同北魏西冊田制陶遺址調查簡報. *Wenwu* 5: 27–37.

Wang Yu 王煜. 2021. "Shanxi Datong Jinmaoyuan mudi rengu yanjiu" 山西大同金茂園墓地人骨研究. MA thesis; Zhengzhou University.

Watt, James C. Y. ed. 2004. *China: Dawn of a Golden Age, 200–750 AD*. New York: Metropolitan Museum of Art.

Wei Jian 魏堅. ed. 1998. *Neimenggu zhongnanbu Handai muzang* 內蒙古中南部漢代墓葬. Beijing: Zhongguo dabaike quanshu chubanshe.

——. ed. 2004. *Neimenggu diqu Xianbei muzang de faxian yu yanjiu* 內蒙古地區鮮卑墓葬的發現與研究. Beijing: Kexue chubanshe.

—— and Wu Yan 武燕. ed. 2015. *Bei Wei liuzhen xueshu yantaohui lunwenji* 北魏六鎮學術研討會論文集. Hohhot: Neimenggu renmin chubanshe

Wei shu 魏書. Compiled by Wei Shou 魏收 (507–572). Beijing: Zhonghua shuju, 1974.

Wei Zheng 韋正. 2011. "Datong nanjiao Bei Wei muqun yanjiu" 大同南郊北魏墓群研究, *Kaogu* 6: 72–87.

——. 2013. "Jindang yu buyao: Han Jin mingfu guanshi shitan" 金鐺與步搖：漢晉命婦冠飾試探, *Wenwu* 5: 60–69.

——. 2015. "Tuoba Xianbei de danguan hezangmu" 拓跋鮮卑的單棺合葬墓, in Neimenggu and Neimenggu, 458–467.

——. 2017. "Datong Bei Wei muzang bihua yanjiu" 大同北魏墓葬壁畫研究, in *Bi shang guan: xidu Shanxi gudai bihua* 壁上觀：細讀山西古代壁畫, edited by Shanghai bowuguan 上海博物館, 96–111. Beijing: Beijing daxue chubanshe.

——. 2018. "Datong Shaling qihao mu Bei Wei bihua jize ticai qianxi" 大同沙嶺七號墓北魏壁畫幾則題材淺析. *Xibu kaogu* 1: 70–79.

——. 2022. "Datong Bei Wei Lü Xu shiguo bihua de yiyi—zai Han Jin Beichao muzang bihua bianqian de shiye xia" 大同北魏呂續石槨壁畫的意義—在漢晉北朝墓葬壁畫變遷的視野下, *Meishu daguan* 4: 56–60.

—— and Cui Jiabao 崔嘉寶. 2020. "Datong Bei Wei pingmin muzang qianxi" 大同北魏平民墓葬淺析, *Xibu kaogu* 1: 128–140.

Wen, Xin. 2016. "What's in a Surname? Central Asian Participation in the Culture of Naming of Medieval China," *Tang Studies* 34: 73–98. http://dx.doi.org/10.1080/07375034.2016.1234994

Whitfield, Roderick. 1996. *Dunhuang: Caves of the Singing Sands: Buddhist Art from the Silk Road.* London: Textile and Art Publications.

Wu Hong 吳荭. 2008. "Gansu Gaotai Digengpo Wei Jin mu" 甘肅高臺地埂坡魏晉墓, in *2007 Zhongguo zhongyao kaogu faxian* 2007 中國重要考古發現, edited by Guojia wenwuju 國家文物局, 84–91. Beijing: Wenwu chubanshe.

——, Wang Ce 王策 and Mao Ruilin 毛瑞林. 2012. "Hexi muzang Zhong de Xianbei yinsu" 河西墓葬中的鮮卑因素, *Kaogu yu wenwu* 4: 75–82.

Wu Hung 巫鴻. ed. 2001. *Han Tang zhi jian wenhua yishu de hudong yu jiaorong* 漢唐之間文化藝術的互動與交融. *Between Han and Tang: Cultural and Artistic Interaction in a Transformative Period.* Beijing: Wenwu chubanshe.

——. 2009. "Enlivening the Soul in Chinese Tombs," *RES: Anthropology and Aesthetics* 55/56: 21–41.

——. 2015. "The Invisible Miniature: Framing the Soul in Chinese Art and Architecture," *Art History* 38.2: 286–303.

—— and Zheng Yan 鄭岩. eds. 2011. *Gudai muzang meishu yanjiu* 古代墓葬美術研究, vol. 1. Beijing: Wenwu chubanshe.

Wu Jiao 吳嬌. 2021. "Datong Bei Wei Shaling qihaomu bihua Zhong cheyu yanjiu" 大同北魏沙嶺 7 號墓壁畫中車輿研究, *Shanxi Datong daxue xuebao (shehui kexueban)* 3: 62–66.

Wu Songyan 吳松岩. 2012. "Cong kaoguxue shiye kan Bei Wei chuqi lisan buluo zhengce" 從考古學視野看北魏初期離散部落政策. *Neimenggu daxue xuebao (zhexue shehui kexueban)* 1: 64–67.

——. 2015. "Qilangshan mudi zai renshi" 七郎山墓地再認識, in Wei Jian and Wu Yan, 110–120.

—— and Zhao Fei 趙菲. 2021. "Shiliuguo zaoqi Tuoba bu yu Murong bu lianyin kao: Cong Neimenggu Damaoqi chutu jin buyao guanshi tanqi" 十六國早期拓跋部與慕容部聯姻靠：從內蒙古達茂旗出土金步搖冠飾談起. *Bianjiang kaogu yanjiu* 1: 299–308.

Xi'an shi wenwu baohu kaogusuo 西安市文物保護考古所. 2004. "Xi'an nanjiao Tang mu (M31) fajue jianbao" 西安南郊唐墓 (M31) 發掘簡報, *Wenwu* 1: 31–61.

Xi'an shi wenwu baohu kaogu yanjiuyuan 西安市文物保護考古研究院. 2014. "Xi'an Fengqiyuan Shiliuguo mu fajue jianbao" 西安市鳳棲原十六國墓發掘簡報, *Wenbo* 1: 10–17.

Xiangyang shi wenwu kaogu yanjiusuo 襄陽市文物考古研究所. 2019. "Hubei Xiangyang Shizhuang Nanchao huaxiangzhuanmu fajue jianbao" 湖北襄陽柿莊南朝畫像磚墓發掘簡報, *Wenwu* 8: 38–48.

Xianyang shi wenwu kaogu yanjiusuo 咸陽市文物考古研究所. 2006. *Xianyang shiliuguo mu* 咸陽十六國墓. Beijing: Wenwu chubanshe.

Xibei daxue wenhua yichan xueyuan 西北大學文化遺產學院 and Yulin shi wenwu baohu yanjiusuo 榆林市文物保護研究所. 2022. "Shaanxi Qingjian Sangshuping Handai shishimu fajue jianbao" 陝西清澗桑樹坪漢代石室墓發掘簡報. *Jianghan kaogu* 6: 36–43.

Xin Long 辛龍, Ning Yan 寧琰 and Wang Yanpeng 王艷朋. 2020. "Xin faxian: Muzang li de caihui tudiao jianzhu sheme yang? Xi'an Shaolingyuan faxian qijin guimo zuida de Shiliuguo shiqi gaodengji muzang" 新發現：墓葬裏的彩繪土雕建築什麼樣？西安少陵原發現迄今規模最大的十六國時期高等級墓葬. http://m.thepaper.cn/wifiKey_detail.jsp?contid=10598028&from=wifiKey#; accessed December 14, 2021.

Xin Xuefeng 辛雪峰 and Geng Qinggang 耿慶剛. 2023. "Xi'an Qin Han xincheng Poliu Shiliuguo muzang yueyong kao" 西安秦漢新城坡劉十六國墓葬樂俑考. *Renmin yinyue* 1: 29–36.

Xiong, Victor Cunrui. 2019. "The Northern Economy," in Dien and Knapp 2019, 309–329.

Xu Bingkun 徐秉坤. 2015. "Buyao yu Murong Xianbei" 步搖與慕容鮮卑, in *Liaoning bowu* 2015, 284–313.

Xu gaoseng zhuan 續高僧傳. By Daoxuan 道宣 (596–667). *Xu gaoseng zhuan jiaozhu* 續高僧傳校注. Annotated by Su Xiaohua 蘇小華. Shanghai: Shanghai guji chubanshe, 2021.

Xu Guangji 徐光冀. ed. 2012. *Zhongguo chutu bihua quanji* 中國出土壁畫全集. 10 Vols. Beijing: Kexue chubanshe.

Xu Ji 徐基. 1985. "Liaoning Chaoyang faxian Bei Yan, Bei Wei mu" 遼寧朝陽發現北燕、北魏墓. *Kaogu* 10: 915–929.

Xu Jiqi 許繼起. 2018. "Lun Cao Wei Liang Jin shiqi de gongting nüyue" 論曹魏兩晉時期的宮廷女樂. *Zhongguo shehui kexueyuan yanjiushengyuan xuebao* 6: 65–76.

Xu Yongli 徐永利. 2018. *Zhongguo gudai muzang siyu xuanjin shi qionglong jizhi yu yuanliu yanjiu* 中國古代墓葬四隅券進式穹窿機制與源流研究. Nanjing: Dongnan daxue chubanshe.

Yang Hong 楊泓. 1999. "Tan Zhongguo Han Tang zhi jian zangsu de yanbian" 談中國漢唐之間葬俗的演變, *Wenwu* 10: 60–68.

Yang Jianhua. 2011. "Gender relationships among the 'Xiongnu' as reflected in Burial Patterns," in Brosseder and Miller 2011, 243–259.

Yao Weiyuan 姚薇元. 1962. *Bei chao Hu xing kao* 北朝胡姓考. Beijing: Zhonghua shuju.

Ye Runqing 葉潤清. 2016. "Anhui Dangtu 'Tianzifen' Dong Wu mu" 安徽當塗 '天子墳' 東吳墓. *Dazhong kaogu* 7: 12–15.

Yin Gang 尹剛. 2020. "Datong Yunbolu Huayu erqi Bei Wei muzang bihua de jiazhi" 大同雲波路華宇二期北魏墓葬壁畫的價值, *Anhui wenbo* 15: 70–83.

Yin Xian 殷憲. 1999. "Bei Wei zaoqi Pingcheng muming xi" 北魏早期平城墓銘析. *Beichao yanjiu* 1: 163–192.

——. 2006a. "Cong Bei Wei Wang Liban qi Yu zhuan, Wang Ban can zhuan shuodao Taihe Liaodong zhengzhiquan" 從北魏王禮斑妻輿磚、王斑殘磚說到太和遼東政治圈. *Zhonghua wenshi luncun* 4: 129–160.

——. 2006b. "Shanxi Datong Shaling Bei Wei bihuamu qihua tiji yanjiu" 山西大同沙嶺北魏壁畫墓漆畫題記研究, in Zhang Qingjie et al. 2006. 346–360.

——. 2007. "'Yang Zhongdu zhuanming' yanjiu" 《楊眾度磚銘》研究, *Zhongguo shufa* 6: 81–84.

——. 2009. "Bei Wei Pingcheng zhuanwa wenzi jianshu" 北魏平城磚瓦文字簡述, *Shanxi Datong daxue xuebao (shehui kexueban)* 1: 38–41.

——. 2012. "Datong Bei Wei gongcheng diaocha zhaji" 大同北魏宮城調查札記, in idem. *Pingcheng shigao* 平城史稿, 50–63. Beijing: Kexue chubanshe.

—— and Liu Junxi 劉俊喜. 2011. "Bei Wei Yuchi Dingzhou mu shiguo fengmenshi mingwen" 北魏尉遲定州墓石槨封門石銘文, *Wenwu* 12: 47–51.

Yishui 易水. 1981. "Han Wei Liuchao de junyue: 'guchui' he 'hengchui'" 漢魏六朝的軍樂: '鼓吹' 和 '橫吹', *Wenwu* 7: 85–89.

Youyang zazu 酉陽雜俎. By Duan Chengshi 段成式 (Tang). Collated by Fang Nansheng 方南生. Beijing: Zhonghua shuju 1981.

Yu Weichao 俞偉超. 1980. "Handai zhuhou wang yu liehou muzang de xingzhi fenxi: Jianlun 'Zhou zhi', 'Han zhi', 'Jin zhi' de san jieduanxian" 漢代諸侯王與列侯墓葬的形制分析——兼論"周制"、"漢制"、"晉制"的三階段性, in *Zhongguo kaogu xuehui di yi ci nianhui lunwenji* 中國考古學會第一次年會論文集, edited by Zhongguo kaogu xuehui 中國考古學會, 117–124. Beijing: Wenwu chubanshe.

Yue Qi 岳起 and Liu Weipeng 劉衛鵬. 2008. "Guanzhong diqu Shiliuguo mu de chubu renshi—jiantan Xianyang Pingling Shiliuguo mu chutu de guchuiyong" 關中地區十六國墓的初步認識——兼談咸陽平陵十六國墓出土的鼓吹俑, *Wenwu* 8: 41–53.

Zadneprovskiy, Y. A. 1994. "The Nomads of Northern Central Asia after the Invasion of Alexander," in *History of Civilization of Central Asia, Vol. II The Development of Sedentary and Nomadic Civilization: 700 B.C. to A.D. 250*, edited by János Harmatta, B. N. Puri and G. F. Etemadi, 448–462. Paris: UNIESCO Publishing.

Zhang, Fan. 2018. "Cultural Encounters: Ethnic Complexity and Material Expression in Fifth-century Pingcheng, China." PhD diss., Institute for the Study of the Ancient World, New York University.

——. 2019. "Chinese-Buddhist Encounter: Synthesis of Fuxi-Nüwa and Cintamani in Early Medieval Chinese Art," *Asian Studies*, Vol. 7, Issue 2 *Meaning and Transformation of Chinese Funerary Art during the Han and Wei Jin Nanbei Periods* (Ljubljana): 87–111.

—— 張帆. 2022. "Datong nanjiao yizhi chutu shidiao fangyan de qingjinghua yanjiu" 大同南郊遺址出土石雕方硯的情境化研究, *Gugong bowuyuan yuankan* 2: 55–69.

Zhang Feng 張峰. 2015. "Bei Wei Pingcheng diqu muzang zushu de guilei" 北魏平城地區墓葬族屬的歸類, *Wenwu shijie* 3, 18–21.

Zhang Guowen 張國文, Hu Yaowu 胡耀武, Pei Deming 裴德明, Song Guoding 宋國定, and Wang Changsui 王昌燧. 2010. "Datong nanjiao Bei Wei muqun rengu de wending tongweisu fenxi" 大同南郊北魏墓群人骨的穩定同位素分析, *Nanfang wenwu* 1: 127–131.

——, Yaowu Hu, Limin Wang, Chenming Cao, Xingsheng Li, Xiaonong Wu, Zudong Shun, Fengshan Chen, Jingsong Bai, Peng Lü, Guoding Song, Changsui Wang, Michael P. Richards. 2015. "A Paleodietary and Subsistence Strategy Investigation of the Iron Age Tuoba Xianbei Site by Stable Isotopic Analysis: A Preliminary Study of the Role of Agriculture Played in Pastoral Nomad Societies in Northern China," *Journal of Archaeological Science: Reports* 2: 699–707. http://dx.doi.org/10.1016/j.jasrep.2014.12.003

——, Xiaogang Hou, Shuyun Li, Yawei Zhou and Michael P. Richards. 2020. "Agriculturalization of the Nomad-Dominated Empires of the Northern Wei Dynasty in Pingcheng City (398–494 AD): A Stable Isotopic Study on Animal and Human Bones from the Jinmaoyuan Cemetery, China." *International Journal of Osteoarchaeology*: 1–16. doi.org/10.1002/oa.2923

Zhang Qingjie. 2005. "Hutengwu and Huxuanwu: Sogdian dances in the Northern, Sui and Tang Dynasties," in *Les Sogdiens en Chine*, edited by Étienne de la Vaissière and Éric Trombert, 93–106. Paris: École française d'Extrême-Orient.

—— 張慶捷. 2007. "Bei Wei Poduoluo shi bihuamu suojian wenzi kaoshu" 北魏破多羅氏壁畫墓所見文字考述. *Lishi yanjiu* 1: 174–179.

——. 2010. "Datong Caochangcheng Bei Wei Taiguan liangchu yizhi chutan" 大同操場城北魏太官糧儲遺址初探. *Wenwu* 4: 53 –58, 95.

——. 2016. "Bei Wei shitang guanchuang yu fushu bihua wenzi: yi xin faxian Xie Xing shitang weili tantao zangsu wenhua de bianqian" 北魏石堂棺床與附屬壁畫文字: 以新發現解興石堂為例探討葬俗文化的變遷, in *Liangge shijie de paihuai: Zhonggu shiqi sangzang guannian fengsu yu liyi zhidu xueshu yantaohui lunwenji* 兩個世界的徘徊: 中古時期喪葬觀念風俗與禮儀制度學術研討會論文集, edited by Beijing daxue Zhongguo kaoguxue yanjiu Zhongxin 北京大學中國考古學研究中心, 233–249. Beijing: Kexue chubanshe.

——, Li Shuji 李書吉 and Li Gang 李鋼. ed. 2006. *4–6 shiji de bei Zhongguo yu Ouya dalu* 4–6 世紀的北中國與歐亞大陸. Beijing: Kexue chubanshe.

—— and Liu Junxi 劉俊喜. 2011. "Datong xin faxian liangzuo Bei Wei bihuamu niandai chutan" 大同新發現兩座北魏壁畫墓年代初探, *Wenwu* 12: 52–54.

Zhang, Quanchao, Xiaogang Hou, Shiyu Yang, Sunzifeng Ruan, Anqi Wang, Pengzhen Li, Xiaofan Sun, Hong Zhu, Qun Zhang, Qian Wang. 2021. "Eternal Love locked in an Embrace and Sealed with a Ring: A Xianbei Couple's Joint Burial in North Wei Era, China (386–534 CE)," *International Journal of Osteoarchaeology*: 1–9. DOI: 10.1002/oa.3009

Zhang Zhizhong 張志忠. 2006. "Datong Qilicun Bei Wei Yang Zhongqing muzhuanming xi" 大同七里村北魏楊眾慶墓志銘析, Wenwu 10: 82–85.

——. 2019. "Datong Bei Wei muzang fojiao tuxiang qianyi" 大同北魏墓葬佛教圖像淺議, in Müller, Höllmann and Filip 2019, 57–80.

——. Jing Xiaoting 靖曉亭 and Li Zhiguo 李志國. 2021. "Datong shi Pingcheng qu Zhijiabao Bei Wei Lü Xu fudiao caihui shiguomu" 大同市平城區智家堡北魏呂續浮雕彩繪石槨墓 https://mp.weixin.qq.com/s/hUMIPDoGZMav9RcJk3vBbg; accessed December 21, 2021.

Zhao Feng 趙豐 and Qi Dongfang 齊東方. eds. 2011. *Jin shang hufeng—Sichou zhi lu fangzhipin shang de xifang yingxiang (4–8 shiji)* 錦上胡風—絲綢之路紡織品上的西方影響 (4–8 世紀). Shanghai: Shanghai guji chubanshe.

——, Wang Hui 王輝 and Wan Fang 萬芳. 2008. "Gansu Huahai Bijiatan 26 hao mu chutu de sichou fushi" 甘肅花海畢家灘 26 號墓出土的絲綢服飾, in *Xibei fengge, Han Jin zhiwu* 西北風格 漢晉織物, edited by Zhao Feng 趙豐, 94–113. Hong Kong: Yishatang.

Zhao Ruimin 趙瑞民, Liu Junxi 劉俊喜. 2006. "Shanxi Datong Shaling Bei Wei bihuamu chutu qipi wenzi kao" 山西大同沙嶺北魏壁畫墓出土漆皮文字考. *Wenwu* 10: 78–81.

Zheng Jingyun 鄭景雲, et al. 2005. "Wei Jin Nanbeichao shiqi de Zhongguo dongbu wendu bianhua," 魏晉南北朝時期的中國東部溫度變化, *Di si ji yanjiu* 2: 129–140.

Zheng Long 鄭隆. 1988. "Neimenggu Baotou shi Bei Wei Yao Qiji mu" 內蒙古包頭市北魏姚齊姬墓. *Kaogu* 9: 856–857.

Zheng Yan 鄭岩. 2012. "Beichao zangju xiaozitu de xingshi yu yiyi" 北朝葬具孝子圖的形式與意義. *Meishu xuebao* 6: 42–54.

Zhongguo renmin daxue lishi xueyuan kaogu wenboxi 中國人民大學歷史學院考古文博系, Xilinguole meng wenwu baohu guanlizhan 錫林郭勒盟文物保護管理站 and Zhengxiangbaiqi wenwu guanlisuo 正鑲白旗文物管理所. 2017. "Neimenggu Zhengxiangbaiqi Yihenao'er M1 fajue jianbao" 內蒙古正鑲白旗伊和淖爾 M1 發掘簡報, *Wenwu* 1: 15–34.

Zhongguo shehui kexueyuan kaogu yanjiusuo 中國社會科學院考古研究所. ed. 2018. *Zhongguo kaoguxue: Sanguo Liang Jin Nanbeichao juan* 中國考古學：三國兩晉南北朝卷. Beijing: Zhongguo shehui kexue chubanshe.

Zhou Yang 周洋. 2017. "Guanzhong diqu Shiliuguo muzang chutu zuoyueyong de shidai yu laiyuan: Shiliuguo shiqi muzang zhidu chongjian zhi guankui" 關中地區十六國墓葬出土坐樂俑的時代與來源：十六國時期墓葬制度重建之管窺. *Xibu kaogu* 3: 119–135.

Zin, Monika. 2003. *Devotionale und ornamentale Malereien*. Vol. I Interpretation. Ajanta: Handbuch der Malereien / Handbook of the Paintings 2. Wiesbaden: Harrassowitz.

Zizhi tongjian 資治通鑒. By Sima Guang 司馬光 (1019–1086). Beijing: Zhonghua shuju, 1976.

Appendix 1. Periodization of the reported Pingcheng tombs*

Periods / Sites	I (pre-398)	II (399–439)	III (440–476)	IV (477–493)	V (post-493)
1. CZ: Chenzhuang 陳莊					M1 (late IV or beginning V)[1]
2. DHC: Dianhanchang 電焊廠[2]	M24, M73, M227	M1, M9, M41, M45, M49, M52, M54, M63, M74, M86, M97, M108, M139, M162, M170, M180, M185, M195, M197, M203, M204, M205, M206, M210, M211, M212, M226, M228, M230, M235, M236, M240, M246	M3, M6, M7, M8, M13, M15, M17, M18, M19, M22, M28, M33, M35, M38, M42, M43, M46, M50, M51, M56, M57, M65, M66, M75, M79, M81, M95, M102, M103, M105, M106, M107, M109, M112, M113, M114, M116, M124, M126, M128, M129, M132, M133, M149, M150, M153, M156, M157, M192, M194, M199, M207, M208, M214, M215, M216, M221, M225, M229, M253	M14, M20, M23, M36, M40, M48, M53, M67, M72, M78, M80, M82, M83, M84, M85, M87, M89, M92, M99, M101, M121, M130, M134, M136, M137, M140, M141, M147, M151, M168, M175, M181, M186, M187, M191, M209, M222, M224, M233, M238, M243	M26, M39, M68, M77, M110, M117, M127, M146, M239

---

* If not otherwise indicated, the chronological attribution of tombs follows the periodization of the ceramics found in the Dianhanchang cemetery; Shanxi daxue et al. 2006: 472. A red shade indicates the presence of paintings, such as murals, or paintings on funerary houses or coffins, a yellow shade indicates that there were clay figurines. The blue shade indicates the presence of both, which occurred only in the tombs of Zhang Zhilang, Song Shaozu (Yanbei shiyuan M5), Jia Bao (in the Yuhe dong District), and the tomb at Chenzhuang (Nos. 1, 2 and 25).

1 Shanxi and Datong 2011. The chronological attribution follows that of the excavators. Based on the pointed arch construction for the entrance, which is a special feature of late Pingcheng brick tombs, the tomb can also be attributed to the late Period IV.

2 Shanxi daxue et al. 2006.

Periods / Sites	I (pre-398)	II (399–439)	III (440–476)	IV (477–493)	V (post-493)
3. EDC: Erdianchang 二電廠[3]		M20, M37 (late)[4]	M3,[5] M33	M1, M4, M5, M11, M16 (Qutu longye 屈突隆業, 490), M17, M36[6]	M2
4. FS: Fangshan 方山[7]				Yongguling 永固陵 (490), Wanniantang 萬年堂	
5.FZC: Fanzhuangcun 樊莊村[8]		Guoliang 國糧 M4		Guoliang 國糧 M1, M6	Guoliang 國糧 M3
6. HAJ: Henganjie 恆安街				11DHAM13 (Han Farong 韓法蓉)[9]	
7. HR: Huairen 懷仁[10]				Danyangwang 丹陽王	
8. HD: Hudong 湖東 / 湖東編組站[11]		2004M13	1986M1 (late III or beginning IV), 2004M1, 2004M4, 2004M6, 2004M11 (late), 2004M15	M2, M3, M8, M12 (all excavated in 2004)	
9. JSMC: Jinshu meichang 金屬鎂廠[12]			M4, M15	M2	M7
10. QJP: Qijiapo 齊家坡[13]			DQM1		

---

3 Datong kaogu 2019.

4 An attribution of Erdianchang M37 to Period II is based on the strong stylistic similarity of its bronze wine warmer *jiaodou* 鐎斗 and bronze steppe-styled cauldron to those from Tongjiawan M7 (No. 17).

5 The pagoda-shaped jug from this burial resembles the one from Yunbolu M10 (no. 26).

6 The glazed tomb figurines from this burial resemble those from the tomb of Sima Jinlong (484; No. 12).

7 Wenley 1947; Datong and Shanxi 1978; Dien 1985; Datong bowu 2007; Okamura and Mukai 2007.

8 Shanxi sheng 2006.

9 Datong kaogu 2015.

10 Huairen xian 2010; Wang Yintian 2010.

11 For Hudong M1: Datong kaogu 2004b. The excavators are of the opinion that the painting style of the coffin painting resembles that of Yungang Grotto 10. Accordingly, they date the tomb in the Taihe 太和 period (477–499). For the preliminary reports on the tombs excavated at the Hudong Railway Distribution Yard *Hudong bianzuyhan*, see Shanxi and Datong 2014 (M11) and 2018.

12 Han Shengcun et al. 1996. The attribution of M2 to Period IV is based on the adoption of the decoration with a band of stamped half-palmette scroll on a jar.

13 Wang and Han 1995.

Periods / Sites	I (pre-398)	II (399–439)	III (440–476)	IV (477–493)	V (post-493)
11. QLC: Qilicun 七里村[14]		2001M20, 2001M28, 2001M29, 2001M36	2001M6, 2001M22 (grave shape unknown), 2020M29, Biguiyuan 2020M831	2001M1, 2001M9, 2001M14, 2001M16, 2001M35 (Yang Zhongdu 楊眾度, 484)	2001M33, 2001M34
12. SJZ: Shijiazhai 石家寨[15]				Sima Jinlong 司馬金龍 (484)	
13. SL: Shaling 沙嶺[16]		M7 Poduoluo 破多羅 (435 or earlier)			
14. SLJS: Shaling Home Depot 沙嶺建材市場東[17]			2018M with a stone house (beginning IV or end of III)		
15. SLXC: Shaling xincun 沙嶺新村[18]			M21	M1, M2, M4, M24 (498), M25 (all late IV)	M22 (496?), M23, M27,
16. TC: Tiancun 田村[19]			1998 Tiancun tomb		
17. TJW: Tongjiawan 仝家灣[20]		M7	M9 Liang Bahu 梁拔胡 (461); Xing Hejiang 邢合姜 (469)		
18. WGT: Wangguantun 王官屯, Yanggao 陽高[21]			Yuchi Ding-zhou's 尉遲定州 wife (457)		

---

14 For the tombs excavated in 2001 (2001M), Datong kaogu 2006a; for Biguiyuan 2020M831, Zhang et al. 2021; for 2020M29, https://www.163.com/dy/article/G6EGM1IS05346RC6.html?f=post2020_dy_ recommends; accessed March 31, 2021. The glazed jug with appliquéd lotus ornament at the base of the neck from 2001M36 resembles that from Tongjiawan M7 (no. 17). The attribution of Biguiyuan M831 and M29 to Period III was based on the shapes of the vessels shown in online news.

15 Datong and Shanxi 1972.

16 Datong kaogu 2006b.

17 Shaling Home Depot 2018a. For dating see Shaling Home Depot 2018b.

18 Datong kaogu 2014.

19 Datong kaogu 2010.

20 58 Pingcheng tombs were detected at this site (Hou Xiaogang 2020: 12). 10 of which were excavated, but only 2 tombs were reported, Shanxi and Datong 2015. For a dating of Tongjiawan M7, ibid., 21. Xing Hejiang's tomb was looted from the same site, but it did not belong to the same Tongjiawan cemetery, see Zhang Zhizhong 2019; Li Meitian and Zhang Zhizhong 2020.

Periods / Sites	I (pre-398)	II (399–439)	III (440–476)	IV (477–493)	V (post-493)
19. WYL: Wenyinglu 文瀛路[22]			M1		
20. XNT: Xiaonantou 小南頭[23]					Yuan Shu 元淑 (507)
21. XSJ: Xiashenjing 下深井,[24] Yanggao 陽高				M1	
22. YBSY: Yanbei shiyuan 雁北師院[25]				M1 (late), M2, M3 (late), M5 Song Shaozu 宋紹祖 (477), M7, M9 (late), M12 (late), M18, M19, M24, M52	
23. YBDD: Yingbin dadao 迎賓大道[26]		M14, M65, M62	M10, M11, M16, M37, M39, M55, M62, M70 (Chigan Kehou 叱干渴侯, 466), M87, M88	M39, M65, M75, M76, M78, M82	M74
24. YCJY: Yuchang jiayuan 御昌佳園				M113[27]	
25. YD: Yuhe dong Shigongan ju 御河東市公安局[28]			Xie Xing's wife 解興妻石堂 (459); Zhang Zhilang 張智朗 石槨 (460)	M13 Jia Bao 賈寶 (477) with a painted wooden house	

21 Datong kaogu 2011c.
22 Datong kaogu 2011b. Based on the historical events and its clay figurines, this report as well as Zhang Qingjie and Liu Junxi 2011 date the tomb to early Taihe period (477–496), i.e., Period IV. However, the typology of the ceramic vessels is similar to that of Tongjiawan M9 (461, No. 17) and Period III of the Dianhanchang cemtery. Therefore, I propose an earlier date for this tomb.
23 Datong bowu 1989.
24 Datong kaogu 2004a.
25 Liu Junxi 2008.
26 Datong kaogu 2006c. M39 is dated based on the resemblance of its grey jar and the stone lamp to those from the tomb of Sima Jinlong (No. 12). Similarly, M76 is dated based on the glazed figurines which bear a close resemblance to those from Sima Jinlong's tomb.
27 Datong kaogu 2021b.
28 Chizhi and Liu 2014 (Stone house of Zhang Zhilang); Zhang Qingjie 2016 (Stone house of Xie Xing's wife); Datong kaogu 2021a (Wooden house of Jia Bao).

Periods / Sites	I (pre-398)	II (399–439)	III (440–476)	IV (477–493)	V (post-493)
26. YBL: Yunbolu 雲波路 / 雲波里路		Painted tomb 09DYM1 (late II/early III)[29]	2019 Huayu II painted tomb[30]; Yunbolu M10[31]		
27. YGZ: Yungangzhen 雲崗鎮[32]				Shitoucun 石頭村 M, 616Chang, Zhangjiawan 張家灣 tomb	Xiaozhancun 小站村 Feng Hetu 封和突 (501)[33]
28. ZJB: Zhijiabao 智家堡[34]		Wang Liban 王禮斑磚銘 (409)	Tomb with a stone bed; 1997 Tomb with a painted stone house; 1997 tomb with a painted coffin; 2021 tomb of Lü Xu 呂續 (456)		

29 Datong kaogu 2011a. The dating of Yunbolilu M1 is based on the technical resemblance of the mural to that of Tongjiawan M9 (461; No. 17). Both murals are painted on a plaster found only on the four walls but not on the roof vaults, leaving them fully undecorated. This special feature suggests a painting technique no later than Period III. However, the murals of Yunbolilu M1 contains motifs of fantastic animals in rectangular frames, which otherwise only occur in the murals of General Podouluo (435 or earlier). Therefore, I propose to date this tomb between Period II and III.

30 Hou Xiaogang 2020 and Yin Gang 2020. Both authors date the tomb between 455 and 465 based on the styles of the lotus scrolls and the assemblage of drinking vessels depicted in the mural.

31 Datong kaogu 2017. The shape of the pottery animal guardians resembles those in the painting of Tongjiawan M9 (461; No. 17). The shapes of the ceramic vessels also match with those of Period III.

32 Datong bowu 2019.

33 Ma Yuji 1983.

34 From Wang Liban's burial only the epitaph is known, see Xin Xian 2006. For the stone bed Wang Yintian and Cao Chenmin 2004 (no information about the tomb); for the tomb with a stone house of 1997 campaign Wang Yintian and Liu Junxi 2001; for the 1997 tomb with a painted coffin see Liu Junxi and Gao Feng 2004, 2005. I have followed the excavators' dating of the Zhijiabao stone house in my 2017 paper. The present analysis suggests an earlier dating. For the most recent finding of the tomb of Lü Xu, in which a stone house with reliefs and paintings, see Zhang Zhizhog et al. 2021.

Appendix 2 Pingcheng tombs containing figurines and lamps*

	Site / tomb / occupant	Tomb type	Period	Human figurines**				Tomb guardians	Lamps	References
				♂	♀ servants and maids	♀ musicians / dancers	Central Asians (all ♂)			
1	Dongxin Square (data incomplete)	?	III (440s–450s)	?	1 with Xianbei-hood, 1 with looped chignons (both glazed)	3 with Xianbei-hoods, 2 with looped chignons (musicians glazed)	1 musician (glazed)	?	?	Datong bowu 2018
2	Tomb of Lü Xu (♂) at Zhijiabao	Earthen chamber; with a painted stone house	III (456)	-	-	-	-	1 warrior and 1 animal guardian	-	Zhang Zhizhong et al. 2021
3	Tomb of Zhang Zhilang (♀); East of Yu River	Earthen chamber; with a painted stone house	III (460)	-	1 servant, 1 maid, both are brown glazed	-	-	-	1 pottery stem lamp	Chizhi and Liu Junxi 2014
4	Yunbolu M10 (♀)	Earthen chamber (3.54 m × 3.8 m), w/ an unpainted stone house	III (ca. 460s)	-	11 servants	3 musicians	3 musicians, 1 acrobat	2 warriors + 2 animal guardians (1 w/ a human and 1 w/ an animal face)	1 multi-armed lamp	Datong kaogu 2017
5	Hudong 2004M11 (♂)	Earthen chamber (2.2–3 m × 3.2 m)	III	1 servant, possibly with a Xianbei hood	3 servants, all with two buns on the head	2 musicians, 1 dancer, all with slicked-back hair	-	-	-	Shanxi sheng 2014

	Site / tomb / occupant	Tomb type	Period	** Human figurines ♂	♀ servants and maids	♀ musicians / dancers	Central Asians (all ♂)	Tomb guardians	Lamps	References
6	Qilicun M22 (data incomplete) (♀, ♂)	?	III	?	1 servant	?	?	?	?	Datong kaogu 2006a
7	Tiancun M1 (♀, ♂)	Single brick chamber (3.5 m × 3.42 m), with a stone bed	III	-	10 servants (all painted)	-	1 (fragmentary, painted)	-	1 multi-armed; 1 emulating an iron rod lamp	Datong kaogu 2010
8	Wenyinglu M1 (♂)	Single brick chamber (2.5 m × 2.5 m), with murals and 2 funerary beds on the north and west walls	III	1 kneeling servant; painted	4 servants; 2 maids; all painted	-	-	-	1 pottery stem lamp	Datong kaogu 2011b
9	Yingbin dadao M76 (data incomplete)	Knife-shaped tomb	IV	?	1 head, with a Xianbei hood, glazed	?	?	?	?	Datong kaogu 2006c
10	Yuchang jiayuan M113, (single burial; no sexing); intact	Knife-shaped tomb	IV	1 equestrian, 1 charioteer, 8 servants, 4 bearers of various objects	2 maids	2 dancers, 6 musicians	6 musicians, 1 acrobat	1 animal-guardian (w/o further information)	2 lamps (deep bowls on high stems)	Datong kaogu 2021b

	Site / tomb / occupant	Tomb type	Period	Human figurines**				Tomb guardians	Lamps	references
				♂	♀ servants and maids	♀ musicians / dancers	Central Asians (all ♂)			
11	Yudong xinqu M13 = Tomb of Jia Bao (477) and wife	Single brick chamber, with a painted wooden house (5.4 m × 4.7 m; H. 4.9 m)	IV (477)	-	3 servants, clothing yellow glazed	-	-	2 warriors and 1 animal guardian w/ a human face	1 stem lamp of stone, w/ motifs of dancers, musicians, acrobats	Datong kaogu 2021a
12	Yanbei shuan M5 (Tomb of Song Shaozu and wife)	Single brick chamber (4.04 m × 4.24 m), with a painted stone house	IV (477)	26 mounted warriors in full armor, 32 mounted warriors with cockscomb-helms (w/ 1 long horn player), 19 standard bearers, 18 armored foot soldiers, 8 servants	6 servants	-	2 acrobats, 2 musicians	2 warriors and 1 animal guardian with an animal face	-	Liu Junxi 2008, 71–162
13	Erdianchang M36 (data incomplete)	Single brick chamber (5.08 m × 5.18 m) with a side chamber	IV	?	1 servant, 5 maids; all glazed dark brown	?	?	?	1 multi-armed lamp, glazed dark brown	Datong kaogu 2019
14	Yingbin dadao M75 (data incomplete)	Single brick chamber (with a pottery horse)	IV	?	?	?	?	?	?	Datong kaogu 2006c

	Site/tomb / occupant	Tomb type	Period	Human figurines**				Tomb guardians	Lamps	References
				♂	♀ servants and maids	♀ musicians / dancers	Central Asians (all ♂)			
15	Xiashenjing M1, with murals; ♀♂ in a coffin	Single brick chamber (3.82 m × 3.92 m)	IV	-	1 servant, 3 maids, all painted	-	-	-	1 stone (octagonal) stem lamp	Datong kaogu 2004a
16	Yanbei shiyuan M2, four coffins (♀, ♂ and 2 children)	Single brick chamber (3.5 m × 3.53 m)	IV	2 servants, painted	6 servants, all painted	2 dancers, 8 musicians (2 are singers), all painted	3 acrobats, 6 musicians, all painted	2 warriors 2 animal guardians (1 w/ a human and 1 w/ an animal face)	1 multi-armed lamp	Liu Junxi 2008, 40–70
17	Qilicun M35 (Yang Zhongdu's 楊眾度 (♂) tomb (data incomplete)	Single brick chamber (4.28 m × 4.62 m)	IV (484)	?	1 servant	1 musician	?	?	1 multi-armed lamp	Datong kaogu 2006a; Zhang Zhizhong 2006: 82
18	Tomb of Sima Jinlong 司馬金龍 (484) and Qinwen Jichen 欽文姬辰 (474)	Double chamber tomb of bricks (ante-bricks (ante-c: 4.56 m × 4.4 m and rear c: 6.12 m × 6.01 m, H. 5.2 m), with a stone bed and a wooden coffin; dromos L. 28.1 m	IV (484)	122 armored warriors on foot, 88 armored warriors on horseback (including a hengchui-band), 113 standard bearers. All glazed and painted	1 maid, 15 servants All painted	12 musicians, all glazed, playing harp, transverse flute, zither, etc.	7 musicians, playing drum, lute, flute, panpipe; 1 camel groom; all glazed. 1 wooden figure	2 warriors and 1 animal guardian with a human face	2 stone stem lamps	Datong and Shanxi 1972

	Site	Tomb type	Period	Human figurines**				Tomb guardians	Lamps	references
				♂	♀ servants and maids	♀ musicians / dancers	Central Asians (all ♂)			
19	Yanbei shiyuan M52 of the General Who Pacifies Distant Lands 平遠將軍)	Single ch. tomb of bricks (4.2 m × 4.18 m) with a side chamber	IV	-	4 servants	2 dancers	?	?	1 stone stem lamp, 1 clay stem lamp	Liu Junxi 2008, 27–39
20	Daxuelu M1, Hohhot, Inn. Mon. ♀♂ in one lacquered coffin	Single ch. tomb of bricks with a brick bed (2 m × 1.94 m)	IV	1 servant 1 horse groom	2 servants	1 dancer, 7 musicians	1 camel groom	2 warriors	1 multi-armed lamp	Guo Suxin 1977
21	Nanmeng Village in Lincheng 臨城南孟村, Hebei	Double ch., of bricks, with murals (3.6 m × 3.5 m and 3.85 m × 3.75 m) dromos L.: 39.25 m	IV	8 servants (smaller than the female ones)	8 servants	-	-	-	-	Hebei and Lincheng 2001
22	Chenzhuang M1 ♀♂ in one coffin	Double ch., of bricks, with murals (4.86 m × 4.4 m and 4.28 m × 4.18 m); dromos L.: 20.5 m	V	head of an official figurine (in report mistakenly interpreted as a female) in Luoyang style	head of a servant, with a topknot, painted	-	1 (maybe a groom, painted)	1 warrior	The stem of the lamp resembles that of a multiarmed lamp but w/o arms.	Shanxi and Datong 2011

* Unless otherwise noted, the tombs are located in Datong and the surrounding areas.

** Unless otherwise noted, the figurines are dressed in Xianbei clothing.

Asiatische Forschungen

Herausgegeben von Thomas O. Höllmann

158: Natalia Yampolskaya

Jadamba

Eight Mongolian Translations of the
Aṣṭasāhasrikā Prajñāpāramitā sūtra

2018. XVI, 284 pages, 19 tables, pb
170x240 mm
ISBN 978-3-447-11157-7
⊙*E-Book: ISBN 978-3-447-19814-1*   *each € 68,– (D)*

Jadamba is the name under which the *Aṣṭasāhasrikā Prajñāpāramitā* sūtra (the "Perfection of Wisdom in Eight Thousand Lines") is widely known in Mongolia. One of the earliest texts of Mahayana Buddhism dating back to the 1st century CE. The sūtra was translated into Tibetan in the 9th century, and in the course of the 17th century multiple Mongolian translations from Tibetan appeared.

The present publication by Natalia Yampolskaya introduces eight Mongolian translations of the *Aṣṭasāhasrikā* as part of the literary process of the 17th century – a period of great significance for Mongolian literary culture. The results of a comparative textual analysis show how a sacred canonical text was handled by the translators of the period, allowing to make observations on the methods and aims of their work. The material is presented in three blocks: the extra-textual data on the eight translations (based on the colophons), the comparative analysis of the texts' structure, vocabulary and style followed by conclusions and observations in a broader context, and the textual material itself in the form of comparative tables that show the overall structure of the eight translations, the text of one chapter and a selection of vocabulary.

159: Shing Müller, Thomas O. Höllmann, Sonja Filip (Eds.)

Early Medieval North China: Archaeological and Textual Evidence

2019. X, 506 pages, 256 ill., 6 maps, 10 tables, hc
170x240 mm
ISBN 978-3-447-11113-3   *€ 98,– (D)*

The Xianbei from southeast Mongolia were the first foreign sovereignty over North China since the 4th century. During the 200 years of Xianbei rulership, the cultures of old and new inhabitants – the Han-Chinese, the Xianbei and diverse steppe peoples, the Sogdians and other Central Asians from the west – confronted and competed with one another.

This volume is one of the first in Europe that concentrates on the cultural conflicts and the emergence of new traditions in North China during the Early Medieval period. Topics include archaeological evidence of the early Fuyu culture in southern Manchuria and early traces of Sogdians in Qinghai, impacts of Buddhism in the formation of new funerary cults and new city planning, the hybridization of diverse funerary traditions such as the use of head rests and stone beds and house-shaped sarcophagi, the emergence of a multiple identity for denizens as an adaptation to a fast changing world, and the militarization of the northern society as seen in murals and in defense lines. Also included are new insights on the Chinese *sabao* and Sogdian *s'rtp'w* titles, and discussions on Sogdian slaves in the Kocho Kingdom as well as on "multi-culture" in Chinese historiographical works.

The papers in Chinese and English have been contributed by renowned archaeologists and historians from China, the USA and Germany.

VERLAG PUBLISHERS
HARRASSOWITZ

Asiatische Forschungen

Herausgegeben von Thomas O. Höllmann

160: Moritz Huber

Lives of Sogdians in Medieval China

2020. Part 1: XVI, 350 pages,
13 figures, 3 diagrams, 11 tables, hc,
Appendices available online, VI, 476 pages,
250 figures, 109 tables, pdf
170x240 mm
ISBN 978-3-447-11380-9
⊙E-Book: ISBN 978-3-447-19956-8   each € 78,– (D)

Sogdians, a group of Central Asians based between the Amu Darya and the Syr Darya, played a significant historical role at the crossroads of the Silk Roads. Travelling the world as caravan leaders, organised in trading networks, they were found from Byzantium to the Chinese heartland. The Sogdian language was a candidate for the *lingua franca* of the Silk Roads for some hundred years and Sogdians acted as polyglot mediators at courts and prominent translators of Buddhist texts. In the Chinese capitals, fire temples were erected for their use and the exotic products they imported were cherished by the people and the court.

This socio-historical study by Moritz Huber provides a translation of the transmitted Chinese records on Sogdians in Sogdiana and China and combines them with archaeological evidence to present a differentiated picture of their presence in China from the 3rd to 10th century CE. Besides the transcription and translation of all epitaphs of Sogdians from an archaeological context, used to tell their interconnected biographies, as well as a detailed discussion of their political organisation in China under the *sabao* 薩保/薩寶, this publication further includes a case-study of the Shi 史 families in Guyuan 固原, Ningxia 寧夏 Province.

161: Ishayahu Landa

Marriage and Power in Mongol Eurasia

A History of the Chinggisid Sons-in-law

2023. XVIII, 424 pages, 7 tables, hc
170x240 mm
ISBN 978-3-447-12052-4
⊙E-Book: ISBN 978-3-447-39421-5   each € 89,– (D)

Since the beginning of his rise to power, Chinggis Khan used matrimonial relations between the members of his family and his allies in order to strengthen his support base and to expand the potential of his army. Whereas research has discussed in detail the history of the Chinggisid women, the role of their male non-Chinggisid counterparts – the imperial sons-in-law (Mon. *güregen*, Ch. *fuma* 駙馬), mostly the powerful military commanders – is still an under-researched topic.

In his monograph, Ishayahu Landa for the first time provides a comprehensive and detailed discussion of the Chinggisid in-laws, approaching them as a separate political institution with its own status, privileges, and ambitions, which played a crucial role in underpinning the Mongol rule across the continent. The monograph is unique in its combined usage of Arabic, Persian, Chinese, Latin and Old Slavonic primary sources as well as its temporal scope, ranging from the early thirteenth century to the period of the Chinggisid Crisis and beyond. The monograph will be of interest for specialists in Mongol, Chinese, Islamic, Russian, and global histories, as well as in the field of Gender Studies, and nomadic history and ethnography. At the same time, it covers an important aspect of the power structure behind the Chinggisid expansion, its maintenance of power from Korea to the Black Sea, as well as its decline.

VERLAG PUBLISHERS
HARRASSOWITZ